The Economics of Public Choice

*This book is dedicated to the memory
of my father, Bill McNutt*

The Economics of Public Choice

By P. A. McNutt

Professor of Political Economy
University of Ulster
 at Jordanstown

Edward Elgar
Cheltenham, UK • Northampton, MA, USA

Published by
Edward Elgar Publishing Limited
8 Lansdown Place
Cheltenham
Glos GL50 2HU
UK

Edward Elgar Publishing, Inc.
6 Market Street
Northampton
Massachusetts 01060
USA

Reprinted 1998

A catalogue record for this book
is available from the British Library

Library of Congress Cataloguing in Publication Data
McNutt, Paddy.
    The economics of public choice : contemporary issues in the
political economy of governing / Patrick McNutt.
    Includes bibliographical references and index.
    1. Social choice. 2. Political science—Economic aspects.
3. Voting. 4. Decision-making. 5. Bureaucracy. I. Title.
HB846.8.M39 1996
302'.13—dc20   96–14168
                                                        CIP

ISBN 1 85278 514 4 (cased)
     1 85898 522 6 (paperback)

Printed in Great Britain by The Ipswich Book Company, Suffolk

Contents

List of Figures   vii

List of Tables   ix

Preface   xi

Acknowledgements   xv

1. An Overview   1

2. Social Choice and Voting   19

3. The Political Economy of Voting   44

4. The Growth of Government   76

5. Bureaucracy and Government Output   99

6. Classic Rent-Seeking   137

7. Economic Analysis of Clubs   178

8. Democracy and Voting   213

References   230

Author Index   245

Subject Index   249

List of Figures

2.1	Representing preferences	29
2.2	Strategy sets	36
3.1	Pareto non-comparability	54
3.2	Non-single peaked preferences	56
3.3	Single peaked preferences	56
3.4	Indifference contours	58
3.5	The contract curve	58
3.6	Indifference contours: three voters	59
3.7	A Condorcet winner, y	59
3.8	The voting paradox	60
4.1	The optimal choice of tax rate	94
4.2	The Peltzman model	96
5.1	The Niskanen model	114
5.2	The Niskanen model	114
5.3	Niskanen's "bureaucratic fat" model	116
5.4	Tullock's model of bureaucracy	118
5.5	Constraints on bureau growth	120
5.6	Bureau-shaping model: top rank	125
5.7	Bureau-shaping model: bottom rank	126
5.8	Monopoly bureau output	127
6.1	Classic rent-seeking model	144
6.2	Basic trade-offs: constant costs	148
6.3	Basic trade-offs: increasing costs	149
6.4	Rent-seeking and monopoly price	155
6.5	Varian's fishtail	157
6.6	Rent-seeking and X-inefficiency	167
6.7	X-inefficiency measures	171
6.8	Change in total revenue	175

7.1	Education vouchers	183
7.2	Income supplement and voucher recipients	183
7.3	External costs of pollution	187
7.4	Optimal provision of a public good	189
7.5	Community costs and provision	190
7.6	Pareto optimality	193
7.7	Pareto optimality and public goods	194
7.8	Gain from joint consumption	196
7.9	Optimal provision of club goods	199
7.10	Costs and benefits of club membership	201
7.11	Optimal club size	201
7.12	Provision with different valuations	206
8.1	The win set, I	221
8.2	The win set, II	221
8.3	Intersecting win sets	223
8.4	Reply and response	223

List of Tables

2.1	Preference profile: Condorcet paradox	23
2.2	Preference profile: Majority outcome	24
2.3	Preference profile and cyclicity	32
2.4	Preference profile and strategies	37
2.5	Preference profile and prisoner's dilemma	38
2.6	Preference profile and top cycle set, I	40
2.7	Preference profile and top cycle set, II	40
3.1	Preference profile: Borda count with voters A, B	51
3.2	Preference profile: Condorcet criteria	63
3.3	Preference profile: Dummett's procedure	67
3.4	Preference profiles and scores	68
3.5	Preference profile: Outcomes of voting procedures	70
3.6	Preference profile: Path dependent	70
4.1	Total outlays of government as a percentage of GDP in OECD countries (selected years)	77
4.2	Structure of government outlays by economic category	84
4.3	Government sector employment	86
4.4	Structure of general government outlays by function	87
7.1	Public goods typology	181
7.2	Collective goods typology	182

Preface

The aim of the book is to investigate the public choice perspective over a range of issues. There is now a burgeoning literature of scholarly research on the subject matter and when the opportunity to write this book on public choice arose I opted to concentrate on a few selected issues. I have tried to develop a different and refreshing approach to many old problems. The theme of each chapter develops ideas and concepts which I have introduced at various conferences and seminar presentations. Writing the book enables me to bring the ideas to a wider and critical audience. This is a book about public choice and Chapter 1 provides an overview of the development of public choice. It is also a book about the political economy of governing or making decisions in a political setting. In Chapter 8, I take a critical look at democracy and voting asking the proverbial question why do rational people bother to vote? Schumpeter had argued that democracy is important because it legitimates the position of authority and that voting entails a belief that the political system or political institutions are accepted, this is, legitimated. I explore the circumstances under which the citizens confer legitimacy, this is, the circumstances under which citizens do things because they think them right, correct, justified or worthy. In newly emerging democracies and in older democracies, once marginalised and disenfranchised groups are beginning to enjoy agenda-access as their unelected representatives are consulted and legitimated in a new political order. Groups evolve which acquire command over the distribution of economic resources, voluntary non-voting becomes a norm. This is the essence of governing.

The rather complex issue of social choice and voting are addressed in Chapter 2 which does not provide an exhaustive survey of the mathematical theory of voting. The reader is referred elsewhere. However, the chapter does attempt to identify the salient issues which are of interest to the public choice scholar. Working from the premise that no unique rule exists which maps individual preferences into a social transitive preference the focus is on voting procedures. Reference is made to voting power as a measure of control over the outcomes of a voting game. Voting is easy in a democratic society although making democracy work is hard. In the chapter, I attempt to introduce a subtle difference between strategic manipulation of votes which invests decisive power in an elite group with the social outcome based on a simple number of voters rule, which appears more unanimous.

In Chapter 3, I explore the political economy aspects of voting by looking at the attempt to either modify or relax the Arrovian assumptions. The argument is made that the social choice mechanism may not be the only method of allocating resources or in making decisions. Is the choice set used in public choice under- or over-defined? Rationality in the context of voting refers to Downsian process of action not to the end-state and its interpretation. In other words, is a transitive social choice the end-state of a rational self-interested voter? In my discussion of the impact of economic conditions on voting I address voting in small committees where the voting outcome will differ according to the political representation of the committee between incumbent and non-incumbent members. I suggest that this differs from vote-trading in that the order of preferences do change and the voter in a committee behaves sincerely in revealing a re-order of preferences which take account of the changes in economic conditions. But how are economic events mapped into the voting arena of committees. The re-order mapping, developed in McNutt (1992), is one possible way. In a rather different context, re-order mapping is introduced in Chapter 8 as a proxy for effective participation in a modern democracy. In other words, effective participation, either through committees, pressure groups, lobbying or protests may best deliver the end-state rather than voting in an election.

Chapter 4 addresses the phenomenon of 'growth of government', a euphemism for increasing public expenditures. Reference is made in the media to 'big government' with the resounding call for less government involvement in the level of the economic activity of modern economies. The chapter paints a picture of growth in both the demand for and supply of public expenditure on a rather large canvas in which issues relating to demography, politics, society and economy have all competed for the reader's attention. A variant of Wagner's Law provided by Stigler argues that, paradoxically, it is the middle and upper income groups which are the major beneficiaries of public expenditure programmes. LeGrand and Winter (1987), for example, corroborated this for the UK. They showed that the families of the professional and managerial classes were, proportionate to the rest of the population, higher users of health and educational services and also major suppliers, through being doctors and teachers of such services. As argued in the chapter, it is not surprising that, in opinion polls, an overwhelming majority of respondents in the ABC1 electors favoured more expenditure to less taxation. That conclusion is the essence of endogenous government, that is, a government which seeks a second term in office and attempts to relax a re-election constraint by choosing to meet the demand for public expenditure because, in part, it is in their political interest to do so. This is governing not government.

However, less government involvement in the provision of public goods has led to a policy of decentralisation. New layers of bureaucracy are put in place. In Chapter 5, the bureau is presented as a private monopolist in this process of decentralisation which is increasingly characterised by a government as a passive sponsor and an active bureaucracy behaving as a private monopolist in the supply of the public good. For example, tax bureaus opt to maximise the tax revenue collected. I suggest that the economic analysis should be directed at conciliatory bureau outputs rather than at output levels diverging from some Paretian social norm. The government-bureaucracy relationship is more clearly analogous to that between shareholders-management with an emphasis on market incentives and objectives. The discussion of rent-seeking in Chapter 6 re-examines the contention that rent-seeking is unequivocally socially undesirable. I look at rent-seeking within a property rights perspective and focus the analysis on a reinterpretation of the geometric measures of rent-seeking. I hope that I have demonstrated that the social costs of rent-seeking whatever that means, and a measure of X-inefficiency introduced in the chapter coincide.

The discussion on clubs in Chapter 7 introduces some of the controversies which continue to appear in the literature in the economic analysis of clubs. Club theory has an important influence in the optimal provision of local public goods and local public finance. Local provision is the inevitable consequence of decentralisation. And in a world characterised by decentralisation, club provision of local public goods is becoming the norm. The Tiebout hypothesis explains the division of society into high income and low income communities. The theory on mixed clubs would support this in as much as it suggests that mixed clubs are not optimal in the provision of the public good. Higher income groups have a higher valuation and use of the public good and are unlikely to share the costs of provision equally with lower income groups with a lower valuation and use. They each represent G-groups, although I would suggest that the higher income G-groups are better represented in the political system at every level.

I have tried to introduce some new ideas into old problems. The book adds one more title to a growing literature on public choice. I hope that my discussion of the issues will add to the applied analysis of current policies.

P.A. McNutt
Moville and Belfast, March 1996

Acknowledgements

Many of the ideas nestled in the chapters of this book have been presented as papers at the annual European Public Choice Society meetings and I am grateful to the many discussants of those papers for their helpful comments. I have endeavoured to use most of the comments in the writing of the book. I would like to extend my thanks to the cohorts of students, graduate and undergraduates, who listened to my ideas in lectures delivered during my career at University College Galway. In particular to the Galway students who opted to take the elective course in Public Choice, when I introduced it at University College Galway in 1985/86. It was the first course of its kind to be introduced at a constituent college of the National University of Ireland and the response of students to it was indeed a testimony to the growing interest in a public choice perspective on economic issues. My thanks also to the undergraduates and graduate students at the University of Ulster at Jordanstown, where I have been since 1994, who continue to attend my lectures on public choice and political economy.

In bringing the book to this stage there are numerous people I would like to thank, without whose support the final manuscript would not have been produced. Early drafts of Chapters 1, 2 3 were typed at the Department of Economics, University College Galway and I would like to thank Claire Noone, Secretary of the Department during my tenure, for her help and advice. The final camera copy was prepared with the expert and professional advice of Maura Carville in Belfast whose expertise and patience helped deliver the final manuscript. Ian Alexander at the University of Ulster prepared the graphics and the figures used throughout the book. Mark Moran at the University of Ulster prepared the index and bibliography. I would like to thank Julie Leppard and her editing and proofreading team at Edward Elgar Publishers for their guidance in bringing the manuscript to published book form. I would also like to thank Dymphna Evans at Edward Elgar Publishers for her help at every stage of the manuscript and particularly for her encouragement and her faith in my ability to produce a manuscript which was long overdue. I am grateful to everybody on the editorial side who have lightened my load as author.

I would like to thank Dominic Lepelley (Caen), Sven Berg (Lund) and Hannu Nurmi (Turku) for the exchange of ideas at different conferences which helped me in the preparation of Chapters 2 and 3. Lecture notes from days as an Oxford graduate student infiltrate the writing of Chapters 2 and 3. Chapter 6 emanates from my DPhil thesis at the University of Ulster and I would like to thank Vani Borooah, Richard Barnett at the University of Ulster, and Peter Jackson at Leicester University for helpful comments in the final writing up of this thesis. I would like to thank Kluwer Academic publishers for permission to use my articles: 'A Note on Condorcet's Probability' and 'Rent-Seeking and X-Inefficiency' which first appeared in the journal Public Choice. In preparation of Chapters 4 and 5 I was able to use the figures which appeared in Peltzman (1980), Mueller (1989) and Brown and Jackson (1992) and I am grateful to their respective publishers for permission to use the figures. The reproduction of the figures was felt to be appropriate in order to prepare the comparative analytical comments on the issue under discussion. Finally, I would like to thank Vani Borooah for his contribution, Chapter 5 and Manfred Holler for the use of one of his figures in my discussion on the win sets in Chapter 8.

Many colleagues and friends have influenced and guided my thought process during the writing of this book. However, I do want to express my gratitude to some individuals who directly, or indirectly through their own published work, have shaped my thoughts. In particular I am grateful to Shanti Chakravarty (Bangor), Manfred Holler (Hamburg), Michael Laver (Dublin) and Martin Paldam (Aarhus) for their comments. I would like to thank Dennis Mueller (Vienna) and Gordon Tullock (Arizona) for their positive comments in endorsing the book and to the external referees at Edward Elgar Publishing for their helpful comments and suggestions. In alphabetical order can I thank Jim Albrecht, Didier Arnaud, Jurgen Backhaus, Richard Barnett, Basudeb Chaudhuri, Don Bathie, Vani Borooah, John Coakley, Oscar Couwenberg, Gaetana Crupiano, Donal Dineen, Leonard Dudley, Eirling Eide, Ken Greene, Magnus Henrekson, Harold Hochman, Douglas Hibbs, Chris Lingle, Isidora Mazza, Oliver Morrissey, Peter Nannstead, Rory O'Donnell, Prasanta Pattanaik, Martin Rama, Gian Romagnoli, Pierre Salmon, Friedrich Schneider, Norman Schofield, Arthur Schram, Ken Shepsle, Frank Stephen, Heinrich Ursprung, Patrick VanCayseele, Martin von Haller Gronbaek, Wolfgang Weigel and Frans vanWinden. I am eternally grateful to you all and I hope you enjoy the read.

I would finally like to thank my wife Maeve Doherty, for her constant support and encouragement.

1. An Overview

Introduction

Modern public choice is a study of the political mechanisms and institutions which circumscribe government and individual behaviour. Mueller (1989) commented that 'public choice can be defined as the economic study of non-market decision-making, or simply the application of economics to political science' (p. 1). Public choice has emerged as a separate school of thought in the past forty years or so; it has developed into a methodology in its own right with distinct influences from both economics and political science. Many of the theoretical constructs underpinning a public choice perspective have evolved from a reaction to developments in the existing literature, notably the Bergson-Samuelson concept of a social welfare function and Arrow's impossibility theorem. The concerns of public choice theorists extend into many aspects of non-market decision making, in their study of the state, the constitutional and democratic model, collective and party behaviour and the state bureaucratic model (Pardo and Schneider 1996).

An objection to the sacrosanct public policy role of government as benevolent dictator, and the adoption of methodological individualism, remains two important hallmarks in modern public choice theory. Generally one accredits Buchanan and Tullock as the intellectual fathers of public choice theory as it developed in 1960's. Their 1962 book 'Calculus of Consent' remains a classic in the literature preceding Olson's (1965) 'Logic of Collective Action' which introduced the collective action problem and its resolution as a central plank in the emerging public choice school. However looking at the earlier origins of public choice, one could argue that there were at least three additional classics that lay the foundations for many of the issues discussed within the public choice school

Arrow produced his 'Social Choice and Individual Values' in 1951 and presented a rather pessimistic view demonstrating the inherent instability of collective decisions. In 1958, Black in 'The Theory of Committees and Elections' injected some optimism into the debate with the stability of the median voter model, introduced a year earlier by Downs in 'An Economic Theory of Democracy'. Downs' approach was to apply economic methodology, particularly the idea of utility income, to the study of political process. By the end of the 1950s the ghost of the Condorcet paradox had been resurrected by Arrow's impossibility theorem and the seeds of a public choice perspective on voting procedures were sown.

The theorem confidently asserted that there was no rule consistent with completeness and transitivity of preferences, Pareto consistency and independence of irrelevant alternatives, for constructing a complete and transitive social preference relation. It cast doubt, for example, on Rousseau's 'social contract' and 'general will' and on the concept of a 'social good' which had appeared in the emerging public finance literature. In fact it cast doubt on all notions that attribute social preferences to a collection of individual preferences; it cast doubt on important areas of twentieth century social thought.

There is little doubt amongst scholars about the procedural aspect of a public choice school of thought as an overlap between economics and political science. If the theory of public goods demand is an integral aspect of contemporary public choice theory, the application of economic methodology to political science is one of explaining the final (optimal) amount and the distribution of that amount of public good. In this scenario the political actions of government are limited by organised interest groups, and the Pigovian interpretation of government as a benevolent dictator no longer obtains. This application of economics to political science does challenge the orthodox basis of modern public finance as politicians and government are increasingly seen as maximising their own self-interest. The challenge to the orthodox approach is that government is no longer exogenous. In other words, the analysis is about a market exchange theory of politics with individual voters (consumers) buying and selling votes and politicians (firms) with an objective (vote) function to be maximised. Within this approach, the required aggregation of individual preferences or decisions undermines the voting process (democracy) by the ever present voting paradox.

Public choice as a discipline gained recognition in 1960s, but its history parallels that of welfare economics and public finance. By the 1950s there was an acceptance of government intervention in the economy; the Pigovian interpretation of government was that of a corrector of market failures. With externalities and the observed failure of the market to attain efficiency, the role of government as an instrument in public policy was secure. Public choice as a school of thought is best interpreted as concerning the relationship between economics and politics, that is, a Downsian emphasis on the 'economic theory of democracy' as espoused by Schumpeter (1976) and analysed by Downs (1957).

There is also the Buchanan approach to public choice which is characterised by a criticism of the Neo-Classical orthodoxy in economic science. It has recently contributed to the school of constitutional political economy. It fits well with the contractarian approach to welfare economics. As a critique of the orthodoxy, in particular the criticisms levelled at the 'social preference' construct in social choice theory and at the criterion of Pareto optimality as an equity criterion, it shares common ground with scholars who otherwise would not be associated with a public choice school.

However reading further back into the history of economic thought, there emerges an element common to the early scholars of public finance and welfare economics, and it is the individualistic methodology. This applies to the behaviour of individuals as tax payers as well as users of public goods, as bureaucrats and as politicians. From the Condorcet paradox to the free rider, this individualism was to play an important part in the intellectual origins of public choice. Wicksell undoubtedly was the most influential representative of this individualistic school of public finance. His material inspired the public goods theory expressed by Samuelson and the economics of political methodology, in other words the public choice school as developed by Buchanan. While both scholars contest to the influence of Wicksell, the public choice approach has developed its own momentum and often finds itself the victim of attack on the realism of the approach, from the Neo-Classical orthodox theory that has evolved from the Samuelson-Hicksian revolution.

It is still not adequately resolved as to whether public choice belongs to the domain of mainstream economics or represents a criticism of and an alternative to, the mainstream Neo-Classical school of thought. Public choice has a positive contribution to make to Neo-Classical microeconomics, enriching our understanding of monopoly, for example, or government behaviour. Likewise, the development of public choice could be interpreted as the generalisation of economics into a political space, the politician is no longer exogenous to the economic events in society. One perception of public choice however, is as an alternative school of thought to the Neo-Classical with historical roots in the Austrian approach as developed in the latter half of the nineteenth century.

That this perception has occurred is an accident of history in that both Buchanan and Samuelson as representatives of the Austrian and Neo-Classical approaches to economics respectively studied the work of early public finance scholars. It is in the division of this earlier work into an Anglo-Saxon Marshallian-Pigovian approach with a concentration on taxes, and an Italian-Scandinavian Wicksell-Lindahl approach that included a public budget determined within a political process, that one can find a historical explanation for the current differences of opinion. This division of early public finance coupled with a sharp methodological difference between the Marshallian approach to value, cost and preferences and the Austrian approach as outlined by Menger and von Mises, set the research agenda for the emerging public choice paradigm.

Collective Action

The collective action problem is particularly acute in the provision of public goods. How best does society allocate the public goods especially in the absence of co-operation? A classic representation of the co-operation problem which is the Prisoner's Dilemma, can be solved by a third party intervention. Two rational individuals will achieve a Pareto inferior outcome, in other words, the Pareto outcome is itself a Prisoner's Dilemma. Within the public choice perspective, Olson (1965) has argued that small rather than large groups are more likely to solve collective action problems co-operatively; McLean (1987) addressed counter-arguments to the normative argument that 'small is beautiful'. One in particular considers a group who have evolved with customs of reciprocal altruism. If individuals on the frontier 'suffer when they meet cheats trying to invade the group' (p. 179), then the larger the group in these Axelrod-type games 'the less vulnerable it is to invasion' (p. 179).

Within the collective action domain there are a few unresolved issues to which a public choice scholar can positively contribute. Taylor (1976, 1987) advocates anarchistic co-operation, arguing that many of the activities undertaken by government in the organisation of society and in the allocating of scarce resources, could be done by an anarchistic community. Advocates of the market mechanism depend on the normative prescription implied by the Pareto improvement, that if somebody gains and nobody loses that society is better off after the change than before.

Let us introduce two caveats to the discussion. One is a respect for individual rights, particularly a right to property. If individuals respect each others rights to private property, rights are important; however if an individual breaks your window there is a violation of your rights to private property. Likewise if he trespasses on your land. Since property rights are essential for market exchange, and given that individuals may not respect the rights of others, a government is necessary to abridge property rights disputes. The individual is dependent on the government therefore as a 'trustworthy external authority'. A second caveat is the formation of government as a co-operative venture for marginal gain. It protects the individual against theft, fraud, negligence and ensures the enforcement of individual contracts.

Buchanan and Tullock (1962) argued for a state in order to carry out 'unanimously approved' activities like taxation. If the individuals in the society agree then there is no violation of rights. Above all individuals could contract in order to specify the extent to which different individuals are entitled to pursue private ends. In this situation could a Pareto efficient outcome be achieved and if so what does it maximise? As Sugden (1981) writes, 'social contract theory tries to answer questions concerned with political obligation'. Essentially society and its political institutions have no natural rights that take precedence over the rights of the individual. He concludes that Paretian welfare economics has no claim on liberal values and that a contractarian social welfare ordering has the same properties as a Paretian ordering. In particular both approaches concur that if an individual prefers x to y and no one prefers y to x then both orderings have the property that x is preferred to y. However he does provide a proof that the contractarian position is stronger, more liberal than the Paretian position. Contractarianism is a special case of Paretian welfare economics and the contractarian social welfare function is derived from the axioms of state preference theory.

He refers to collectivist egalitarianism which suggests that equality is inherently good in itself. It is a mistake to attempt a reconciliation between Paretian welfare economics and collectivist egalitarianism; in the end-state model of public choice, a liberal must be individualistic and the appropriate social welfare ordering is a contractarian one. It is very much the absence of individual co-operation and contracting that occasions the need for government, particularly in an allocative and distributive capacity. The public goods paradox could be resolved by deferring the optimal provision of the public good to a government - the end result however if it occurs, is a sub-optimal provision. Buchanan (1965) introduced the idea of clubs, with homogenous individuals forming a club and providing a non-rival excludable public good. Optimal provision at least in the Buchanan model can be achieved by determining the optimal number of members, vide Chapter 7. But the collective action problem is at the heart of public choice theory in that if individuals co-operate there is always the free rider possibility. Can this be overcome by determining an optimal group size for co-operation as in the literature on groups outlined by Olson (1965)? The overlap here between game theory and public choice has strengthened the argument that co-ordination amongst individuals in a Prisoner Dilemma-type situation may be possible in the absence of government.

Government itself may be an externality *vis-a-vis* the macroeconomics literature on the 'crowding-out effect' of government. An interpretation of government, for example, as an open set of metric politicians, allows for the very real occurrence of political trade-off between efficiency and equity. Politics is essentially about the distribution of benefits and burdens and *metric politicians* are faced with a re-election constraint that can be relaxed by currying favour with interest groups. To a limited extent the role of government may be supplanted by interest group activity on issues with a populist dimension.

A decision on distributive justice is a decision on the distribution of rights. Nozick (1974) has argued for the right to liberty, Dworkin (1976) has argued for the right to equality while Rawls (1971) ranked the right to equity over the right to liberty. Within this minimal government scenario liberals and libertarians clash and one wonders if the outcome is sufficiently different from a government outcome or indeed from an anarchistic co-operative outcome.

Taylor (1976) has commented that individuals resolve their differences more amicably in the absence of third parties such as institutions (lawyers) and governments. Many writers believe that co-operation is better than competition. Our problem here is whether co-operation is exclusively political or whether competition is exclusively an economic concept. The Prisoner's Dilemma characterisation of co-operative behaviour does offer some insight. In the original dilemma, had the prisoners co-operated a miscarriage of justice would have taken place; it is the lack of trust, even amongst prisoners, that forces each rational individual to follow his self-interest. If competitiveness and co-operation in a barter economy arrive at a similar allocation of resources, a fundamental theorem, that eludes the public choice literature, may be nascent.

The factor which contributes to the analysis is information, in that the competitive environment is defined with perfect and indivisible information. If individuals have the information and make the decision, then no rights are violated and the decision is fair. This accords with the line of argument expressed rather succinctly by Buchanan (1983, 1996). Co-operation however requires information gathering by the co-operative members, that is, free riders, asymmetries and divisibility. This can be alleviated by a third extraneous authority, for example, the planning (prices) board, or a government, but in the absence of that public goods characterisation of information, both competitiveness and co-operation arrive at the same barter (contracted) outcome. A public choice perspective would suggest that if the barter society ranked a state of nature II over I, then they should contract to be in state of nature II; institutional barriers may prevent this. However, the institutional barriers in this situation not only include bureaucracies but the initial allocation of goods, educational opportunities, equal access and opportunity, the laws and legal system and the effectiveness of political representatives.

Voting Systems

An area of overlap between mathematics and political theory which has become a hallmark of public choice writings is the study of voting systems. In a democracy, one of the most evident social collective choice rules is that of majority voting. It had been established by Condorcet as early as the eighteenth century that majority voting rules could lead to inconclusive outcomes given certain applications. Arrow's impossibility theorem goes much further than this. It is not only the case that the majority rule produces an intransitive social ordering, but there does not exist a social choice rule that will satisfy all of the voters' preferences. However, in reality, the probability of this voting paradox occurring is so small that it makes no practical difference (Tullock, 1967). Given the number of individuals and the number of alternative possibilities presented, the probability of the paradox occurring is very small.

The assumption therefore that individuals, be they voters or politicians, act rationally in their own self interest is the underlying theme of public choice analyses of the political economy.

A major concern for public choice scholars has been the inadequacies of liberal democracy. As such, their concerns are similar to those of the Austrian school. However, they differ greatly in their methodology. Hypothesis formulation and testing of political phenomena and their respective economic underpinnings, has taken on a strong positivistic influence. Theories are conceptualised first of all by making the assumption that individuals are utility maximisers, always attempting to maximise their gains while minimising their costs. Following a deductive logic, precise testable theories are then subjected to empirical testing to verify their findings. Public choice theorists favour the operationalisation of rules, thus emphasising the need for mathematical and statistical models. For them, the economic analysis of political institutions must be by means of a quantifiable variable. Precise universalistic hypotheses are explained by the strong economic influences that comprise their make up, initially derived from the assumption that the economic agent in the model is a self interested, utility maximising individual.

The public choice perspective on democracy has placed great emphasis on the market organisation of the political system where downsizing government is the modern analogue of classical political economy. The areas analysed in the main have been the search for a restructured democratic constitution, the imperfection of the interest group process and an over-expanded state system. Public choice theorists have been highly vocal on the issue of democratic voting arrangements. They regard the principle of one vote per person as an inadequate expression of individual preferences compared with a system that allows a multiple number of votes per person depending on the issues, parties and candidates that have to be decided (Downs, 1957).

The suggestion stems from the economic methodology that allows individuals to allocate their budget to their perceived consumer rankings in accordance with their most desired commodities. This process could not be aggregated into a single decision since it could not deal with the complete information of an individual's needs. Thus, it can be argued, why should the voting system be aggregated in such a fashion? A single vote cannot encompass all the views of the people and their future development of the democratic state. Another proposed model that exhibits the intensity of voting preferences is the process of vote trading or log-rolling. This refers to the tyranny of the majority outcome whereby the sum of the benefits to the majority (in a majority outcome) may be less than the value of the costs to the minority. In such a situation, the minority may be willing to trade votes to prevent this situation occurring. Vote trading is in effect an extension of the economist's rational, self-interested utility-maximising model. Buchanan and Tullock have demonstrated that vote trading makes majority voting more efficient in terms of the allocation of resources and the distribution of welfare. By enabling individuals to exchange their votes, the system establishes a more acceptable outcome in terms of Pareto efficiency.

Log-rolling and pressure groups influence the distribution of the costs and benefits of public policies. The outcomes of any vote trading games will depend on the voting system and the coalitions formed between different actors in the game. Moreover, log-rolling can result in the public sector (as measured by the size of public spending) being larger than it might have been in the absence of log-rolling. This view would not equate very well with empiricism. As vote trading takes place through time, the size of the public budget increases. This growth in public budgets calls into question the overall efficiency of vote trading. New-right political views are distinctly evident in public choice accounts of electoral competition. The voter/consumer, as before, has been categorised under the rational actor model. In the Downsian world of political economy, the behaviour of the political parties and politicians is also characterised by self-interest.

Party leaders are viewed by public choice theorists as vote maximisers, motivated not by ideological considerations, but instead by a desire to gain political power. This electoral model means in theory that general elections do not necessarily produce a government close to the choice of the median voter. The assumption that voters can be characterised along bipolar dimensions is dropped and instead voter preferences on multiple issues must be considered. The strategy of the potential political leader is to be of a catch-all nature across as many issues as possible, without contradicting the ideological basis of the party. With a multitude of parties competing on the same issues, it is imperative that they position themselves in n-dimensional space, inevitably forming a coalition of different ideological interests (Laver, 1993), From a new right perspective, voting is seen as a clear cut process, in the sense that voters know best what they want. Thus rational actors choose their product (candidate) assuming it correlates closely with their revealed preference (vote). Therefore, the electoral system for public choice theorists is a machine finely-tuned in determining a citizen's revealed preferred position.

Endogenous Government

The Downsian vote maximising model of government has found its greatest expression in the public choice literature of the political business cycle. Since voters are concerned with the short term economic indicators such as the level of inflation, unemployment changes, promotion of growth and income distribution objectives, it behoves government to consider the manipulation of the economy as an election winning objective. Instead of being passive in economic affairs, the actions of vote-maximising governments may generate business cycles in the economic indicators. Where strategies for economic management are influenced by politicians' concerns with election strategy, then one may witness a Phillips-type trade off between electioneering and economic efficiency. In the aftermath of an election, the government can emphasise the need for fiscal rectitude and the vote winning measures may be reversed. Therefore, government actions may tend to disguise the realities of the economic and fiscal situation from voters, ensuring that each time a voter faces an electoral decision, they are furnished with insufficient or misleading economic information.

The incumbent government thus has the power to disguise the effect of past electoral competition by expanding national debt to meet voters' electoral expectations. Deficit spending spreads the costs of current account spending over future time periods, which means the present government can conceal these transition costs from the electorate. In their analyses, public choice models correctly show a long run tendency for state expenditure to grow. Party competition is assumed to be influenced by 'Wagner's law', as government expenditure increases in real terms - citizens in an industrialised democratic society will demand better standards of social services and an extension of the public service as a prerequisite to electoral support. The public choice school has joined with political commentators in their criticisms of the role played by Keynesian counter-cyclical policies in electoral competition. Consider the following quote, attributable to Buchanan, quoted in Brown and Jackson (1990): 'The post war Keynesian period let to a generalised erosion in public and private manners - explosion of the welfare rolls, widespread corruption in both the private and the governmental sector and observed increases in the alienation of voters from the political process.'

The policy outcomes of government have been viewed in terms of the political inputs. From a public choice perspective, we could argue that although governments deliver policies in line with voter preferences, party competition is not in the interests of economic management. Supply side public choice methodology contains little reference to these influences. It places an emphasis on the state as a monopoly supplier of goods and services. Public choice concerns lie in the potentially exploitative nature of state bureaucracy and institutions. Demand-side models treat state institutions as a unit which cannot be analysed internally, but its workings are instead analysed from a knowledge of the political/economic processes that influence the workings of these institutions (Dunleavy, 1991, p. 112 and Chapter 5).

In negotiating the size of the budget from the state, for example, the bureaucracy has the advantage of an incomplete flow of information, due to the principal-agent problem. Bureaucratic officials (agents) know the budgetary needs of their bureaucracy. In a democratic system of government, it is unlikely that the ministerial head of a bureaucracy (principal) can have the same knowledge of the initial workings as the agent, since his portfolio is usually limited to the lifetime of the government. It is therefore in the agent's rational interest to provide the principal with an incomplete flow of information or misinformation in order to obtain a greater discretionary budget. The bargaining process between the legislator and the bureau is never played in a situation of perfect information. The political heads of departments are usually sympathetic to the aims of the department, so seek to gain finance to boost their political prestige (Tullock, 1974). Given this structural model public choice theorists correctly conclude that western democratic governments have very little control over their allocations to bureaus (Niskanen,1971).

Political crises and especially those caused by the decline of Keynesian consensus are central to this area of supply side methodologies. The emergence of crises has been largely due to the creation of X-inefficiencies in government monopolies relative to private producers. In economic terms, these crises have been seen (as in the 1970's in Western Europe) to increase inflation and to lower public expenditures which in the long run slows economic growth. Olson considers that economic growth is a public good for pressure groups, as political organisation is a collective commodity for individuals. He argues that the strategic groups in society have a long term political interest in the expansion of their share of national income rather than in expanding the growth rate of society. Each group will devote its resources towards organising the impact of the market on its members and will attempt to externalise the costs of restrictive practices on the rest of society. Therefore, a public choice methodology provides a case for arguing that political instability can be examined using micro-economic underpinnings. If public choice is to concern itself with political methodology, then it will have to temper its conservative approach.

Impossibility Theorems

In any discussion of the impossibility theorem reference is made to preferences. One makes the assumption that individuals are their own best judge: individuals know what they like and can choose from a selection of alternatives. In order to impose some order on the individual's set of preferences we introduce a few axioms. The order assumes that an individual can rank preferences, for example, prefer apples to bananas. Preferences have the following properties: *Completeness:* for any number of alternatives (xyz) the individual can rank the set of alternatives, either preferring any two (xPy), or being indifferent between any two (yIx). *Ordering:* this may be strong (xPyPz) or weak ordering (xPyIz). The latter is generally sufficient for a choice.
Transitivity: for a complete set of three alternatives, (xyz), transitivity can imply either [xPy and yPz => xPz], [xPy and yIz => xPz], [xIy and yPz =>

xPz] and [xIy and yIz => xIz]. Preferences are quasi-transitive, if only the first holds and the property of acyclicity arises if: [xPy and yPz => not zPx].

Utility represented by U reflects the direction of preferences; if for example xPy then $U(x) > U(y)$; an individual is choosing his/her best alternative and is assumed to be rational. There is a utility function U which exactly reflects the individual preferences, such that $U(x) > U(y)$ if and only if xPy. If this can be proved, then the best alternative, either x or y, reduces to a mathematical problem of maximising the utility function. And important ingredient in the proof is that individual preferences are complete and transitive. One of the more striking contrasts between nineteenth-century utilitarians and recent treatments of utility is the concern with inter-personal comparisons. The modern use of preferences includes no basis for comparison.

The use of cardinal numbers in the utility index is generally associated with the Bentham philosophy of utilitarianism. The greatest happiness principle, which is the cornerstone of utilitarianism could be translated into the maximisation of the society's total utility index U. The index U is the sum of individual utilities whereby the total may increase without an increase in all the individual utilities. The utilitarian philosophy maximises the utility (happiness) of the greatest number. Utilitarianism and the Paretion criterion represent two possible criteria on which to base policy decisions. Are they an acceptable value premise? Collectively they are the basis of modern welfare theory and distinguishing between what is good and what is bad, both from the individual and for society, can be supported by reference to these criteria.

For example a decision A is good, and a policy B is good for society if in the implementation of the policy from the status quo, nobody loses and somebody gains, i.e. a Pareto improvement occurs and total utility is maximised. And here we have, through the fundamental welfare theorems, a support for the private market economy, which supports such an improvement. The voting paradox as evolved by Arrow, Chapter 3, reveals the impossibility of translating individual preferences into a collective preference. An important issue is the possibility of multiple preference orderings. As Brandt (1967) emphasised in his reply to Arrow 'some choices are motivated by the prospect of enchanted personal welfare... whereas others (paying taxes) are motivated by considerations of moral principle'.

The argument that people are moved by either self-interest or benevolence has an established history from Hume and Smith. Goodwin (1980) outlines the distinction between 'ethical preferences' as distinct from the private preferences addressed by Arrow. Paralleling this argument is yet another paradox - the Downs' paradox that anyone bothers to vote at all. While it may be irrational to express private preferences through voting, why people bother to vote in the context of ethical preferences, can be explained in terms of taking a moral stand. In reaction to the seminal work of Arrow, Buchanan and

Tullock (1962) argued against the realism of an analogy between individual and social preferences. They suggested that the paradox may be overcome by a constitutional contract, whereby individuals knowingly allow less-than-unanimous decisions. Their introduction of log-rolling and side payments enabled Pareto optimal voting outcomes. By the mid 1960s the stage had been set for the establishment of a public choice approach to public policy. Whether it proffers an independent methodology or not is left to the reader.

The developments since Arrow's seminal work define the vast literature of social choice (Sen, 1986). On the one hand there is the literature on strategic voting and in particular on vote trading. It requires that individuals vote contrary to their true preference on an issue. Social choice theorists have argued that strategic voting is an inherent feature of voting methods; the Gibbard-Satterthwaite theorem proves that any voting methods can be manipulated. Much of the research in this area has been conducted by political scientists familiar with the rigors of game theory. Necessary and sufficient conditions for vote trading have been established. The Schwartz theorem for example, states that if preferences are separable and if a Condorcet winner exists, sincere voting yields that winner.

This development tends to suggest that we cannot rule out the possibility that everyone in society has the incentive to reveal their preferences strategically. By doing so individuals can manipulate the outcome of (say) a committee, a legislature or some other social process. But it also asserts that individual actions are interdependent and in particular that one makes assumptions about what another would do in the (similar) circumstances. Interdependence and conflict go hand in hand, and the literature which explores this area of strategic voting uses the theory of non-cooperative games. The work in this area of direct relevance to public choice is the development of a concept of equilibrium in order to resolve the interdependent choices.

Another development is with respect to the manipulation of social choices, agenda control. It is rewarding for the individual or group in so much as strategic voting is not observable. An interesting dimension to this is the property of path dependency where the social choice depends on the sequence in which the alternatives were considered. The committee chairman has a control over the sequence of items on the agenda; Ordershook (1986) shows how a chairperson with complete information and sophisticated voting, could lead the committee to choose any alternative he or she desired. Hence the literature concentrates on the disequilibrium that arises under majority rule. Arrow's impossibility theorem created a literature on the manipulation of voting outcomes, strategic voting and in particular on vote trading and on the consequences of disequilibrium under majority rule. It raises problems for political theory and political philosophy, it challenges the political process on which democracy is built and it forces an alliance between economics and politics that really is the essence of public choice. The impossibility theorem has survived the Little-Samuelson criticism and many others have attempted to either relax the initial assumptions or replace them.

Normative Criteria

The 1930s saw the arrival of the New Welfare Economics, and many economists under the influence of logical positivism, followed the lead given earlier by Pareto. It represented an important intellectual shift away from Edgeworth and Pigou and the utilitarian argument that individual utilities could be added together to give a measurable total welfare. The idea of preferences were introduced, buttressed by the concept of an indifference curve, and as Gibbard (1986) commented: 'quantitative utility has been purged from it (theory of rational choice) and replaced by preference orderings which cannot be added together' (p. 166).

He further commented that 'the switch to preference satisfaction as a standard of personal welfare has been a mistake' (p. 166). The Pareto criterion based on such preferences prevents any interpersonal comparisons of differences in utility that were allowed under utilitarianism. This rather difficult literature on the search for an ethic that can be satisfactorily applied to economics, concentrates on the concept of a person's good, what Gibbard called 'the intrinsic reward of his life' (p. 192). Utilitarianism required some interpersonal comparisons and although this has been perceived as a weakness by the New Welfare Economics the existence of Pareto non-comparable states restricts the Paretian ethic that underpins the new welfare theory.

A concept of ethical fairness or indeed unanimity as outlined by Buchanan (1978) and Buchanan and Tullock (1962) respectively, can equally represent alternative ethical criteria to utilitarianism and the Paretian ethic. As alluded to earlier the developments in contractarian welfare economics can accommodate the development in the Buchanan approach to public choice, and vice versa. The one unresolved issue across the public choice literature discussed in Chapter 8 is why do rational individuals bother to vote. The paradox of voting concludes on the inability of a voting rule to translate transitive individual preferences into a social preference. Downs (1957) thought it irrational to vote but Goodwin (1980) has argued that 'only people bother to vote ... can be explained in terms of taking a moral stand' (p. 89). The argument suggests that the ethical tastes evoked by voting are less diverse (indeed less selfish) than tastes evoked by ordinary events.

That search for an ethical standard is very much within the domain of any school of thought and particularly within the public choice school. The basic premise is an efficient and equitable way of allocating scarce resources; the history of political science and economics, and social science generally, has offered us anarchy (Taylor, 1976, 1987), market and government. An alternative is altruism (Titmuss, 1970, Margolis, 1982 and McNutt, 1988), which works quite well in commodity specific markets such as blood transfusions. But what about care for the elderly? If Titmuss (1970) is correct, that people give blood because there is no market, is there an analogy with the elderly, who should be cared for by their relatives in the absence of either market or government support? What is a fair outcome and in this context McLean (1987) has commented that: 'public choice should not cut itself off from questions like should the able bodied be taxed for the benefit of the disabled, and if so how heavily - it can and should enrich the debate' (p. 182).

Welfare economics texts and public finance texts in general, open with passing overviews on normative criteria but in the wake of new overlaps between economics and philosophy, many scholars have begun to re-evaluate the need for equity criteria within economic policy making. Public choice could have a lot to offer to this debate in at least proffering an alternative and fresh outlook on old recurring problems. There is a relativist argument embedded in the traditional statement that '£1 to A is worth more than £1 to B', and a deeper investigation into that relativism may question the policy of taxing B. Ethical statements easily translate into ethical standards and any controversy about these standards will manifest themselves in the application of the standard to policy analysis. In the last resort normative criteria must defer to the ethical consensus in society, and it is in arriving at that consensus, that public choice may continue to contribute. For example, in the 'Calculus of Consent' both authors concurred that if individuals can agree on an issue that there is no violation of individual rights, in other words, a government can do 'unanimously approved' activities such as taxing and spending.

The rationale for welfare economics as a separate topic within economics could be found in Pigou's (1920) 'Economics of Welfare' where he commented on the need in economics for a 'practical usefulness of some sort'. How can we decide whether policy decisions by government are right or desirable? How can we argue for the existence of a better alternative on social issues? How can we indeed without recourse to some set of criteria? That is the essence of welfare economics, a pot-pourri of welfare criteria applicable in public finance and within the domain of public choice.

We have to accept basic value judgements before we adopt the set of criteria. With utilitarianism, for example, not every boat rises with the tide, but the value judgements implicit in utilitarianism are better highlighted by reference to Pigou's equalisation of marginal utility of incomes and Sen's Weak Equity Axiom (WEA). The Pigovian Criterion was quite revolutionary and may have unwittingly buttressed the income transfer from rich to poor that is the basis of modern direct taxation. But it essentially makes an inter-personal comparison of the sort alluded to earlier, that' £1 to a poor guy is better than £1 to a rich guy'. By measuring hypothetical marginal utility of incomes, the income transfer increases the net utility of society. More interestingly it presupposes an unfair initial distribution of income, an issue not considered by the Paretian ethic and connects the welfare of a society with the distribution of its income.

The WEA outlined by Sen (1973) not only contradicts the utilitarian outcome, but introduces a quality non-utility dimension to the relative 'richness' or 'poorness' of an individual. Using interpersonal comparisons it asserts that income should be distributed in an income redistribution to those individuals with relatively lower welfare. Individual i may be extremely rich and j poor, but if individual i were rich and severely handicapped, j may prefer, relatively, to be poor and healthy. In general if person A derives more utility than person B for any given level of income, then any redistribution of that income should favour B. The Pigovian criterion of equalising the marginal utility of incomes earned utilitarianism a reputation for being equality conscious.

The marginalist reasoning did emanate from utilitarianism and remained the dominant theme of the old welfare economics, pre-1932. The advance of the 'New' post-1932 theory of welfare economics with an emphasis on ordinal utility and indifference curves had a ready made precursor in Pareto. The implicit difficulties in interpersonal comparisons can be somewhat overcome by the Paretian guideline of 'someone gained and nobody lost'. With the use of indifference curves constructed for constant utility and the use of the Edgeworth-Bowley diagram the scene was set for the conditions of Pareto efficiency. In a two good-two consumer world Pareto efficiency in exchange occurs with the equalisation of marginal rates of substitution for the two consumers across the two goods produced.

Equalisation of marginal rates of technical substitution establishes efficiency in production, and the third property requires that the marginal rates of substitution be equal to each other, and equal to the marginal rate of technical substitution. Such equalisation of marginal rates of substitution, which are essentially the slopes of the indifference curves and the isoquants, occurs at the tangency point between (say) any two indifference curves. The locus of all these tangency points is called the Edgeworth contract curve and any movement away from the contract curve will make somebody worse off. Exactly where the economy is located on the contract curve depends on the initial allocation of goods, the final optimal position is attained by bargaining either by exchange in barter or through the price mechanism.

Herein lies the fundamental theorems of welfare economics. The first or direct theorem states that a perfectly competitive market economy will arrive at a Pareto optimal outcome; the second or converse theorem states that if a Pareto optimal outcome exists it can be supported by a perfectly competitive market economy. By combining both theorems we can state that the price-market system with modifications can be used to bring about an optimal allocation of resources. But the initial allocation may be inequitable; this may lead to an inequitable yet optimal competitive outcome. And this is one major objection to complete reliance on the market mechanism. Also on the contract curve any two Pareto optimal points are non-comparable. Society therefore cannot rank states or allocations on the contract curve; the existence of Pareto non-comparable states represented an impasse briefly overcome by the Kaldor-Scitovsky compensation tests. The tests are an attempt primarily to overcome the problem of Pareto non-comparability, but their weakness is that the redistribution from gainer to loser is a potential redistribution, and not an actual transfer.

At this juncture, recall the impossibility theorem which argued that there was no rule which would translate individual to social preferences. In other words, if there is a collective choice rule R satisfying the Arrovian conditions outlined earlier one could translate individual preferences into social preferences. The utility function is a ranking of individual's welfare, likewise a social welfare function is a ranking of a society's welfare. If there is a collective choice rule R, then there is also a social welfare function W which is like a collective choice rule defined across the commodities. So in a sense the Pareto non-comparable points on the contract curve are mapped into a utility space, generating the utility-possibility frontier. The point at which the social welfare function is tangent to the utility-possibility frontier is the preferred point for society; it is the point which has maximised the social welfare function of society subject to the utility levels of the individuals in that society. However there is an important weakness in this argument in respect of the utility possibility frontier. It is not always the case that a movement from an initial position on the frontier to an end position represents a Pareto improvement.

An alternative to the Paretian perspective is what Sugden (1981) has defined as contractarian welfare economics. It is of particular interest given the works of Rawls (1971) and Nozick (1974) and also the liberal re-writing of welfare economics as in Peacock and Rowley (1974). From a public choice perspective, however, it raises an interesting question: if individuals could contract, why is there a need for government or for state? The answer to this question in the writings of Hobbes is to avoid anarchy, that is, the Leviathan represents discipline in order to achieve a common purpose. Hobbes assumed that human beings were sufficiently rational to recognise their own interests. For example in order to avoid anarchy they formed a state. The public choice theorist as in Buchanan's interpretation of constitutional rules, could argue that individuals would not vote for a decision that bestowed no individual benefits. The social choice paradox, however, suggests that each individual would obey the social choice rule (no insincere voting) and trust that the outcome from the social choice is beneficial.

However such obedience and trust exist only because they are (implicitly) assumed; however one can only assume them as long as the social choice outcome coincides with individual egoistic outcome. Rationality as introduced by Hobbes set up a Leviathan; public choice ought to argue that rational man would see that the social choice outcome would not be individually beneficial. The social choice mechanism may not be the only method of allocating resources or making decisions. Voters interpret voting as a game of strategy, and game theorists extend their concern beyond the normative search for voting criteria and into the prediction (equilibrium) of individual and group strategic choices in committee decision making with many interdependent voters. The attitudes of many individuals have been analysed as egoistic. As Downs (1957) commented 'rationality thus defined refers to the process of action, not to their ends or even to their success at reaching desired ends' (p. 6). The argument is advanced in the later chapters of his work 'men are not always selfish ... frequently do what appears to be individually irrational because they believe it is socially rational' (p. 27).

This would recast the paradox of voting into a search as to whether or not there was popular support for the initial set of Arrovian conditions. If the rational individuals in society do not accept the Arrovian conditions the foundations on which the paradox of voting stands could crumble. Furthermore, one could deduce that vote trading and insincere voting were rational responses in a competitive self-interested voting world. Therein lies a challenge for public choice scholars.

We shall argue later in Chapter 8 that voluntary non-voting is rational. Such behaviour, insincere voting in committees and voluntary non-voting amongst the electorate, has meaning for voters because they are in effect participating in the political process. Voting is so central to democracies that the business of voting - insincere voting, voluntary non-voting, lobbying, elections - only makes sense because it relates to effective participation in an ordered (democratic) political market. Chapters 2 and 3 review the primary problem of social choice which is to understand the logical relationship between individual (voting) action and collective choices. There is a burgeoning literature of research focused on the relaxations and extensions to Arrow's original conditions. Chapter 2, in particular, reviews voting rules and examines the impossibility theorem. The chapter looks specifically at the calculation of Condorcet probabilities in small committees.

In modern economics the total amount and the composition of public expenditure is determined by a variety of public choice mechanisms, in particular government discretion, growth in bureaucracy, voting and pressure-group activities. In Chapter 4, however, we argue that a considerable part of the growth in government expenditure in the OECD countries might be explained by demographic and social factors. The role of bureaucracies is examined in Chapter 5 wherein the Niskanen model is juxtapositioned with the Dunleavey bureau-shaping model. The chapter explores the principal-agent relationship between government and its expenditure proposals and the bureaucracy intent on redistributing public output to targeted interest groups.

Chapter 6 relies heavily on an essentially static framework in order to re-evaluate the welfare losses brought about by rent-seeking. The firm in the classical textbook model of monopoly pricing is a nexus of contracts with the possibility of quasi-rents. It is argued that rent-seeking overlaps with X-inefficiency. The author accepts that a more appropriate framework for studying directly unproductive profit-seeking (DUP) activities is a dynamic framework wherein rent-seeking is in the nature of investment in rent-creating projects. However, the chapter focuses on a property rights perspective to rent-seeking and on the compensated nature of transfers. The addition of a monopoly's profit to the social cost of monopoly depends on the nature of the firm, that is, on the assignment of property rights within the firm and on the sources of the monopoly. The latter point is by no means a novel insight. Demsetz (1988), for example, pointed out that in cases where the monopoly is the result of buying out rivals 'the only real resource cost of rent-seeking behaviour is the cost of negotiating the exchange of ownership' (p. 110).

Chapter 7 introduces an approach which deals with the characteristics of public goods, the theory of clubs, pioneered by Buchanan (1965) and Olson (1965). Club theory accounts for the many 'voluntary groups deriving mutual benefit' (Sandler and Tschirhart, 1980, p. 1482), which serve the explicit purpose of influencing government and political institutions. The most visible arrangements are trade and industry associations; in Chapter 8 we introduce a G-group of individuals as a club, arguing that a modern democracy may be interpreted as a coalition of G-groups which seeks a rational negotiation of property rights.

A variety of institutional conditions influence the nature of the political process, the opportunity costs of voters the relative abundance of political officers, the fiscal capacity of the economy, specific interest groups with privileged access to government and government decision-making. In our final Chapter 8, we evaluate the concept of democracy against the background of public choice inefficiencies associated with the democratic political markets - misrepresentation of voter preferences, anarchy and the ascendancy of G-groups - where the performance of the political system has been supplanted by political innovations in the business of voting.

2. Social Choice and Voting

Any discussion on voting can be rather misleading as to what to expect on content. This chapter does not provide an exhaustive survey of the mathematical theory of voting, but rather peruses through the subject matter identifying areas of direct interest to public choice scholars. The term voting is widely used across the public choice literature, referring as it does to the rather complicated and intricate nature of voting. Scholars realise that voting is a mosaic, made up of different voting procedures applied in many different circumstances from small committees to large elections. However, apart from the ubiquitous voting cycles, there is a common denominator, the idea that voting is both representative and fair and an important requisite in a political system. Even so, we run into problems about the fairness of the outcome and since the work of many scholars have established sets of different criteria, including Arrow's original conditions, the daunting task is to find a unique rule that satisfies all criteria. No such rule exists (Miller, 1988, p. 827).

Quite frankly, there are many voting procedures, there are many variants of the same criteria and there are different criteria. This very well may be the essence of the theory of voting. But what does voting mean in a democracy? The answer to this simple question has generated a debate which subdivides methodologically into (a) the Madison inspired liberal interpretation of voting and (b) the more populist interpretation of voting *a la* Rousseau. Riker (1982) in an overview of both approaches suggests that in the liberal view the function of voting is simply to control officials while the populist view believes, rather naively we might add, that by popular participation 'democratic governments embody the will of the people and cannot therefore oppress' (p. 9).

The theme of this chapter revolves around the voting paradox and the attendant impossibility theorems. The impossibility result simply states that if each citizen has a transitive ordering of preferences the outcome of a simple majority voting procedure will not be transitive. One intuitive meaning of transitivity is that individuals generally prefer more to less. While this is easily understood in the context of rational consumers buying commodities, for voters it is conceptually more difficult to understand. In the interim, imagine that Downs' expected utility income is embodied in the vote on each alternative; transitivity ensures that the highest utility generating alternative is ranked first by the voter. Although regarded as one of the more difficult areas of the public choice literature one could argue whether or not a discussion on the impossibility theorems is appropriate in a public choice text. We believe it is.

However, a proper understanding of the origins of what has become social choice theory and the important overlap with the theory of voting, prepares one for the inclusion of elements of social choice into a public choice discussion. Both approaches to the theory of voting do share some common ground. The reconcilability of a social choice insistence on transitive social preferences and the public choice insistence on the irrelevance of a voting paradox is important for a complete understanding of the complicated nature of voting. The Arrow impossibility theorem had an important impact on liberal democratic political thought. Quite simply, it ruled out populism, which is best illustrated in a political system by a referendum which reflects the Roussean will of the people. The stark conclusion of the impossibility of a collective outcome attacked the very fundamentals of the political process, a process with which public choice theorists were becoming increasingly identified.

THE THEORY OF VOTING

The bewildering scope of the subject matter of voting is amply illustrated by the many books and monographs, listed in our bibliography, which have appeared during the past years. The principle of democracy is founded on voting procedures; Riker (1982) comments that 'voting which is the main subject in the theory of social choice, is at the heart of both the method and the ideal of democracy' (p. 8). Arrow's theorem was a direct challenge to the theory of democracy, and the controversy which it unfolded deserves a central place in a chapter on voting. Riker (1982) envelopes voting with the conceptual and ideological meaning of democracy, proffering voting as a method *a la* Downs by which citizens can 'seek self respect and self control' (p. 8). In other words, voting and the process of voting is central to democracy; he comments that 'the democratic method is the process of participation, specifically through voting, in the management of society, where voting is understood to include all the ancillary institutions (like parties and pressure groups) and social principles (like freedom and equality) that are necessary to render it significant' (p. 8).

The voting process, by which a democratic society composed of individuals with different preferences decide upon a course of action, has been analysed since the earliest writings of Borda in 1781 and Condorcet in 1785. Condorcet in writing his essay arguing that, if one candidate can beat the remaining candidates by majority rule, then the candidate should be elected, unwittingly pioneered the theory of voting. More than a century and a half later, Arrow (1951) crystallised the theme of the Condorcet essay into the voting paradox, which highlighted the absence of a rule or method of aggregating individual preferences. In a similar tradition, Downs (1957 pp. 36-40), in defining his logical structure of voting comments that 'if (the citizen's expected party differential) is positive, he votes for the incumbents; if it is negative, he votes for the opposition; if it is zero, he abstains'. Downs' rational voter computes the expected utility income before and after an election, the difference in the expected incomes is the expected party differential. However, the Downsian voting procedure becomes more complicated as the rational voter realises that no one party will be able to do everything 'hence he cannot merely compare platforms: instead he must estimate in his own mind what the parties would actually do were they in power'.

Political scientists were aware of the voting paradox and of the contributions from Borda, Condorcet and Dodgson, but it was not until Arrow's (1951, 1963) formulation of the paradox, that disturbing questions about voting were raised. As this chapter evolves, we shall explore some of the mathematical properties underpinning the impossibility result and examine the relaxations and extensions of the original Arrow theorem. Many of the relaxations and extensions which are examined substantiate Arrow's original position regarding the intransitivity of social preference. A public choice perspective is developed which principally attacks the methodological foundation of the paradox, that is, the concept of social preference. Historically the early writings of both Black (1948) and May (1952), both contemporaries of Arrow during his initial writings, had an important contribution to make to the debate and to preparing the ground work for an eventual public choice perspective.

In a different context, Farquharson (1969, p. 9), who pioneered the idea of sophisticated voting, defines a voting procedure as 'the process whereby an outcome is selected as the result of the voting'. In his characterisation of voting, we identify at least two important aspects *vis-a-vis* (i) that voting stops once an outcome has been selected and (ii) that 'votes are directly in accordance with their (voter's) preference scales ... call the "top" outcome of a subset that outcome highest on a voter's scale. A voter votes sincerely, then, if he chooses the subset with the highest-ranked top' (p. 19). His monograph introduced the concept of a sophisticated voter who 'makes the best use of his vote, to attempt to predict the contingency likely to rise: that is to say, how the others are likely to vote' (p. 38). Dodgson (1870), in many of his pamphlets on voting, referred to a tendency of voters to adopt 'a principle of voting which makes an election more a game of skill than a real test of the wishes of the electors' (p. 10). The game of skill is also played in committees where individual committee members adopt a rule or strategy on how to vote. The difficulties confronting committee members who play this game of skill is looked at in our discussion on strategy sets.

The theory of voting occupies a central place in the public choice literature. In the last forty years or so since the publication of the seminal work of Arrow (1951), economists, political scientists and mathematicians have explored every analytical angle on the theory of voting. This impressive body of literature that is now the mathematical theory of voting, is sub-divided into two different groups, namely the social choice theory group which attempts to rescue the voting paradox and the public choice group which has no truck with the fundamental concept of social preference. It is helpful to distinguish between a group of public choice scholars who attack the assumptions underpinning the Arrovian result and a second group of public choice scholars who object in principle to the methodology that leads to the impossibility conclusion. The latter group takes the lead from the early writings of Buchanan (1954) on the relevance to society of the voting paradox. The essence of what has become known as social choice theory endorses the point that individual preferences cannot easily translate into a social preference. Social choice theory raises questions about voting that are as unresolved as the many issues raised by the liberalism-populism dichotomy. Social choice theory reinforces the voting paradox which simply states that the social outcome of voting procedure is not transitive. As Riker so eloquently put it 'what makes all this so democratically unpalatable is that, apparently, the only way to make "society" choose coherently is to impose a dictator' (p. 18).

The Voting Paradox

The voting paradox, also referred to as the Condorcet paradox, is best illustrated in the following example of three individuals A, B and C, ranking their preferences across the alternatives x, y and z. Throughout this Chapter we shall restrict our examples to a 3 X 3 scenario with 3 alternatives or candidates and 3 voters. Each column in the subsequent tables may be read as a preference profile with each individual preference ordering ranked from top (most preferred) to bottom (least preferred) in the table. Hence, for individual B we can write the preference ordering as yPzPx, where P represents the preference operator in Chapter 1.

Using individual A as a representative voter, we can establish transitivity across individual preferences with xPy and yPz which yields xPz. Likewise for individuals B and C with yPx and zPy respectively. In other words, a majority outcome in favour of x, xPy (by A and C) and of y, yPz (by A and B) yields the social preference x, xPz. However, with the majority outcome z, zPx (by B and C), a cycle in x is generated with xPz and zPx. The theoretical implication of this cycle is that neither x nor y nor z emerge as the social preference as no alternative can defeat the remaining two alternatives in a straight pairwise majority vote. The public policy implication is rather more ominous. While collective decisions are taken on policy alternatives, the methodological issue for public choice scholars is to defend and untangle the eventual decision from a web of compromise and deals.

Table 2.1 Preference profile: Condorcet paradox

A	B	C
x	y	z
y	z	x
z	x	y

It is quite clear from the preferences in Table 2.1 that, although the individual preferences accord with individual voter transitivity there is no transitive *social* preference. What we require is an alternative which can defeat all other alternatives by simple majority rule in a pairwise vote. This is the original Condorcet condition, now referred to as the Condorcet criterion. It is a rather strong assumption given the many combinations across individual preference orderings. The completeness property ensures that all combinations are considered; even with a complete weak preference ordering (xPyIz => xPz), across individuals a transitive social preference may not materialise.

Theorem 2.1: There is no collective choice rule satisfying the simple majority criterion which can generate a transitive social choice. In other words, unless a strong majority rule exists, social preferences are cyclical.

This is the essence of the paradox of voting which will be presented later and rather more formally as the Arrow general possibility theorem. Before embarking on that adventure let us now continue with a public policy dimension to the voting paradox. We have three policy makers A, B and C considering expenditure changes across the housing, health and education budgets. The policy areas on which the budget cutbacks fall are represented by three alternatives x (housing), y (health) and z (education). The expenditure committee is allowed to decide by majority rule. In the real political world of the Commons Select Committees in the UK or House Committees in the US more complicated voting rules are adhered to in decision making. The different procedural rules refiect the omnipresence of the voting paradox. If the individual preferences are ranked as in Table 2.1, no decision will be taken. Policy maker A ranks (xyz), indicating that the changes should impact first on the housing budget, then on the health and the education budgets in that order. Both B and C have a rank which together with A's preference, generates a cycle.

Table 2.2 considers an order of preferences which with the exception of the first column, is a repetition of the preference order in Table 2.1. However the significance of the change in the A's preference order is in securing a consensus, that is, a majority outcome. The majority outcome is in favour of budget changes in education. This public policy decision was the result of a decision rule which embodied a misrepresentation of the preferences of one individual. Ironically, if you look at the pairwise votes in Table 2.2, there is no cycle. While the Arrovian impossibility of a transitive social preference is subject to a set of criteria which any democratic society would find acceptable, what may have been overlooked is a criterion of simply making a decision.

Table 2.2: Preference profile: Majority outcome

A	B	C
x	y	z
z	z	x
y	x	y

A majority decision is made in this situation. For example, both B and C rank zPx, both A and C rank xPy, and by transitivity zPxPy => zPy which is the preferred ranking of the A and C majority. The policy makers collectively decided to change budget expenditure on education. The arrival at a majority decision was possible by the change in the vote of policy maker A. We must remember that the preference order of policy maker A remains the same in both preference profiles. In Table 2.2 policy maker A ranked changes in the health budget higher than changes in the education budget. In so doing, policy maker A is said to have vote traded with either B or C (C being the more likely candidate) in return for a similar gesture in the next round of voting. This is the very essence of pork-barrel politics as epitomised by voting decisions in the US Congress.

Buchanan and Tullock (1962) referred to this 'log-rolling' procedure in the US Congress as an example of vote trading, which apparently offers a solution to the paradox of voting. Although vote trading has been criticised, it still remains in the real world that vote trading enables a collective decision to be made. It is an illustration of strategic voting. However, Arrow has criticised log-rolling and Ng (1979) has concluded that log-rolling violates the independence property addressed by Arrow. This property allows the choice from a specific set of alternatives to depend on how the alternatives are ranked in that preference profile independent of other preference profiles. The rather strong independence property states that if we were to add a fourth alternative, w, to the alternatives in either Tables 2.1 or 2.2, that the preference ranking across the triple (xyz) will not change by the presence of w. Hence for policy maker B, yPzPx could read as yPwPzPx or yPzPwPx. Vote trading or log-rolling is very much within the domain of public choice theory. But does it proffer an escape route from the voting paradox? The answer is in the affirmative, in so far as any cardinal representation of voting allows an escape from majority cycles. We shall address this issue in our discussion of the Borda method in Chapter 3.

Vote trading is a re-ordering of the preference rank not of the preference. In other words policy maker A prefers budget changes on health to budget changes on education. This is the sincere preference. Vote trading, like single-peaked preferences discussed in the next chapter, does offer an escape from the voting paradox, but not without violating the Arrovian conditions. Buchanan and Tullock (1962) demonstrated that majority rule was efficient under vote trading. One consequence of vote trading where policy decisions are decided sequentially rather than on an either/or basis, is a much larger public budget outlay than without vote trading. Vote trading is a form of strategic misrepresentation of preferences and if the misrepresentation was a reaction to external influences on the policy maker such as intensive lobbying by interest groups, one would have to question the optimality of the majority outcome. From a public policy perspective, the optimality of the outcome must be weighted against a social cost composed of private rent-seeking resources and the opportunity cost of the public resources denied to education in our example.

In a very real sense there is an opportunity cost to the citizen for each alternative. Alternative z may have been the preferred citizens' choice but alternative x was the compromise alternative agreed by majority vote by the representatives of the citizens. The gain, denoted by G and computed (say) in terms of party stability, hung parliaments or loyalty to the ruler, to the political system in returning x must be weighted against the high opportunity cost of x, denoted by C, from the citizens' perspective. The lesson of the 1798 French Revolution is that representatives, no matter how dictatorial, cannot afford to disregard what we label the *Bastille constraint*, $C(x) \geq G(x)$. In other words, no compromise on voting rules to secure a majority outcome should be tolerated in a democratic system. The fact that the Bastille constraint has been relaxed in modern democracies, reflects more on the citizens than on the political system *per se*.

Does vote trading secure a Condorcet outcome? In reply we need to focus attention briefly on sincere voting. Schwartz (1977) developed the concept of separable preferences which contributed to the success of sincere voting in arriving at a Condorcet outcome. Individual preferences are separable if the preference on one issue is independent of the preference on another issue. It is regarded as a strong assumption and somewhat unrealistic in the real world of legislative committee decision making where vote trading and sophisticated voting are common.

Theorem 2.2: If individual voter preferences are separable and if a Condorcet winner exists, sincere voting yields that winner. This would imply that vote trading will exist only if a Condorcet winner does not exist.

The implication of the Schwartz theorem on vote trading has been summarised by Ordershook (1986) who offered a more robust interpretation of Theorem 2.1, when he commented that 'if all voters possess preference information about each others preferences, if there are no impediments to trading, then vote trading is pointless'(p. 85). However, in the public policy arena where recurrent decisions are made on funding allocations and where allocative decisions, by their very nature, are interdependent, voters would be unlikely to self impose a constraint of separating their preferences.

Voting is Easy

Before we proceed to discuss the Arrovian perspective on the voting paradox, we would like to advance one basic acceptable criteria for a voting result. In a democratic society voting is easy, although making democracy work is hard because of the fair requirements attached to voting rules. In particular a majority criterion which states that if a majority of voters have an alternative x as their first choice, a voting rule should choose x, would be deemed acceptable and fair. In our opening example in Table 2.1, assume that A represents a group of 5 voters, B a group of 4 and C a group of 2 voters in an 11 member committee, then the housing alternative x would be the majority outcome by a simple number of voters (NVR) rule. It satisfies both a majority rule and a fairness criterion. A variant of this rule, we contend, has entered the voting literature in two rather interesting ways. Firstly through the historical development by Condorcet of his strong majority criterion, the Condorcet criterion, which requires an alternative to defeat all others in a pairwise campaign by simple majority rule. This was alluded to earlier in Theorem 2.1. And secondly through the weak majority preference (WMP) criterion of Ng (1979) which requires that 'if I, the number of individuals is even, at least I/2 individuals prefer x to y, if I is odd at least (I-1)/2 individuals prefer x to y' (p. 129). The Condorcet (winner) criterion generates the Condorcet paradox as outlined earlier and the main objection to a WMP criterion is the resulting Bethamite social welfare function, which may 'lead to a very unequal distribution of income' (p. 131).

The implications of weak majority preference are spelled out in Ng (1975) and Ng (1979). The criterion in many respects evokes the tyranny of the majority debate outlined in Riker (1982). This translates into a concern for the welfare of the minority, the 49 percent who preferred y to x. In our example in Table 2.2, policy maker A by voting insincerely resolved the paradox. An equivalent outcome would be possible if a number of voters rule was adopted. The choice is simply between a number of voters rule outcome and an outcome arrived at by strategic manipulation of the votes. There is a subtle difference: strategic manipulation invests decisive power in an elite group while the social outcome based on NVR is more unanimous. But it is not as simple and straight-forward as this surely; if it were there would have been no need to develop an entire literature on voting rules and a companion set of acceptable properties that they must satisfy.

THE IMPOSSIBILITY THEOREM

The social choice literature has attached itself to an esoteric analysis of acceptable properties grouped together as the Arrovian conditions for a collective choice rule. Arrow's celebrated theorem shows that certain value judgements which society find fair to incorporate into a voting rule are logically inconsistent. Let us abstract here: there are two issues which are important in any search for acceptable criteria, (i) that in any choice situation there is the problem of the independence of the final choice from the path in which comparisons are made and, (ii) that if an alternative is rejected in a pairwise comparison should it be excluded or included in a larger comparison? A third issue which will be discussed later, is the requirement that social choice rules satisfy Pareto optimality. The requirement is a compelling one as long as the analytical framework of social choice theory is based on individual preferences. Otherwise as with the numbers of voters rule, a fair outcome can be achieved. The economics literature in general, with notable exceptions in Sugden (1981) and Sen (1987), has been reticent to acknowledge alternatives to the Paretian ethic.

Our first point of departure looks at the cornerstone of Arrow's (1951, 1963) theorem, the transitivity condition, about which he states quite clearly that 'the importance of the transitivity condition ... (involves) ... the independence of the final choice from the path to it' (p. 120). It has been recognised by scholars that Arrow had compared this to the integrability problem in consumer theory. In this context there is one important observation to note (which in many ways has been at the root of public choice attacks on social choice theory), and it is this: can we impose conditions of choice behaviour devised for individuals on society? Buchanan (1956) and others say no. While disputing the property of transitivity, public choice scholars would wish to retain the independence property or some variant thereof. For example, in a jury rule, which is the quintessential fair rule, independence would require the same verdict whether a jury composed of 7 men and 5 women, was divided or not into separate sets (7 men and 5 women) and subsets (4 men and 3 women; and 3 men and 2 women).

But a jury rule, with which Condorcet was originally concerned, is also neutral which means that it does not favour either alternative, consequently it does allow for the possibility of a tie. This is not very satisfactory when a decision has to be taken. Both the Condorcet winner and the Borda winner satisfy neutrality in guaranteeing that no alternative has an advantage. However as Riker (1982) noted, neutrality 'is inappropriate, when either decisiveness or delay is desired' (p. 58). Neutrality is a technical base for equality in voting rules when applied to either candidates or alternatives in a binary context. Otherwise, path independence may be appropriate as a base for equality. May

(1952) had shown that a collective choice rule which satisfied independence, strict monotonicity, anonymity and neutrality is a rule that chooses alternatives on the basis of majority decision.

Our second point refers to the exclusion of an alternative if defeated in a pairwise vote. Within the social choice literature the original Chernoff (1954) condition requires that all alternatives defeated in a pairwise vote are to be excluded in a larger comparison. However weak path independence provides inclusion of some alternatives in the overall choice set. Plott (1973) defined his property of path independence as a combination of both weak path independence and the original Chernoff condition. According to Bandyopadhyay (1986), 'the impossibility results with the Chernoff condition (has) led the social choice theorists to conclude that any consistency conditions related to the Chernoff property is the main culprit for paradoxes in social choice' (p. 110). So why proceed with a property that perpetuates the voting paradox? Specifically because it guarantees a Pareto optimal outcome, ensuring that society is not faced with an alternative which had earlier been rejected unanimously. Ferejohn and Grether (1977) showed that the original Chernoff condition contributes to an oligarchy.

Theorem 2.3: With three alternatives and a finite number of voters, the Chernoff conditions, together with weak path independence and the Arrow conditions generate an oligarchy.

In the absence of the Chernoff condition, society may end up with a Pareto suboptimal outcome. The oligarchic outcome identified in Theorem 2.3 is equivalent to our number of voters rule outcome; it differs significantly in that power is concentrated in the Ferejohn and Grether oligarchy.

Arrow's Theorem

A key point in the understanding of Arrow's impossibility theorem is a review of the set of assumptions that underpin the impossibility result. The conditions pertaining to the original theorem are very much a part of securing a paradoxical result. Relaxation of many of the conditions has enabled the social choice literature to expand. First we have the *ordering conditions* of reflexivity, completeness and transitivity (C,T). The social preference generated by the collective choice rule must be complete and transitive. For every pair set of alternatives (xy), either xRy or yRx and for every triple (xyz), there must be an ordering (say) xRy, yRx and xRz. The social ordering completely orders all alternatives. The transitivity assumption ensures that if xRy and yRz, that xRz.

An ordering of the preferences with a real valued representation of the preferences yields the social welfare function $W(x)$ which we can write as $W(x) = f(U_1[x_1], \dots U_N[x_N])$. The social ordering R, depends on individual orderings of the social state x, such that $R = f(R_1 \dots R_N)$, where f is the social welfare function (SWF) referred to by Arrow and R translates into the Bergson-Samuelson social welfare function. In other words, when all three properties hold for the binary operator R, the function f is a social welfare function which is a special case of a collective choice rule (CCR). In addition to the ordering conditions, there are the related properties of quasi-transitivity, defined as (xPy & yPz) => xPz and P-transitivity defined as (xPy <=> [xRy & ~ yRx]). With these additional properties we can define a quasi-transitivity social decision function (QT SDF) which requires R to be reflexive, complete and quasi-transitive. As illustrated in Figure 2.1 each of the collective functions are subsets of each other.

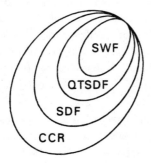

Figure 2.1 Representing preferences

The one-step interpretation of the underlying assumptions in Arrow's theorem reads as follows: universal domain (U) which means that the social choice procedure can cope with any permutation of the preferences, Pareto condition (P) which means that if for all individuals who prefer xPy then the social choice is x and the social choice rule should return x. The independence condition (I) states that the social ranking of any pair depends only on the individual ranking of that pair while the non-dictatorship (ND) property states that there is no individual or group whose preference becomes society's preference. The Arrow theorem therefore states that there is no collective choice rule that satisfies all the four properties outlined. The theorem established the impossibility of translating individual ordered preferences into a transitive and complete social ordering.

The voting paradox has a celebrated history from the early writings of Borda and Condorcet to the general possibility result attributed to Arrow (1951) in his original manuscript. Historically the theory of social choice arose out of the paradox of voting. The rule adopted for translating individual preferences into social preferences was majority rule. It was the basis for the evolving theory of democracy and political representation. Any rule or method, including simple majority rule, is now referred to as a collective choice rule. One can think of voting rules as examples of collective choice rules which enable us to arrive at a social preference. The eventual social outcome is referred to as the winner, scaled into Condorcet winners, Borda winners and plurality winners. Our basic task at this juncture is to argue that there is no rule or method for translating individual preferences into a transitive social preference.

The next property is *unrestricted domain* (UD). Often referred to as universality, it assumes that the collective choice rule should sort all individual preferences no matter what they are; hence all possible individual preferences profiles must be ranked by the rule. For one individual and 2 alternatives there are two profiles xRy and yRx; but as we generalise to one individual and 3 alternatives (xyz), then there are 6 profiles, and for two individuals and 3 alternatives, there are a possible 36 profiles. It is a significant assumption. The third requirement is the ubiquitous *Pareto criterion* (P). A collective choice rule must obey the Pareto criterion, in that if both individuals prefer y to x, then the collective rule should rank y over x. If two individuals prefer y to x and somebody is indifferent as between x and y, then the rule should return x likewise. In the tradition of normative welfare economics this is taken by many, but not all economists, as a fundamental requirement of any rule or method.

The property of *non-dictatorship* (ND) is appealing and remains a fundamental property of any voting rule. Its avoidance is regarded as a fundamental test of any collective choice rule. Finally we have the *independence condition* (I). Properly entitled the independence of irrelevant alternatives, this is perceived as an important criterion for a collective choice rule. If individuals alter their preferences over the alternatives x and y, but do not change their preferences over the set a and b then the collective choice rule should rank a and b in accordance with individual preferences, independent of the preference over the (irrelevant) x y alternatives. It excludes the possibility that the binary ranking of (say) xPy, could change if a third alternative was present (say) z, so that xPzPy. By transitivity this yields xPy whereas in the binary preference xPz. The Arrow theorem may be stated as follows (Sen, 1986).

Theorem 2.4: Consider the general form of the collective choice rule: $R = f(R_1, \dots R_N)$; we assume at least 3 distinct social states, $X \geq 3$, and that the set of individuals H is finite. For f to be a quasi-transitive social decision function we require that R be quasi-transitive, reflexive and complete. There is no social welfare function satisfying the properties of universal domain, Pareto principle, non-dictatorship and independence when the choice function for society is based on $R = f(R_1, \dots R_N)$.

Relaxations and Extensions

A complete statement of the Arrow theorem, from a public choice perspective, states quite eloquently that there is no collective choice rule, satisfying the properties of transitivity and completeness across preferences, unrestricted domain, the Pareto criterion, non-dictatorship and the independence of irrelevant alternatives, that translates individual preferences into social preferences. There is however the possibility of a dictatorial collective choice rule. The theorem excludes majority rule as a voting rule, even though it apparently abides by all the acceptable properties. As a voting rule it initiates the voting cycle. This was a blow to the liberal democracies who pioneered the use of this rule across committees, and argued for its fairness characteristics. As would be expected the reaction to the Arrovian possibility theorem became intense. Some scholars criticised the relevance of the theorem to social welfare decisions, other scholars concluded that the paradox was irrelevant to the real world where majority and collective decisions are a regular occurrence. Vote trading is a case in point. However there is a genuine concern over the voting paradox; if it can be shown to exist under rigorous assumptions, the question must be asked as to how collective decisions are arrived at in the real world? The reply that agenda manipulation, vote trading, log-rolling and the complicated procedures and rules of committee decision making contain the answers has created a burgeoning literature to which public choice scholars contribute. Riker (1982) and Ordeshook (1986) offer an excellent treatment of the complicated issues.

At this stage we would like to review some of the relaxations and extensions of the original assumptions that have entered the social choice literature and are of direct relevance to public choice scholars. The reader is referred specifically to Sen (1986) and the references therein for a comprehensive and lucid account of the developments of social choice theory since the inception of Arrow's proof. We shall content ourselves with a discussion of points of interest to the theme of the chapter, namely, the voting paradox and the possible resolution of the paradox. The public choice scholar is more content to unlock the paradox and consider the implications of the proverbial key whereas the social choice theorist considers the endemic nature of the paradox. In this respect social choice theory analyses the very nature of the cycling problem which is ubiquitous not only in public choice but also in political science. On the other hand, the median-voter theorem and strategic voting procedures have offered the public choice scholars a welcomed reprieve from the paradox.

The first set of conditions to which scholars turned their attention were the properties of completeness and transitivity. Arrow had argued for a concept called R-transitivity, using the R (as least as good as) operator, xRy and yRz => xRz. This is a definition of (strong) transitivity as the R-operator includes both strict preference (P) and indifference (I) as outlined in Chapter 1. In other words xRy is expressed as either xPy or xIy. However the relation xRy will rank x over y, since xRy => xPy. Sen (1986) has suggested a weaker preference operator, the P-operator defined as xPy; with transitivity xPy and yPz => xPz. This is referred to as P-transitivity or quasi-transitivity. Using quasi-transitivity and the remainder of the Arrovian assumptions, Sen demonstrated that a social order based on P-transitivity can exist. The rule, however, is government by consensus.

Gibbard (1973) proved a variant of Arrow's impossibility theorem; he showed that with quasi-transitivity across preferences and the Arrovian assumptions, an oligarchy rather than a dictatorship arises. Within the logic of the preference orderings transitivity implies P-transitivity but not vice versa, and P-transitivity implies acyclicity. If transitivity is dropped altogether from the set of required properties agenda manipulation and vote trading ensure an outcome. Consider the preference profile in Table 2.3:

Table 2.3: Preference profile and cyclicity

A	B	C
x	x	y
w	z	x
y	w	z
z	y	w

There are two points of interest in this particular profile, namely (i) there is a cycle across the triple (yzw) as follows: wPy by A and B, yPz by A and C, which yields wPz, but zPw by B and C, which creates the cycle wPz & zPw; (ii) alternative x defeats all other alternatives in the profile, that is, xPy, xPz and xPw. The social preference is x without reference to transitivity across the pairs (xy), (xz) and (xw). The collective rule which generates x is referred to as a social decision rule which is less restrictive than a social choice rule. The social choice outcome cannot be predicted form the preference profile because of the cycle. When transitivity is weakened to acyclicity, which is defined as xPy and yPz => ~ zPx, Brown (1975) using the Arrovian assumptions proved the existence of a collegial polity. The collegium acting alone were unable to form a social preference over any pair.

Theorem 2.5: A quasi-transitive social decision function with universal domain, Pareto principle and independence will yield an oligarchy rather than a dictatorship. In other words, there exists a decisive group G such that xP_iy for each ith member of the group => xPy and xP_iy for some members of the group => xRy.

The latter condition in Theorem 2.5, which relates directly to some members of the group, allows us to define an almost decisive group as ($[xP_GY \& YP_{H\text{-}G}x]$ => xPY), which is a particularly strong strategy position in a committee of size H. A group G can be almost decisive over a pair and then decisive over the complete set of alternatives. The completeness assumption has been considered in the context of its relevance and requirement along side the Pareto criterion. In other words, if the Pareto criterion cannot rank the alternatives x and y, why should a government or committee attempt to do so. In order to demonstrate decisiveness one must assume the Pareto principle, since the Pareto principle implies that if one group is decisive then so is one individual. This means that if a group of 13 is decisive, then there exists a group of 12, a group of 11 and eventually one individual, all of whom are decisive. This is referred to as the group contraction lemma.

Theorem 2.5 indicates how members of an oligarchy acting in unison can translate the group preference into the social preference. Feldman (1980 p. 192) comments that 'acting apart, each member of the oligarchy has veto power over a y he regards inferior to x'. Completeness ensures a ranking across all available alternatives and a weak ordering, xPyIz ensures xPz. If x and y represent two states of the economy, the fundamental welfare theorems suggest that the market mechanism will decide between x and y. The alarming outcome from Gibbard is that a group of individuals may decide upon x. An earlier version of the oligarchy outcome was delivered by Mas-Colell and Sonnenschein (1972) with the additional properties of strong monotonicity and a special case of Arrow's independence property restricted to pairs of alternatives. Their social decision function, in Theorem 2.6, is not quasi-transitive, which should, alas, imply an acyclical decision function.

Theorem 2.6: With alternatives $X \geq 3$ and number of individuals $H \geq 3$ and H finite, a social decision function satisfying universality, Pareto principle, independence and strong monotonicity, is oligarthic.

Theorems 5 and 6 imply that both preferences and voting procedures are manipulable, which does not augur well for the voting process. Universality, or unrestricted domain, like freedom of choice or expression, is a property that ideally should describe any collective choice rule. However if everybody has a freedom of expression over an issue, one can easily see how a cycle in the preferences could likely occur. Each individual's preference ordering on an alternative may be diametrically opposite. For example, in the preference profile illustrated in Table 2.1 earlier voter A had the ordering xPyPz, which is diametric to individual C's ordering zPxPy. If the range of preference orderings can be limited there may be a way around the property of universality. Single-peaked preferences, for example, ensure a majority outcome, but single-peaked preferences (see the discussion in Chapter 3) if they existed, are precluded by the universality assumption.

We are left with the pivotal properties of the Pareto criterion and the independence of irrelevant alternatives. Very few public choice scholars have attacked the Paretian ethic, and unless we as scholars introduce alternative normative criteria, there does not seem to exist a ready alternative to the Pareto criterion. Not every rule abides by the independence assumption; for example, the Borda rule violates the independence assumption. The impossibility result can be further relaxed if some of the underpinning assumptions are relaxed. For some, in the case of relaxing transitivity, the result produces a curate's egg, neither firm nor soft evidence for either quasi-transitivity or acyclicity. Mueller (1989) comments that 'one considers the restrictions which must be placed on the patterns of individual preference orderings to ensure that either quasi-transitivity or acyclicity holds' (p. 141). But in reality, and especially in small committees, the cyclical preferences created by transitivity can be overcome although rather arbitrarily (say) by drawing lots.

Domain restrictions do offer a possible escape route from the Arrow paradox. Arrow himself suggested that Black's concept of single-peaked preferences was a possible contender. If the individual preferences are single-peaked and the number of voters is odd, majority rule yields a transitive social preference. Consider the following example on public expenditure cutbacks, with alternatives x, y and z in descending order representing less severe cutbacks. The right wing will rank xPyPz and the left wing will rank zPyPx, and a centrist would rank yPzPx, which generates the social preference: yPz & zPx => yPx. However by ranking the alternatives as zPxPy, the centrist exhibits what is referred to as double-peaked preferences at alternatives z and x. Glance forward to the illustrations in Chapter 3 on peaked preferences.

There is an interesting dimension to this, in particular if we consider policy maker's preference profiles with respect to public expenditure. There is always a worst alternative in everybody's complete set of alternatives. In the case of public expenditure cutbacks policy makers may have a worst alternative in (say) harsh cutbacks in child support. In the social choice literature, that worst value of the alternative is restricted from the individual's preference ordering. Value restriction requires that for any triple (xyz), there is at least one alternative (say) x, and at least one value (worst, best, medium) 'such that in no one's preference ordering does that alternative have that value' (Sen 1986, p. 1138). By introducing a set of concerned voters, who are not indifferent across the triple (xyz), Sen concludes that if individual preferences are value restricted, and the number of concerned voters is odd, then majority rule is a social welfare function, yielding transitive orderings.

In the social choice literature the condition of neutrality is often relaxed thus permitting the use of non-utility information. The property of neutrality refers to the voting rule *per se* ensuring that the rule-based outcome remains unchanged. If pairs of two alternatives get permutated so that x becomes a while y becomes b, the rule-based outcome remains unchanged, that is, (if for all individuals $xR_iy <=> aR_ib => xRy <=> aRb$). The condition will reappear in our later discussion in Chapter 3 of the contribution of May to the voting paradox. The importance of the neutrality assumption is highlighted in the following theorem due to Blau and Deb (1977).

Theorem 2.7: With number of alternatives X ≥ 3 number of individuals H ≥ 3, then any social decision function satisfying unrestricted domain, neutrality, independence and monotonicity, gives someone veto power.

An important observation, which is embedded within the social choice theorems and worth remembering, is that a combination of the Pareto principle and the independence property yields the neutrality condition. Can we expect a decision making committee to disregard any permutations that may arise in the alternatives on the agenda? The argument is made that many issues in public policy are resolved with reference to data on incomes, inequality, and violation of rights such as liberty and hunger. Do these additional pieces of information have a status which outweighs the richer utility information discussed elsewhere? The discussion of the Paretian liberal in Sen (1986) reveals an impossibility result arising from the incompatibility of a utility based criterion (Pareto principle) and an allowance for individual rights expressed as the condition of minimal liberty.

GAMES AND VOTING POWER

This issue of agenda manipulation has forged links between game theory and the theory of voting. If x defeats y in a pairwise vote, game theorists comment that x dominates y while political scientists speak of the coalition of voters who support x. The Condorcet winner is therefore undominated, defined as the core alternative in that it defeats all other pairwise comparisons. The theorem identified in Ordeshook (1986) states that 'for strong simple majority rule voting games, the Condorcet winner is the core, and the strong core and Condorcet winner are equivalent' (p. 347). In this literature voters interpret voting as a game of strategy, and game theorists extend their concern beyond the normative search for voting criteria and into the prediction (equilibrium) of individual and group strategic choices in committee decision making with many interdependent voters.

The very absence of a Condorcet winner under majority rule opens up the possibility of strategic voting. In addition, there is the acknowledged interdependence across voters and across committee members which allows their respective behaviour to be characterised as a non-cooperative game. Public choice scholars would readily admit to this. Non-cooperative games according to Ordeshook (1986) in its traditional interpretation assumes that although fates are interdependent, people cannot coordinate their choices' (p. 97). The essential character of non-cooperative games is outlined in Ordeshook (1986) and Binmore (1992) and the interested reader is referred to both texts and the readings contained therein.

Suffice to state here that the two representations of non-cooperative game behaviour, the extensive and the strategic form, are widely applied in political science. As with probabilistic voting discussed in Chapter 3 the concept of equilibrium and its definition play a crucial role in game theory. In both approaches it is the concept of equilibrium which links the theory with the real world of politics. Ordeshook defines an equilibrium as 'a strategy n-tuple, such that each persons strategy is a best response to the choices of the other (n-1) players' choices that the equilibrium implies' (p. 143). The usual problem of existence and uniqueness have allowed this literature to flourish.

Strategy Sets

Individual voters are interpreted as agents (1, ... i, ... N) in the voting game and each individual voter chooses a behaviour bi, which depends on other voters behaviour, represented by b_{-i}, such that bi = $f(b_{-i})$. We can define an equilibrium as follows:

$$\text{for all } i, bi^* = b_i(b_{-i}^*)$$

so that if agent i chooses the position or behaviour (for example, voting for alternative x) bi, then so does everybody else and b* is defined as an equilibrium. There is a mutual dependence issue particularly in smaller committees, in that voter i must know the behaviour of other voters and vice versa.

There is the strategy set S_i. The strategic behaviour of each voter is a subset of what is available and this available behaviour is a strategy. By observing the strategy we can determine the behaviour S_i. We assume that individual strategy sets depend on the strategy set of other voters, hence $S_i = f(S-i)$, often written as Si(S-i). The strategy set is $S = (S_i, ..., S_N)$, and D(S) is an outcome, where Z is the set of outcomes and D(S)ε Z. One can think of Z as states of the world or possible outcomes from a voting procedure. For each individual voter we have a set of preferences $\geq_i$ over Z where $(\geq_i)$ is the set of preferences. The relationship between all concepts is shown below.

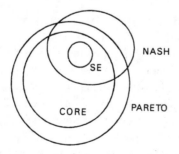

Figure 2.2 Strategy sets

We have a composite mapping, f, which is like a social choice rule in that f informs us on how different preferences link into a particular outcome from the voting process. If we knew f we could (i) determine outcomes given preferences, (ii) the responsiveness of outcomes to changing preferences and (iii) given any f* with complete knowledge of what is going on we could find Ø* such that:

$$f^*(.) = \text{Ø}^*([Zi], \text{Ø}^*(.))$$

Given individual preferences over strategies, we are interested to know how would individual voters act in a given situation with $bi = bi(b-i, \geq_i)$. In this case, bi is an equilibrium b* given $(\geq_i)$ and this $S(\{\geq_i\})$ is a strategy which defines that equilibrium. An equilibrium b* exists and the S function is defined if one individual continually change preferences as other voters change their respective preferences.

Table 2.4: Preference profile and strategies

		A	**B**
i's strategies	A	0	2
	B	1	3
		j's strategies	

We can remove the Ø function and replace it with a utility function such that $U_i(S) > Ui(S')$ iff $\text{Ø}(S) \geq \text{Ø}(S')$. Individuals i and j are said to be in strict competition if for all strategies S and S'

$$Ui(S) > Ui(S') \Rightarrow Uj(S') > Uj(S).$$

and the possibility of cooperation is not possible under strict competition. Si* is defined as a dominant strategy if for all S_{-i} and Si:

$$Ui(Si^*, S_{-i}) \geq Ui(Si, S_{-i}).$$

In Table 2.4, strategy B is the dominant strategy of the ith player; if the ith player knows that player j will always oppose her, then if she plays B, j plays A and only if she plays A does j play B. Player i has a choice of outcomes 1 and 2 so she chooses 2 and A is her strategy but not her dominant strategy. But this outcome rests on the assumption that each player knows the strategy of every other player, S-i; conversely if the ith player does not know the strategy of every other player then she should always choose her dominant strategy. In other words, the importance of a belief structure in the voting system is not to be overlooked.

The simplest belief structure of others is that they choose strategies independent of you, if we have S-i and Si* then:

$$Ui(Si^*, S_{-i}) \geq Ui(Si, S_{-i})$$

where $S_i(S_{-i})$ is defined as a best reply function. The individual voter seeks S^* such that $Si^* = Si(S-i^*)$. In other words S^* is an equilibrium iff

for all i, $Ui(S_i^*, S_{-i}^*) \geq Ui(Si, S_{-i}^*)$ for all Si.

Theorem 2.8: if Si is a compact convex set and if the Nash reply functions are continuous then a Nash equilibrium exists, that is:

there exists S^* such that $Si^* = S_i(S_{-i}^*)$ for all i.

Proof: Allow two Nash equilibria S' and S".

$$U1(S_1', S_2') > U1(S_1'', S_2') \tag{2.1}$$

$$U2(S_1'', S_2'') > U2(S_1'', S_2') \tag{2.2}$$

by strict competition

$$U1(S_1'', S_2'') < U1(S_1'', S_2') \tag{2.3}$$

=>

$$U1(S_1', S_2') > U1(S_1'', S_2'') \tag{2.4}$$

by transitivity.

Likewise it follows that:

$$U1(S_1'', S_2'') > U1(S_1', S_2') \tag{2.5}$$

Since equations 2.4 and 2.5 are contradictory, arising from two equilibria, then only one Nash equilibrium exists.

The V-Set

Our interest is principally with co-operative games, the quintessential example of the calculus of consent. The individuals evaluate their respective strategy choices in terms of utility payoffs. The characteristic function v(C), of a coalition C, summarises at least a given level of utility from adopting a joint strategy. Is there a solution concept for co-operative games? The core represents a particular type of stability in co-operative games; as defined by Ordeshook 'the core of a game in characteristic function form is the set of *undominated* payoff vectors' [our italics] (p. 341). A Pareto optimality outcome was earlier defined as an outcome which dominates all other outcomes. Consequently, if alternative x is in the core it must be Pareto optimal. The Pareto optimal outcome may not be selected by two players as witnessed by the Prisoners' Dilemma. In co-operative equilibrium agents do act together in order to produce mutually beneficial outcomes. In Table 2.5 which records different utility payoffs for different strategies we show that individual players by their actions can lead to Pareto inefficient points like (AA).

Table 2.5: Preference profile and Prisoners' Dilemma

		A	B
		A	**B**
player 1	A	1,1	0,3
	B	3,0	2,2
		player 2	

If player 1 does not cooperate with player 2, 2 plays A and 1 plays A, and if 2 plays B, 1 plays A. Hence (AA) is a dominant strategy. The actions of other players does not depend on your behaviour. If player 1 believes that he has a follower then he plays B; all dominant strategy equilibria are Nash equilibria. However by co-operation both are better off with strategy B, since (BB) is Pareto superior to (AA). In searching for an equilibrium it was important for game theorists to link the core with the Condorcet Winner criterion. If a Condorcet winner exists, it is an equilibrium; it has been established in the literature that if a Condorcet winner exists in a simple majority voting game, that it is the core. Game theory has also concluded that if a Condorcet Winner exists it is an equilibrium strategy for each candidate. It soon became evident that a core equilibrium may not exist in voting games simply because of the strong stability conditions required. In reply, game theorists offered alternative solution concepts.

The oldest solution concept is the von Neumann-Morgenstern V-set or stable set. The attractiveness of the V-set is its geometric representation of winning coalitions. However, in the real world of applied politics the V-set representation is unable to predict coalitions. It has now been supported by a new set of coalition formation solution concepts which have made significant advances in political science (Laver and Schofield 1990; Laver and Shepsle 1990 and Laver 1993). In the world of small committees the V-set however, still retains its throne.

Solution Concepts

We now turn our attention to some solution concepts in finite voting games. The solution concepts can be classified into (i) solutions based on simple majority rule including the Condorcet winner, the Copeland winner, the Banks set, and (ii) those using the size of the majority, including the Pareto set and the Borda winner. It has been shown that all group (i) solutions reduce to the Condorcet winner when one exists as witnessed in Banks (1985), Moulin (1982) and Nurmi (1987). For group (ii) the Borda winner solution may not include the Condorcet winner, when it exists, as shown as early as Black (1958). Nurmi (1983) has argued that the Condorcet winner has to belong to the Pareto set; otherwise it would be considered worse than some other alternative by the voters. The Pareto set is a very inclusive solution concept including all group (i) solutions. However it does not include the top cycle set as proved by Nurmi (1983). The top cycle set is equivalent to the Condorcet set, since a Condorcet winner ensures it is the top cycle set. The following example in Table 2.6 is borrowed from Nurmi (1987); what we notice is a majority cycle aPb, bPd, dPc, cPa which contains c which is Pareto dominated by d. This preference representation indicates the possibility that the top cycle set contains elements which are not in the Pareto set as first suggested by Miller (1980). Miller, Grofman and Feld (1986) extend this possibility to show that if a solution is not included in the top cycle set that it is also distinct from other group (i) solutions.

Table 2.6: Preference profile and top cycle set, I

Voter 1	Voter 2	Voter 3
a	d	b
b	c	d
d	a	c
c	b	a

However in the case when the Condorcet winner exists, the Borda winners may not be members of the top cycle, hence the interest is in another solution concept, the max-min set, first introduced by Kramer (1977) which belongs to group (ii). The profile in Table 2.7 is again from Nurmi (1987); it shows that the max-min set does not always belong to the top cycle set. The max-min solution is d but there is a top cycle consisting of a, b and c. The Pareto set contains both the max-min and Borda winners.

Banks (1985) showed that the Banks set is always a subset of the top cycle of the uncovered set. With so many different solutions and ramifications, is there a right solution? One resolution of this dilemma is to choose a solution which has Condorcet winner characteristics, that is, one which reduces to a Condorcet winner, where it exists. Indeed Fishburn (1973) and Riker (1982 p. 82) had earlier presented situations where the Borda winner is more plausible than a Condorcet winner. But what about the Bank set? Nurmi (1987) argues that the Banks set is too inclusive to be of much practical value. If the uncovered set is large, for example, the Banks set will be large. Are there subsets of the Banks set? He argued a case for looking at the Copeland winner as a subset of the Banks set, commenting that 'this solution would have the support of the strategic consideration in the sense that one could always build an agenda resulting in that alternative via sophisticated voting' (1987, p. 21).

Table 2.7: Preference profile and top cycle set, II

Numbers of voters			
5	3	2	5
a	b	d	c
b	c	b	d
d	a	c	a
c	d	a	b

Voting power

In a game theoretic context, power is a measure of different actors degree of control over the outcomes of a voting game. The influence or power that actors may have on other actors is not considered. There exists a variety of power indices based on the characteristic function $v(C)$. The most common are the Shapley-Shubik and Banzhaf indices. Both measure the a priori ability of a voter to affect the outcome of the game. The actual numerical values are often similar and the two measures can be regarded as equivalent. However since they are associated with different probability models there are different axioms associated with each. The Shapley-Shubik index turns out to be an additive measure with some useful theoretical properties; in other words, the sum of individual power indices will be plausible measure of coalition power. The Banzhaf index does not have this additive property but is associated with a more appealing probability model. It originates from empirical studies of weighted voting in multi-member electoral districts and it captures the fairness of representation in voting situations. Conversely, the Shapley-Shubik index, relies on axioms established by Luce and Raiffa (1958).

The Shapley-Shubik index relates to a probability model where the set N of players is arranged at random in order. Let S denote the set of players that precedes the ith player in the ordering and let i be awarded the amount (g) which is the gain that the ith voter brings to the coalition consisting of all predecessors. It can be shown that i's expected gain is precisely the value of the index. The Shapley-Shubik index sums to one allowing one to speak of the relative power of different groups or the proportion of power of different groups. The Banzhaf index has been maximised in order to allow a comparison between the two indices. The power index is defined as the number of swings for a particular player of the set N. The probability of a swing is based on a model where each player randomly votes 'yes' or 'no' with equal probability. Two types of swings are possible: in the first swing, the winning set turns to a losing set if the ith player leaves the coalition, while in the second swing, the losing set turns to a winning set if the ith player joins the coalition.

The Banzhaf index may be interpreted as the theoretically possible number of times a group is a member of a distinct minimal winning coalition. Since the principal interest lies in comparing ratios rather than magnitudes, the Banzhaf index is often normalised to add to one. In its normalised version, it has been argued (Berg, 1990), the index has lost its original meaning of a probability measure. In addition, a normalised Banzhaf index score is lower than the non-normalised score giving a different interpretation of the underlying model. The indices are intended for games with N finite players; developments with infinite players have revealed limiting properties of the indices (Shapiro, Shapley, 1978 and Dubey and Shapley ,1979). The value for Banzhaf, however, coincides in both games. Irrespective of the number of players, the Shapley-

Shubik index may be interpreted in terms of power proportions while the Banzhaf index may be interpreted as the probability that a group is part of a winning coalition. This remains the fundamental difference between both indices.

Voting power is the chance than an individual's vote within a committee or indeed a block of votes controlled by an interest group, will change a losing coalition into a winning coalition. If so, the individual or group is said to be pivotal. The best known measure of voting power is the Shapley-Shubik value. To illustrate this value we use a four member committee in which each member has one vote. With four votes a tie is possible (2:2) so the committee decides to nominate individual A as chairman. In so doing how much power does committee member A have? Shapley and Shubik (1954) argue that it is equally likely that all four members will be pivotal. To arrive at their value, we have to argue that the members differ in the intensity of their support for the alternative, so a ranking of the members (abcd) would suggest that d is least in favour, but that if a and b could persuade c, the vote would be carried 3:1. In this case c is pivotal. But with a as chairperson, we must deduce the number of occasions in which a is pivotal. With four members there are $4! = 24$ arrangements of (abcd). Straffin (1980) concludes that the chairman is pivotal in 12 out of the 24, with b, c and d pivotal in 4 each of 12. With the following calculations for a $= {}^{12}/_{24} = 0.5$ and for b,c and d $= {}^{4}/_{24} = 0.16$ we deduce that the chairman has three times as much power as the other committee members.

If a committee had (say) three members and four votes required with votes allocated as (4,3,2), an application of the Shapley-Shubik measure tells us that there are $3! = 6$ permutations of the votes (4 3 2), (4 2 3), (3 2 4), (3 4 2), (2 3 4) and (2 4 3) and four pivots in four cases, with power indices as (${}^{4}/_{6}$ ${}^{1}/_{6}$, ${}^{1}/_{6}$). The member with four votes has four times as much power as the other two members. Even if they formed a coalition with five votes, this member remains pivotal in the voting process. Since its appearance the Shapley-Shubik index of power has been widely accepted by political scientists. The ability to calculate a power index indicates the strength of a particular voting rule. In our example do we wish to design a voting rule, which circumvents the voting paradox, but gives the chairman that much power? It has found widespread use in the evaluation of the fairness of various voting rules and in conjunction with Banzhaf-Coleman has been used by many scholars in the past including Straffin (1977) and Leech (1990) to ascertain when a particular procedure might advantage or disadvantage voters.

As an alternative index the Banzhaf-Coleman index looks at the swings of each committee member; briefly if Si denotes the number of coalitions for which member i swings, and if n is the number of players, then the index $Bi = S_i / \Sigma S_j$. For example if only the coalitions (1,2), (1,3) and (1,2,3) are winning, member 1 has three swings, both 2 and 3 have one swing each, hence the index B = $(^3/_5, ^1/_5, ^1/_5)$. To convert this into a power index, we assume a $(0, 1)$ normalisation, and the equivalent power indices are $(^2/_3, ^1/_6, ^1/_6)$. This power index and the Banzhaf-Coleman index are not equivalent. Straffin (1977) in particular has shown that the Shapley-Shubik and Banzhaf-Coleman indices give quite different interpretations of a proposed legislation because the former assume voters have homogenous standards of judgements and the latter assume that each voter's judgement is independent of the judgement of other voters. The question of dictatorship translates readily into power indices which question voting procedures that may satisfy acceptable criteria.

3. The Political Economy of Voting

In this chapter we explore the political economy aspects of a relaxation or modification of the Arrovian assumptions outlined in our previous chapter. What does the relaxed property actually mean in the real world? How different is the modified condition and how significant a difference does the modification make to the voting outcome. Riker (1982) subtitled his work rather appropriately as 'a confrontation between the theory of democracy and the theory of social choice'. An interesting discussion is presented in Riker wherein he suggests that the impact of Arrow's theorem forces one to accept either 'intransitivity for society or to achieve transitivity at the cost of creating a kind of dictator' (p. 18). The essence of the Riker position really focuses attention on the recurrent fact that 'the *outcome* of voting is not transitive' (p. 18) [our italics], rather than on any one specific flaw in the democratic method. However, a relaxation of the Bastille condition, as argued in Chapter 2, may hint at undemocratic methods.

Like Feldman (1980) earlier, Riker's (1982) main concern is whether or not there is a way, a method or a rule subject to the set of properties U, P, I and ND, in which to transform individual preferences, which are transitive and complete, into a collective preference. Our earlier illustration in Table 2.2 of Chapter 2, where the alternatives translate in realistic cutback options on either health, education or housing, indicated a majority rule yielding a non-transitive social preference. The transitivity condition is weakened, or fails, albeit a social decision is taken. The completeness property is rather strong for the social preference. It requires that society ranks all the alternatives either by strict preference or indifference. As noted earlier a complete weak ordering across these alternatives ($xPyPz => xPz$) generates a binary preference. This raises issues regarding the information which the rule enacting committee has on the triple set (xyz). One could for example, re-interpret the indifference, yIz, as information-neutral.

A primary requirement in social choice is that the social preference generated by the rule be transitive and complete. This requirement is of particular interest in that there are accepted criteria in economics which do not generate a transitive social preference. The Pareto criteria for example generates Pareto non-comparable points in the Edgeworth contract curve. Classical welfare economics sought to remedy this distributive problem by recourse to the Kaldor-Hicks-Scitovsky compensation tests and the Samuelson social indifference curve. There is a strong feeling across the literature against relaxing the Pareto criterion; as Ng (1979) argued, it would take an unusual ethic to argue against the Pareto criterion which boldly states that xPy if x makes someone better off and nobody worse off. We could argue that an inclusion of externality in consumption, and envy may make someone worse off even if income remained unchanged. Alternatives to the Pareto condition is the majority rule criterion and Ng's weak majority preference criterion (WMP). Two acknowledged concepts which may underpin the Paretian ethical premise are fairness (envy) and altruism.

The property of universal domain (UD) requires a rule mapping for every possible individual ordering. Samuelson (1977) has noted that the number of individual orderings may be quite large. For a triple and n individuals there are 13 different transitive contributions, and therefore logically 13 raised to the power of n possible combinations of the orderings. What occurs here in the literature is the imposition of restrictions on all these orderings, in order 'to investigate the nature of the combinations which do lead to social transitivity' (p. 58). One restriction which we shall look at later is Black's concept of single-peaked preferences. Black's (1948) theorem shows that if individuals have single-peaked preferences, the majority rule will lead to a social ordering, and the outcome is the median-individual optimum. The later assumption on convexity of preferences used by Downs (1957) is equivalent to Black's single-peakedness. The property of convexity has the usual representation of a smooth downward sloping indifference curve. If we take one point on that curve, $x \varepsilon I$, convexity focuses on the set of points X, $x \varepsilon X$, regarded by the voter as at least as good as x. This set, R(x), consists of all points x' ε I such that x'Rx. Since x'Rx => x'Px, the voter will not rank x' above x, which is equivalent to the property of single peakedness in preferences. Black's condition of single-peakedness is over-sufficient in establishing majority rule as a collective choice rule. Mayston (1974) defined weakly single-peaked (WSP) triples as 'a triple (which) contains an alternative, say x1, such that every concerned voter over the triple strictly prefers x1 to one or both of the other two alternatives in the triple' (p. 60).

The Inada (1969) conditions of single cavedness (SC) and separation into two groups (STG), complimented Sen's (1969) property of value restrictions (VR), which is a necessary and sufficient condition for majority rule to be a collective choice rule. Sen's VR condition states that each triple must satisfy either WSP, SC or STG. And further Sen and Pattanaik (1969) extend Inada's conditions into the condition of external restrictedness (ER), which allows individuals to be unlimited and the individual orderings to be either weak or strong. One can see from this complicated literature that relaxation of the UD property offers no easy escape from Arrow's theorem. Arrow's property of non-dictatorship (ND) is welcomed; it precisely means that there is not a 1:1

relation between the social preference and an individual's preference ordering. It also rules out any independent arbitrators, even if the arbitrator took cognisance of the group of individuals' preferences. This links into a path-dependence problem, in that selection of some information or the choice from a binary choice may preclude a particular outcome. Ironically, the existence of a cycle allows an agenda setter or chairperson to influence the choice of alternative.

In Arrow's initial formulation of his theorems, completeness and transitivity were two axioms, additional to the set of properties. The completeness axiom has been questioned on the extent to which it is necessary with the Pareto condition. The ideological issue on whether or not the Pareto outcome should be left untouched trespasses on the fundamental theorems of welfare economics. The resolution in favour of the Pareto outcome no matter how unfair the allocation may affirm a free market outcome. One has to search the public choice literature again for agreement on this. However, transitivity has been weakened to quasi-transitivity and acyclicity by Sen (1986) who has argued that the transitivity property is not required. He proceeded to introduce his a α and ß-properties. If we replace transitivity with quasi-transitivity and retain completeness, Pareto condition, UD and I, Gibbard (1973) proved that an oligarchy arises rather than a dictatorship. If we replace transitivity with acyclicity we arrive at Brown's theorem on the existence of a collegial polity.

Extensions to the original conditions laid down by Arrow is indeed another avenue of fruitful research. Early in the appearance of Arrow's theorem Murakami (1961) replaced the ND property with a property of strong dictatorship, the violation of which according to Ng (1979) 'implies that there is a dictator for every choice' (p. 117). Kemp and Ng (1976) replaced ND with anonymity, referred to also by the property of undifferentiatedness, which can easily translate into a one man one vote. What arises from these extensions is a new and more robust set of impossibility theorems namely the Arrow-Murakami and Kemp-Ng impossibility theorems. This raises the intriguing question can the paradox of voting, indeed the paradox of social choice, be resolved? We refer the interested reader to check on the numerous excellent texts and articles in our bibliography in a search for the answer if indeed it can be found. But has social choice theory developed in the most rewarding way? In the following section we look at an alternative approach to social choice theory to the problems encountered in voting, an alternative approach which may challenge the sacrosanct position of the median voter theorem in voting.

PUBLIC CHOICE PERSPECTIVE

At this juncture we thought it appropriate to develop the reaction to the impossibility theorem from the public choice literature. Since the arrival of the original theorem by Arrow (1950) Buchanan has objected to the methodology implicit in the theorem. Buchanan (1954) had initially criticised the idea of translating individual preferences into a social preference. As Feldman (1980) comments 'it is quite silly in the first place to think that there might be social preferences that are analogous to individual preferences' (p. 19). The general reaction that is exclusively within the parameters of social choice theory, either attacks or extends Arrow's axioms and five properties, and a particular reaction to the methodology or logic that ascribes to a collective choice rule is very much within the public choice domain.

This still remains the case forty years later, with the development, principally from the Austrian school of public choice based at George Mason, of constitutional political economy. Buchanan (1983a) has argued that individuals could agree to a social outcome or decision, and that by agreement an unanimous decision is made. Implicit here is a concept of fairness: if a group of individuals agree to alternative x then x is fair. We would offer a word of caution; because if x is fair this does not guarantee an agreement on x (McNutt, 1992). If a set of constitutional constraints were introduced to the decision making process, the arrival at a consensus may rank fairness higher as a criterion than transitivity. Whether by agreement or by bargaining, a contract is made (e.g. a written constitution) and the impasse of the impossibility theorem has apparently been overcome (Brennan and Buchanan, 1985). The emphasis on contracts is in the spirit of the science of exchange attributable to both Buchanan (1983a) and Hayek (194). A related methodological issue is whether or not the institutions within which collective decisions are made, are Rawlsian-just institutions. In many respects, the debate on a just social contract presupposes agreement (consensus) on a just contract (outcome).

In Buchanan (1954) and Buchanan and Tullock (1962) the existence of an entity called social preference is critically questioned. Social preference is a misnomer, they contend, as individuals vote and not the societies *per se* in which they live. We have looked selectively at the criticisms levelled against the conditions and assumptions that underpin Arrow's theorem and the concept of social preference. But there is no clear solution on the agenda. Others have argued that the binary operator R is unfair; a pairwise comparison along with the I condition does restrict the individuals' choice space. This had left some of the earlier scholarly work, notably Schick (1969), accepting social preferences but dropping transitivity and forced others such as Pattanaik (1968) and Sen (1970a) to focus on the R-maximal elements.

Does a public choice perspective support the advocacy of simple majority rule? The majority rule allows for social indifference and is analogous to the R-operator, hence majority rule is complete, that is, either x defeats y, or y defeats x or they tie. Therefore as a voting rule it is both complete with respect to preferences and consistent with the Pareto criterion. Its main weakness is its non-transitivity (the creation of cyclical preferences) as a rule. The non-transitivity is inherited from the Pareto condition which is unable to rank alternatives across a finite number of individuals' H, on the Edgeworth contract curve. Figure 3.1 illustrates the contract curve CC as the locus of all points of tangency between the indifference curves of two groups of voters, G and H-G. While the Pareto condition can rank x, the off-contract curve point with y on the contract curve yPx, it is unable to rank y and z on the contract curve. The social preference for either y or z would depend on either (i) the absolute numbers in each group to ensure a majority or (ii) the relative bargaining strength of G and H-G. If G has the greater bargaining power or more members, alternative z will be the majority outcome.

An alternative way to overcome the non-transitivity is to impose Black's (1948) condition of single-peaked preferences. In his original work, which pre-dated the bargaining literature, Black considered the novel idea of peaked preferences across voters. His basic theorem remains an important contribution:

Theorem 3.1: Black showed that, with three alternatives, if the number of individuals, H, is odd, and if the single-peakedness property is satisfied, then majority rule is transitive.

It indicates as Feldman (1980) suggested that 'majority rule should give rise to sensible results' (p. 171). The Black theorem generally only holds with a uni-dimensional alternatives set; in a multi-dimensional set, as will be shown later, majority voting leads to the median preference becoming the social preference. This result is a consequence of restricting the individual choices, and turning the multi-dimensional set into uni-dimensional one. The persistence of majority rule and its variants as rules for collective decision making continued with the work of May (1952), a contemporary of Black, in establishing majority rule as a fair criterion. Writing just after Arrow (1950) had revealed his general possibility theorem, May identified three criteria that would be required for a fair collective choice rule.

His first criterion, monotonicity, requires that an increase in the vote of one alternative implies an increase, at least not a decrease in its vote. As Riker (1982) pointed out 'it would be perverse in the extreme if increased votes for an alternative contributed to its defeat' (p. 45). Arrow had used this property in developing his positive association concept. The second criterion is anonymity, often referred to as undifferentiatedness, which embodies the principle of 'one man, one vote' that is, one vote cannot be differentiated from another. It does not allow any weights to be attached to a particular individual's vote. Finally the property of neutrality, often referred to as duality, ensures that the rule does not favour any one alternative. However neutrality does allow for the possibility of a tied outcome, which may not be appropriate if a decisive vote has to be taken. We return later in this chapter to a consideration of the work of both May and Black, who along with Downs were contemporaries of Arrow.

Theorem 3.2: May proved that simple majority rule was the only method that simultaneously satisfied the three fairness criteria of monotonicity, anonymity and neutrality. Hence one can conclude that simple majority rule is fairer than other methods of collective decision making.

Tullock (1967) introduced sufficiency conditions for transitive majority rule, which have since been generalised by Grandmont (1978). His paper is very much in the spirit of our discussion on domain restrictions within social choice, wherein certain alternatives, for example the worst alternative, were ruled out from individual preference orderings. As an alternative Tullock pioneered the idea of looking at the domain restrictions that have to be satisfied in taking into account the actual number of people holding different preference orderings. Using the following characterisation of Tullock's idea, let (a), a point in the Euclidean space, represent the best alternative, and all other alternatives are ranked by their distance from a,1. Tullock assumes that the sets of a1 are symmetrically distributed over a rectangle with centre a*. The majority relations which emerge are then shown to be transitive. An interesting dimension to this is the public choice consensus that majority decisions are made in the real world, either by vote-trading or agenda manipulations. There is then the concern from other scholars on the transitivity of the social preference given Arrow's (1963) adamant defence of the property, which insures 'the independence of the final choice from the path to it' (p. 120). Combining transitivity of the social preference with binary choice will most definitely ensure path-independence as argued by Plott (1973). Graff (1965) considered the ratio of the probability of a majority winner to the probability that the majority preference relation is transitive, a ratio he concluded that goes to zero as the number of voters is increased.

In our later example on public expenditure, one would find it difficult to accept the rigor imposed by the Arrovian independence property, whereby we would have to interpret the triple as containing three independent pairs rather than having one of the pairs dependent on a combination of the other two. In other words, public expenditure allocation is interdependent and evolves from a wide domain of individual preferences. Rather than proceeding in this direction, social choice has introduced the property referred to as independence of irrelevant characteristics (IIC). According to Mayston (1974) this requires that social choice preferences with respect to some characteristics of the social state, for example the provision of public transport, can be formulated independently of the levels of other characteristics, for example, the allocation of broadcasting channels, if individual preferences are correspondingly separable with respect to the relevant characteristics (p. 75). Theorem 3.2 proffered separable preferences and sincere voting as an alternative to vote trading.

There has been no public choice development on the line suggested above; for the moment we refer to the interdependence of public expenditure votes and note the absence of research in this esoteric area. However we do develop the rudiments of a minimal choice theory for those committee members who take cognisance of unfavourable (that is, unfavourable for the citizen) economic developments in the political system. Tullock on a different note has argued that the theorem is not important in reality. No decision process meets all the requirements exactly and works, but there are many practical workings (social choice) rules. The literature does tend to agree on the cyclical behaviour of voters on small committees, a fertile bastion of Arrow's impossibility. A more important development within the public choice paradigm is of course the May-Black theorems on voting. In the interim let us look at the contribution of an earlier scholar, Borda.

Borda Numbers

The cyclical nature of majority rule outcomes can be overcome by vote trading especially at the committee stages of voting. If you glance back to Chapter 2 at the ranking (xyz) in Table 2.1, a cycle evolved with zPx, xPy and yPz. However, if individual B were to alter his ranking from yPzPx to zPyPx, no cycle would occur and a social preference in favour of z would be the outcome. Alternative z was the first preference of individual C. Although B changed his ranking in the pair (yz), possibly through a vote-trading deal with C, he did not change his true preference order. This rather simple example, of what public choice theorists address as log-rolling, is heralded as an escape route from the majority rule cycle, as indeed in the Borda numbers rule. Principally, the Borda method uses cardinal numbers in order to rank preferences, a method which does violate the Arrovian independence property. For Arrow, independence requires that every subset of alternatives be independent 'in the sense that whenever the individual preference relations between the alternatives are known, the social choice is unaffected by individual rankings of alternatives not in the original subset'. In Table 3.1 we have two individuals whose respective preference orderings are xPzPy for A and yPxPz for B. Borda proposed his 'method of marks', which has come to be known as the Borda Count, in 1781. An alternative receives no points for being ranked last and (n-1) points for being ranked first. By this method, Table 3.1 returns x from the triple set (xyz) with $x = 5$, $y = 4$, and $z = 3$. When z is excluded the Borda count is indifferent with x = 3 and y = 3. The Borda count simply sums individual points for each alternative, as illustrated by the following preference profile.

Table 3.1: Preference profile: Borda count with voters A, B

	x	y	z	x	y	
A	3	1	2	2	1	A
B	2	3	1	1	2	B
	5	4	3	3	3	

On the left-hand side of Table 3.1, the social choice is alternative x by the Borda count method since 5 is the greater cardinal number. However, if alternative z is excluded, as illustrated on the right-hand side of the Table, the Borda count method yields a social indifference between x and y, an outcome which violates the independence assumption. Sugden (1981, p. 140) provides a neo-utilitarian defence for the Borda count method. His argument is couched within the social contract theory where individuals have an extended ordering of the kind 'it is at least as good to be person i in end state x as it is to be j in y' (p. 141). The Borda method as a cardinal scoring method is supportive of a re-ranking of (information available) alternative end states.

However there are a number of arguments in its favour as a voting rule. Straffin (1980) develops two arguments in particular that the Borda method chooses the alternative which occupies the highest position on the average in the voter's preference ranking. He further comments 'that the Borda count of an alternative x, divided by the number of voters, is just the average number of alternatives ranked below x' (p. 27). So in our example x has an average rank of 1.5 from the bottom, higher than y with (1) or z with (0.5). The second argument extends from this but depends on the voters having a strict preference ordering, that is, votes. But we have shown the Borda violates the independence property. Straffin's second argument is that 'the total number of votes that alternative x (in our example) would get in pairwise contests is exactly its Borda count'. This does not occur in the preference orderings in our Table 3.1 precisely because with two voters there is no strict preference ordering. In general the Borda count satisfied the Pareto condition and the monotonicity condition but it fails to satisfy a majority rule criterion. For example if A in Table 3.1 was a group of four voters and B a group of three voters, y would be the plurality winner, but x remains the Borda winner.

Alternatives to Pareto

Within this section we would like to explore some alternatives to the Paretian ethic, which is not only the fundamental normative concept underpinning modern welfare economics, but it is also one of the principal assumptions of the Arrow impossibility theorem. Contractarian welfare economics does present itself as an alternative to Paretian ethic within normative economics, but here we wish to focus on the relevance of the ethic to the arrival at the voting paradox. The Paretian ethic enters the social choice debate as the condition of Pareto consistency which requires that a collective choice rule respect unanimous opinion.

Let us remind ourselves of the components of the Paretian ethic. The Pareto principle states that if two individuals prefer alternative x to y, then society must prefer x to y; and if two individuals prefer x to y and a third is indifferent across the pair (xy), then society must still prefer x to y. It is as Feldman (1980) comments 'a very mild requirement for a collective choice rule' (p. 181). Pareto consistency as used in the social choice literature is stronger however than the Pareto principle since it requires strong preference for all individuals. It was introduced by Arrow (1963) to replace his original assumption of positive association (not unlike monotonicity), a requirement which Blau (1957) revised to free orderings (all possible orderings are admissible) and in so doing exposed a weakness in Arrow's original proof. The Pareto consistency could also be interpreted in the following way; if somebody prefers x to y and nobody prefers y to x, then society should prefer x to y. Ng (1979) has introduced the idea of weak majority preference, that is, if the number of individuals m prefer x to y is greater than the number of individuals n who prefer y to x, then society using the weak majority preference (WMP) criterion (m > n) prefers x to y. As Ng (1979) argued 'WMP states that if at least half of the people say "yes" and no one says "no" then a change must be recommended' (p. 131). But as a value premise could it replace either that Pareto principle or majority rule? Ng argues that accepting the Pareto principle implies accepting WMP; if a majority prefer x to y and there 'is no individual in the minority who feels any worse off', then society should prefer x to y.

The degree of feeling worse off (better off) has entered the literature under the auspices of the concept of finite sensibility. Used in pair analysis, it generates an intransitive indifference for an individual, such that xPy xIy^* $y^*Iy^\wedge$ but $xPy^\wedge$, where each y (superscript) for example reflects degrees (of pain). Utility functions representing this preference ordering have to be scaled, such that $xPy => |U(x) - U(y)| > a$. Ng (1975) shows that using this utility function, and the WMP value premise, the social welfare function (SWF) is the Bentham SWF. The arguments in this part of the literature are very much within the domain of utilitarianism which predated the ordinal utility theory on which the Pareto conditions depend. Liberalism has had an impact on the Pareto principle, in the guise of Sen's (1970b) Paretian liberal. It argues that there are certain choices over which an individual should have a decisive say irrespective of society's Paretian preference. The weak Pareto principle is contrary to this, which led Sen to argue that both principles are inconsistent, in his formal proof of the impossibility of a Paretian liberal. As Sen (1970b) commented 'whether you should sleep on your back or on your belly is a matter in which the society should permit your absolute freedom, even if a majority of the community is nosey enough to feel that you must sleep on your back' (p. 152). This has led to a flurry of articles on the technical side, but it has allowed the use of more than just utility in considering social orderings. The income distribution might provide useful information, access to commodities, personal rights, and enable us to move away from utility based preference orderings.

Sen (1986) reiterates the proof that there is no social decision function satisfying the properties of (i) minimal liberty, that is, at least two persons are strongly decisive over one pair of social states each (reading a book, on which side to sleep), (ii) unrestricted domain and (iii) the Pareto principle. If individual 1 has the ranking $bPxPyPa$ and individual 2 has the ranking $yPaPbPx$ then by minimal liberty xPy and aPb, likewise by the weak Pareto principle yPa and bPx. The strict preference cycle indicates the impossibility result ($aPbPxPyPa$). A corollary of this result since SWF is also a social decision function is that there is no Bergson-Samuelson SWF satisfying these conditions. The general approach within the social choice framework is to retain the weak Pareto principle; it is required as a condition to determine whether or not there are reasonable rules to aggregate individual preferences. Public choice queries the aggregation of preferences asking if there is some conceptual meaning attached to the aggregate.

The ethic that is implicit in the Pareto principle is accepted by most scholars as a fundamental normative criterion for any rule of aggregation. However, the use of non-utility information indicates the incompatibility of Paretian values and liberal values, and the development of alternative normative criteria such as the core, equity, justice and fairness, proffer alternatives to the normative criterion of Pareto optimality. The optimality result is questionable. In Figure 3.1 alternatives y and z are defined as Pareto optimal to x. However, if the G group dominates, alternative z will emerge as the social outcome. The position of y *vis-a-vis* z on the contract curve, where each position indicates a relative distributive share (say) of public funds, is inherently inequitable. The fundamental theorems of welfare economics, the pillars of the Neo-Classical school of thought, have been built on the foundations of a Paretian ethic, particularly Pareto optimality. But Paretian welfare criteria restrict the outcome to a contract curve where points are non comparable (although Pareto efficient) and inequitable.

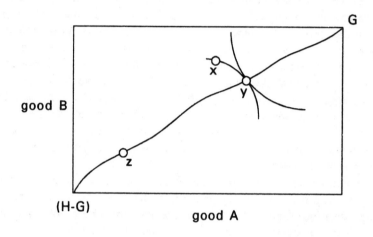

Figure 3.1: Pareto non-comparability

But can these alternatives be introduced in the analysis of the general possibility theorem? The answer embedded in the literature is apparently no; the general possibility theorem builds on combining utility information, that is, no interpersonal comparisons with a ban on non-utility information through the property of neutrality. Within the social choice debate there have been improvements on the utility-based information, with such concepts as ordinal non-comparability, cardinal non-comparability, level, full and unit comparability and ratio scale comparability which, as noted in Sen (1986), establish that the social welfare functional is of a utilitarian type which implies a utilitarian strict preference. The enrichment of the utility information does have some effects on eliminating the impossibility result. The criteria of justice (as in Rawls' maximin rule) and equity did enter the formal rigour of social choice theorems in the earlier halcyon days of an equity conscious welfare economics. Suppes (1966) introduced the grading principle of justice and Hammond (1976) introduced several equity criteria, in particular his Axiom E. The Suppes' principle extends the Pareto principle by using dominance, that is if each person in x is at least as well off as the corresponding person in y, then xRy, and if someone is better off in x then the corresponding person is y, then xPy. One must remember that the Pareto principle like the Suppes principle, builds on dominance (D) of utilities (xDy => xRy) and that the weak Pareto principle guarantees the decisiveness of all ranks put together. Hammond's Axiom E, however, demands that if A is worse off than B in both states x and y, and A prefers x to y, while B prefers y to x, with everybody else indifferent across x and y, then society ranks xRy. Likewise the relative majority rule in Dummett (1984), declares the alternative with the greatest number of vote as the winner.

Rawl's (1971) maximin violates the strong Pareto principle but when redefined across lexicographic preferences, creating the leximin rule, it not only satisfies the strong Pareto principle, but also Suppes' principle and Hammonds Axiom. Both maximin and leximin incorporate the dictatorship of a particular rank, for example, the worst off group. Sen (1986) showed that although such rules on comparability provide an informative base for relaxing the Arrow impossibility result, it is at the expense of possible rank-dictatorship. The rank dictatorship theorem states:

Theorem 3.3: A social welfare functional satisfying unrestricted domain, independence of irrelevant alternatives, with Pareto principle and anonymity and the invariance restriction, must be ranked dictatorial (Sen, 1986).

Leximin may satisfy anonymity, the strong Pareto principle, neutrality (which is equivalent to a property of non-dictatorship), Suppes' principle, and the Hammond Axiom but it implies that each rank has dictatorial power as lower ranks remain indifferent. By introducing the property of separability, which simply states that if the utility numbers for all states remain unchanged for all non-indifferent individuals, then the social ordering should not change either, the rank dictatorship result can be modified according to d'Aspremont and Gevers (1977) if the weak Pareto principle is replaced by the strong Pareto principle. As Sen (1986) commented 'one of the unappealing features of leximin is that it permits the interest of one person (if relatively badly off) to override the interests of a great many others' (p. 119).

BLACK'S THEOREM AND SINGLE-PEAKEDNESS

Arrow was not alone in his study of the voting paradox. He has acknowledged, in particular, the influence of Black (1948). May (1952) established the necessary and sufficient conditions for simple majority rule (SMR). Black (1948) in an earlier article before the appearance of Arrow's theorem, introduced the concept of single-peaked preferences as a solution to the paradox. The graphical representation of the preferences maps the alternatives as ordered against the ranks on the vertical axis of the graph. For example, the preference profile in Table 2.1 in the previous chapter can be illustrated by

Figure 3.2, and the representation is said to be non single-peaked. Likewise Figure 3.3 illustrates the preference profile in Table 2.2 and the representation is said to be single-peaked. In the latter preference profile there is no voting cycle unlike in the profile in Table 2.1. Riker (1982) has commented that the property of 'single-peakedness implies transitivity and hence ensures the existence of a Condorcet winner' (p. 126).

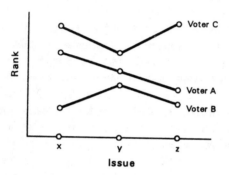

Figure 3.2: Non-single peaked preferences

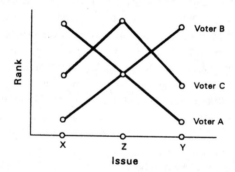

Figure 3.3: Single peaked preferences

   May and Black had independently considered the collective decision making process and had arrived at less pessimistic conclusions than Arrow. The May and Black contributions warrant an inclusion in the school of public choice. At the time of their writing a school of public choice had not formally been adopted, but their contributions indirectly contributed to that corpus of works that shaped a public choice perspective on voting. May proved that simple majority rule between two alternatives is fair, as it is the only method or rule which satisfies the properties of monotonicity, undifferentiatedness and neutrality. These latter set of properties he concluded are criteria for fairness.

The theorem is restricted to binary decisions only and Riker has noted that the arrival at a binary choice may have in itself been unfair. The property of undifferentiatedness is equivalent to anonymity introduced by Parks and Ng (1976), neutrality (duality) asserts that the rule or method favours neither x nor y and the property of monotonicity is best understood as a property of positive responsiveness, that is if an individual's preference moves in the direction x, that x should not lose the majority vote (i.e. weak unanimity).

It is essentially a technical requirement although as Riker points out monotonicity is an essential part of any voting rule, but the relative degree of monotonicity depends on the morality of the voting rule. For example a two-thirds majority is monotonic while a simple majority is strongly monotonic. Doran and Kronick (1977) devised an example to show that the single transferable vote method violates the property of monotonicity. Finally monotonicity implies unanimity and monotonicity implies weak unanimity. Black's contribution with the introduction of single-peaked preferences, also supported the simple majority rule method.

There is no cycle with the single-peaked preferences. Black's theorem states that if the number of voters is odd and if the single peaked property is satisfied then the majority voting rule is transitive. This does not mean that single-peakedness is a necessary condition of transitive social preferences. For example we noted that vote trading secures a transitive social preference as does other cardinal criteria which are outlined in Sen (1986). The attraction of single-peakedness as suggested by Ordershook (1986) is its geometric simplicity.

How restrictive is the single-peaked property? Ng (1979, p. 122) has argued that the assumption of single-peakedness violates the Arrovian assumption of free triple. Voters who rank (zxy) and (yxz) agree that x is in the middle allowing some common ground between them. It is not surprising therefore that there is some link between Black's theorem and Downs' (1957) median voter theorem - introduce a third voter with a ranking (xzy) and convince yourself that there is a double peak for individual 3 at x and z. This preference ordering generates a cycle. A more correct interpretation of the requirements of single peakedness property would be as follows: there is no constraint on how one arranges the alternatives (xyz) in a one dimensional space as long as there exists one way of arranging them which gives a single peaked preference order for every individual. The property restricts the domain of the individual and therefore violates the Arrovian UD property.

In the real world of committees or indeed in electoral voting generally, individuals behave in a multi-dimensional space. One dimension is the political dimension of the right:left continuum. Before we extend Black's theorem into a two-dimensional space we introduce the concept of circular indifference contours as illustrated in Figure 3.4. For any two points on a given contour the individual is indifferent as between them, that is, both x^ and x~ in Figure 3.4 gave the same level of utility. The individual prefers a point closer to a bliss point x* in the centre, hence x^Px. If we consider the contours for two individuals as in Figure 3.5, with an initial point at y both individuals prefer a point like y* in the shaded intersection of their respective contours. All points of tangency between their contours span a locus of points on which they both agree called the contract curve CC.

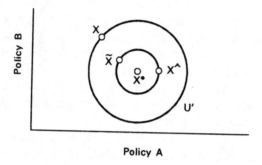

Figure 3.4: *Indifference contours*

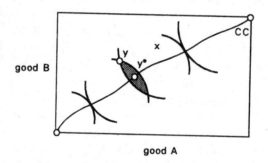

Figure 3.5: The contract curve

In other words if there is any possibility of a majority decision with these two individuals the decision will lie on the contract curve. If we expand to three individuals in Figure 3.6 with point s as the initial point, a majority of individuals 1 and 2 will prefer s* to s but at s* a majority of individuals 2 and 3 prefer s^ to s*, but at s^ a majority of individuals 2 and 3 prefer s~ to s^ and so on in a cycle. With three individuals can we escape the voting cycle? The affirmative answer requires that the third individual's preferred point, y, should lie on the contract curve between the other two, x, z as illustrated in Figure 3.7. The multi-dimensional equivalent of the Black theorem requires this unique

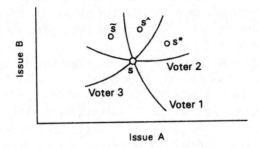

Figure 3.6: Indifference contours: three voters

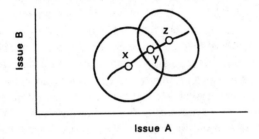

Figure 3.7: A Condorcet winner, y

occurrence as it guarantees that alternative y is the Condorcet winner. The rarity of this occurring suggests that Black's theorem may collapse in an n-dimensional set of alternatives. If we return to Figure 3.5 the shaded area, for example, would correspond to the intersection of the Pareto optimal outcomes for the minimum winning coalition 1 and 2.

For two individuals the shaded area in Figure 3.5 would lie near the centre of the diagram in a median position where neither can do worse but can do better. The shaded area is defined as the core and for strong simple majority voting games the Condorcet winner is the core. The link between Black's single-peakedness and Hotelling-Downs' median voter theorem can now be established as follows: if preferences are single-peaked then the median preference is a Condorcet winner and the social preference order under simple majority rule is transitive.

Figure 3.8 illustrates the voting paradox as a contour diagram. The positions of the alternatives (xyz) reflect the rank order of the three sets of individual preferences; for individual A the rank xPyPz is illustrated with x in the centre, y on the circumference and z furthest from x. The resolution of the paradox requires the location of one of the alternatives in the shaded intersection of the indifference contours which would reduce the illustration in Figure 3.8 to one equivalent to that in Figure 3.7. Plott (1967) and Kramer (1973) independently explored the problem of multi-dimensionality in Black's theorem with a general conclusion that simple majority rule creates cycles and that the single-peakedness theorem fails.

The development of Black's theorem along these lines has initiated an exchange between public choice theory and game theory which we alluded to in Chapter 2. Questions on the stability of voting outcomes and on the existence and uniqueness of such an outcome are of interest in this literature. The absence of a Condorcet winner opens up the possibility of strategic voting. Ordershook (1986) contends that the same applies for co-operative game theory without a core. Black's contribution is inextricably linked with Downs (1957) median voter argument. It is in the interest of political parties to secure the median position on an issue as predicted by Black's theorem; consequently political parties appease the median voter. The growth of centrist parties in European democracies is an example of this phenomenon. The Gibbard-Satterthwaite results on the impossibility of a strategy-proof voting procedure and the description of social choice as an n-player strategic game, has put a wedge between public choice and social choice that may not have been intended by the pioneers in search of a solution to the voting paradox. While the developments in the respective literatures may appear parallel there are interesting areas of overlap. One concept in particular which is used by both approaches is the Pareto set.

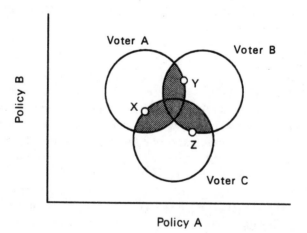

Figure 3.8: The voting paradox

PROBABILISTIC VOTING

Rational voter and social choice theories *a la* Arrow, Black and Downs as enunciated in this chapter apply mathematical analysis to solving what appears to be an intractable theoretical problem, the voting paradox. Elster and Hylland (1986, p. 2) in a rather critical attack on developments in social choice theory commented that 'social choice may be approaching the baroque stage. Breakthroughs are dwindling, while minor embellishments are accelerating. Formalism is gaining the upper-hand'. Lafay (1991, p. 23) has argued elsewhere that this direction in social choice has created a gulf between social choice theorists and political scientists. With this background he advocates probabilistic voting as the bridge across which political scientists may cross to experience 'a new vision of the optimal strategy of the politicians, allowing a deep re-evaluation of the welfare properties of the electoral system and offering large new possibilities for empirical analysis of voters and government behaviour'.

A central tenet in understanding the attack on social choice theory is in its refusal to include formally uncertainty and imperfect information in the theories. Although mentioned by Downs, Arrow himself refused to include probability calculations in his social choice. Alternatively the developments in strategic voting may have replaced any interest in imperfect information while the emerging literature on political lotteries indicated that uncertainty was a source of instability for the majority rule while Shepsle (1970) and Fishburn (1973) independently show that although a lottery can never be an equilibrium point, it can defeat a Condorcet winner under certainty and thus create cycles. McKelvey showed that voter uncertainty about the location of candidates does not change the equilibria. Contrast this with an earlier result from Davis, Hinich and Ordershook (1986) who concluded that the location of the equilibrium is no longer the median, a result which contradicted the Black-Downs basis of social choice theory. Later Hinich (1977) concluded that the median voter is an 'artefact' which holds only in the case of certainty.

It is the central conclusion regarding the median voter that has contributed to the demise of probabilistic voting in the literature. One has to think through the impact of this result on (say) the Meltzer-Richards theory of government growth. The result that majority voting maximises the likelihood of unanimity (Coughlin and Nitzan, 1981), runs counter to the social choice theorems. According to Ledyard (1984), probabilistic voting is not based on a rational choice behaviour of voters. At a different level, however, we need to ask whether an equilibrium can exist under (i) uncertainty and (ii) under imperfect information. Davis, Hinich and Ordershook (1970), Hinich (1977), Coughlin and Nitzan (1981) find equilibrium results with imperfectly informed candidates, while Enelow and Hinich (1984) assure the researcher of 'special equilibrating properties' and that 'prospective uncertainty among voters . . . are all stabilising factors in two candidate elections' (1984, p. 111).

Downs (1957) showed that in deterministic voting, if an equilibrium exists it is Pareto optimal; Coughlin (1982) has shown the same for the probabilistic case and further demonstrated that every outcome in any sequence of elections remains Pareto optimal. A final result, due to Wittman (1984), states that if the policy space is compact and convex, a Nash equilibrium exists. We developed a similar proof with respect to a compact strategy set for voters in Chapter 2. Within the probability model approach there is an interesting phenomenon called the Condorcet Loser, which we would like to present in this chapter, as a minimal requirement which a voting rule should meet. In addition, we look at the computational method used to calculate Condorcet probabilities and offer a refinement when applied to small committees. Notwithstanding escape routes from the voting paradox, it is our contention that cyclical preferences are endemic to smaller committees with (say) a finite membership of less than seven.

The Condorcet Loser

Among the numerous criteria that have been formulated for evaluating alternative voting systems, the Condorcet criteria are the most often used. Whether in an election or in committee an alternative or candidate is called the Condorcet winner (CW) if it can obtain a majority of votes in a pairwise contest against every other alternative. In some cases there is no CW as evident by the existence of the Condorcet paradox, illustrated by the preference profile in Table 3.1. With respect to the profile in Table 3.2, there is what Straffin (1980) referred to as 'a reverse Condorcet criterion' (p. 22), which is more popularly known as the Condorcet Loser (CL) criterion. This criterion states that if an alternative, such as alternative c in Table 3.2, would lose in pairwise majority contests against every other alternative then a voting rule should not choose c as the winner. The Condorcet Loser is beaten by all remaining alternatives in pairwise majority comparisons. Such alternatives do not always exist but when they do a voting system should choose the CW criterion and reject the CL criterion. Do voting systems violate either or both criteria?

Sequential voting looks at the sequence in which votes are taken in binary choice situations. Committee chairpersons frequently determine in what sequence pairwise alternatives are voted upon. In other words, the chairperson sets the agenda and unless individual preferences are sequence independent *a la* Sugden (1981, p. 137), the selected outcome will depend on the agenda (sequential voting apparently creates a vacuum in which an agenda setter can operate). The agenda setter therefore has inordinate power in selecting the winning alternative. The extent of that power depends on two important conditions, namely, (i) that individual preferences are not separable and (ii) that all other voters vote sincerely. The absence of a Condorcet Winner in agenda manipulation remains in the black box of committee decision making. Readers will find the discussions on agenda control in Farquharson (1969) and Riker (1982) of interest.

After sequential pairwise voting, plurality voting (PV) is probably the most widely used voting rule. In PV each voter votes for one alternative and that alternative with the largest number of votes is deemed the winner. PV has the added advantage of abating the agenda effect of sequential voting while satisfying the Pareto criterion. However, the PV system has its weaknesses; it violates both Condorcet criteria. In Table 3.2 we illustrate the problem with PV. We have 9 voters and a triple of alternatives (abc). The preference orderings are as follows:

Table 3.2: Preference profile: Condorcet criteria

3 voters	2 voters	4 voters
a	b	c
b	a	b
c	c	a

Under PV alternative c wins with four voters ranking c as the top preference. The inequity of this result is shown by the five to four majority who rank c last in their preference ranking. There are five voters who would prefer either a or b to alternative c. In a pairwise contest b is preferred to a, b is preferred to c and alternative a preferred to c. This translates into bPa and aPc => bPc by transitivity and bPc in a pairwise contest. Hence alternative b, the Condorcet Winner, which lost in a PV against c, is the preferred alternative in a pairwise contest. The plurality winner c is a Condorcet Loser, beaten by all other alternatives in a pairwise vote. The example in Table 3.2 above, illustrates that PV violates both Condorcet criteria. A common attempt to overcome this weakness is to combine PV with a run-off between the top two alternatives if no alternative receives a majority of votes on the first ballot.

In recent years a great number of studies have evaluated various voting systems on their propensity to violate the CW criterion. Surprisingly much less attention had been given to the likelihood of the CL criterion violation. The CL criterion is however a more paradoxical situation than the CW non-election since in the first instance the election winner would be beaten in majority pairwise contests by any of the other alternatives. In the second case the election winner would be beaten by at least one and perhaps only one other alternative. The CL election is disturbing enough to consider the CL criterion as a minimal requirement that a voting system should meet. It seems reasonable to rule out the system which can lead to the CL election unless one can demonstrate that the occurrence of the paradoxical result is extremely rare. It is therefore of some interest to compute the probability of the CL election for the voting systems given rise to such a result.

Lepelley (1986) considered two specific voting systems; the first one is PV and in contrast his second system selects the winner as the alternative with the fewest last place positions in the voters' preference ordering, a system called the negative voting system (NV) *a la* Boehm (1976), Brams (1977) and Brams and Fishburn (1983). Both voting systems, like the Borda method, belong to the general class of cardinal number (k) scoring rules in that every voter votes for his preferred alternative and the winner is the alternative receiving the largest number of votes. We get the PV system by selecting the alternative most frequently placed first as with alternative c in Table 3.2. We get the NV system for m alternatives by taking a score $k = (m-1)$ and assigning the largest k to the lowest ranked alternative. NV suggests alternatives a and c from the single-peaked preferences in Table 3.3. NV is indecisive when preferences are single-peaked.

The NV system used by Lepelley is different from the system proposed by Boehm (1976) where each voter is allowed one vote either for or against an alternative but not both and the winner is the alternative with the largest net vote. Lepelley (1986) found that (i) when all preference profiles are admissible in three alternatives elections with large electorate both PV and NV systems have about a 3 per cent chance of electing a CL (ii) when the preference profiles are single peaked the NV system never selects the CL and this result is independent of the number of alternatives, and (iii) the probability of electing the CL in a three alternative election when PV is used is not substantially modified by the single peakedness property. It would appear that results (i) and (iii) provide a very strong argument against the use of PV. Since PV is the most widely used voting system the resulting problem is then to find an alternative voting system. In this respect Lepelley notes that despite the result (ii) that NV does not appear to be a realistic alternative to PV. He considered approval voting, where each voter can vote for as many alternatives as she wishes and the winner is the alternative with the largest number of votes. Many authors including Brams and Fishburn (1978, 1983) consider approval voting as superior in many respects to PV. Riker (1982) remains unimpressed defining approval voting as 'somewhere between plurality voting and the Borda count' (p. 89). The result in Lepelley, however, augurs well for approval voting.

Calculating Condorcet Probabilities

Probability voting models arrive at important conclusions on the paradox of voting as witnessed by Lepelley (1986). The computation of the probabilities in these models uses the Selby relations for sums of powers of integers. The integers are essentially the number of voters with linear preference orderings. With an ordered set of integers the equation implicit in these calculations may have to be amended. Numerous articles have been devoted to computing probabilities for simple majority winners and the Condorcet paradox. In particular, the classic paper by Gehrlein and Fishburn (1976) has made a significant and well-cited contribution. This section amends the algebraic equation used in the method of computing probabilities for the Condorcet paradox, originating in the Gehrlein and Fishburn (1976) article. The proof is outlined in McNutt (1993a).

Working from the premise that studies of the paradox are based either on preference profiles or anonymous preference profiles, that is A-profiles, Gehrlein and Fishburn further comment that 'examination of the spaces of profiles and of A-profiles as they relate to Condorcet's paradox can provide new insights into the paradox'(p. 2). Assuming only three alternatives or candidates and further assuming that the number of voters is odd, mathematical expressions are derived for the proportion of A-profiles that avoid the paradox. They continue to show how the likelihood of the paradox can be computed on the basis of a probability distribution over A-profiles.

Let the set $A = \{a, b, c, ..., m\}$ denote a set of m alternatives and n represents the number of voters assumed to be odd; each voter is assumed to have a linear preference order on A. A profile is an n-tuple of individual linear orderings. A profile is single-peaked for example iff there exists a linear ordering P over A such that either aPbPc or cPbPa implying that for each voter j, aPb => bPc. If applied to the three alternatives case (m = 3) the definition simply says that a profile is single-peaked iff at least one alternative never appears in last position in the individual orders. In the three alternatives case there are six linear orders:

Let n_i be the number of voters whose preference order is i. Let n be the odd number of voters who have six linear preference orderings on the m = 3 alternatives; hence the vector $(n_1, ..., n_6)$ gives the distribution of n voters over the six orderings. There is one important inequality in this literature:

$$n_1 + n_2 + n_3 \leq (n + 1)/2. \tag{3.1}$$

Recall that n1 is the number of voters with (say) the preference ordering aPbPc and likewise for n2 and n3. A Condorcet Loser exists if it is defeated by all remaining alternatives in pairwise majority votes. So for example in this literature a Condorcet Loser occurs if:

$$n_1 + n_2 + n_3 \leq (n-1)/2 \text{ and } n_1 + n_2 + n_4 \leq (n-1)/2. \tag{3.2}$$

These equations are important to the probability voting models in arriving at their conclusions. For example, Lepelley (1986) argued that when preferences are single peaked that the negative voting system never selects a Condorcer Loser but the plurality voting system does select a Condorcet Loser. Berg (1985) argued convincingly that with anonymous profiles there was a lower probability of the Borda effect. The conclusions are arrived at with the use of equations 1 and 2, in conjunction with the probability values that are computed by using the Selby (1965) relations for sums of powers of integers.

The issue addressed here looks at what happens if the number of voters with a linear preference profile, n_i, can be interpreted as an ordered set of integers. That they are integers is not the issue really, since this is assumed by the direct use of the Selby method. The result in McNutt (1993a) hinges on the fact that an ordered set of voters F which has the least upper bound property contains a sub-field G. Small committees are a proper subset of the larger committees with which these probability models are concerned. In other words, the calculation of probabilities for the paradigmal small committee, the case of three members and three alternatives, may require an amendment to equation 1. In effect this may require replacing the $\leq$ inequality sign with $<$ in calculating Condorcet Loser probabilities and replacing $\geq$ with $>$ in the calculation of Condorcet Winner probabilities, particularly when applied to smaller committees. The question remains just how small?

VOTING PROCEDURES

Voting plays an important part in political affairs from small committee decision making to national elections. A collective decision in the absence of unanimity requires a voting procedure but as Dummett (1984) so cleverly argued 'the voting procedure employed often has a critical effect upon the outcome' (p. 1). An interesting example of the intricacies of voting procedures was found in the rules and procedure governing the election of the conservative party leadership in the UK. In the first round of voting, candidate Thatcher as the plurality winner failed, however, by two votes to acquire the necessary two thirds majority of 187 votes. This necessitated a second round of voting with a winner declared if 187 votes were secured. Three candidates entered the agenda, candidate Major, candidate Hurd and candidate Heseltine. When votes were counted in the second round candidate Major was two votes short. Then the two rival candidates, candidate Heseltine and candidate Hurd, unilaterally withdrew from the next stage of the complicated voting procedure which consisted of vote transfers based on the equivalent to a proportional representation type rule. The withdrawal of the two candidates returned candidate Major as the majority winner. Ironically, candidate Major assumed the leadership with significantly less aggregate votes than candidate Thatcher in the first round of voting.

In addition to the voting procedure, the recurrent possibility of cycles is a serious problem in a three member committee voting on three different issues. In this context, fairness of the voting procedure is an important criterion. This has been established since the May (1952) theorem on the fairness of majority rule. May, by his characterisation of fairness by the properties of anonymity monotonicity and neutrality, contributed to the identification of majority rule as a fair voting rule. Dummett (1984) comments that 'a voting procedure is fair if it reflects as accurately as possible the preferences of the voters' (p. 29). The difficulty here is the inability to deduce voter preference from empirical studies on voting. In particular we do not know whether the individual voted sincerely or insincerely, and the preference of the voter may not necessarily translate into choice. In the latter sense voter A may prefer x to y, but the social choice may be y.

The paradox of voting illustrates that majority voting generates a cycle across individual preferences, hence majority rule in intransitive, and this is a special case of the Arrow impossibility theorem. It is the connecting link between social choice theory and the mathematical theory of voting, but as Dummett (1984) comments 'it would be a hysterical reaction to interpret it as meaning that there is no rational method of determining the fairest outcome from the preference scales' (p. 54). He argues that the Arrovian assumption of independence 'conflicts with the more compelling principle that whether x would be a fairer outcome than y depends not only on how many (or which) voters prefer x to y ... but on how strong their preferences are'(p. 54). Manipulating an idea in Dummett, we consider the following preference scales for five voters across the four outcomes (abcd).

Table 3.3: Preference profile: Dummett's procedure

Voter	1	2	3	4	5
	a	c	b	b	a
	b	d	d	d	c
	c	a	a	a	b
	d	b	c	c	d

In Table 3.3 there are three voters who prefer d to a, but a is the first choice of two voters and is the only outcome which is not ranked last (that is, regarded as the worst outcome), while d is ranked worst by two voters and it is the only outcome not ranked first in any preference ordering. The three voters who rank d to a, do so across their second and third preference scales and for these three voters there is a majority of two in favour of b; across all five voters there is a majority in favour of b against d. Both b and a are the first choice of two voters. Dummett (1984, p. 124) introduced the idea of a preponderance score to which the reader is referred. Essentially the role of the chairperson may help to resolve the dilemma as long as the chairperson is not voter 2 in our particular case.

What is a fair outcome in this situation cannot be determined with the independence assumptions, the principle has no plausibility, according to Dummett (1984) who concluded, as illustrated in our example above, that 'in deciding which of two possible outcomes x and y are out, several would be the fairer, the voters' preferences between either of them and the remaining outcomes are not irrelevant' (p. 56). In order to expand on the Dummett example, we add a sixth voter with the same order of preferences as voters 3 and 4, that is, (b) (d) (a) (c). In this case we now have three voters with the same preference ordering. Two interesting points emerge from this preference profile with the addition of a sixth voter, namely (i) independent of pairwise voting, a number (above a critical number) of voters do have identical preferences, and (ii) that their first preference b, could translate into the social preference. Is there a voting criterion embedded in the preference profile satisfying conditions (i) and (ii)?

Arrow's original search, according to Dummett, was to determine a criterion 'for deciding from the preference scales (in Table 3.3), whether the outcome produced by the voting procedure is the fairest one' (p. 50). Dummett (1984, p. 115) later argued for a complimentary fairness criteria to majority rule decision making. He proffers two criteria, namely (i) no outcome can be fair if it has a lower majority number than some other outcome (if there are r outcomes, a majority number is defined as $(r - 1)$) and (ii) if b has a lower preference score then a, b cannot be a fair outcome. For our preference ordering in Table 3.4 we compute both the majority number and the preference score as follows:

Table 3.4: Preference profiles and scores

	a	b	c	d
Majority number:	2	2	1	1
Preference Score:	9	9	7	6

In the preference profile the majority numbers add to 6 which is greater than $(r - 1) = 3$, and this is principally due to the cyclical majorities between the outcomes as alluded to in a different context by Dummett. However, the preference score criterion which is essentially the Borda count, has apparently generated an indifference between outcomes a and b. This requires different voting rules to supplement the Borda count but nowhere in the voting literature have we come across the situation where the Borda count fails to return an unanimous winner. The possibility of a *Borda paradox* can be seen in the preference profile in Table 3.3. Both alternatives b and a have the same Borda number 9. With the addition of our sixth voter, b emerges as the Borda winner.

However, if the sixth voter had the preference order (adbc), alternative a would have emerged as the Borda winner. Ordershook (1986) alludes to a related problem which he refers to as the *inverted order paradox* (p. 68), where the alternative ranked lowest in its score is ranked highest when one alternative is removed from the profile. Ordeshook (1986, p. 70) continued with an interesting variation of the Borda count method. Instead of awarding 3 points (number of outcomes, n, less 1) to the first preference, consider an arbitrary number k < 3. In our particular example in Table 3.4 if k = 2, b is the winner with 5 points, a gets 4 points and both c and d get 3 points each. If k = 1, which is the special case of plurality voting, both a and b tie with 2 points each. The choice of winner varies with the choice of k, a condition which has become known as the *truncated-point total paradox*. It emerges from voting procedures that either the intransitivity of a rule or the existence of a paradox appear to be unavoidable in a general voting case.

Miller (1988) in an excellent précis on voting, grouped voting procedures into three broad categories, namely: (i) aggregation procedures where the individual transitive preferences are aggregated in one step into a single winner, examples include plurality voting and the Borda count method; (ii) elimination procedures whereby individual preferences are aggregated with the weaker (less voter support) alternatives eliminated at each stage until a winner is arrived at (examples include plurality plus run-off, where all alternatives are eliminated except those with the first and second preferences and the Coombs exhaustive procedure which eliminates the alternative with the most last-place rather than fewest first places votes), and (iii) sequential binary procedures whereby a sequence of binary choices is put to the voter and the sequence convergences to an eventual winner. Some examples of sequential binary procedures include Black's (1948) committee procedure which Miller (1988) referred to as standard amendment procedure, and the successive procedure discussed at length in Dummett (1984), where each alternative according to Miller is 'voted up or down as a single majority vote [and] the first alternative to receive majority support is selected' (p. 827).

Let us turn our attention to Table 3.5 which illustrates the various winning alternatives, from the preference profile in Table 3.3, generated by the different voting procedures each of which offer a possible social preference.

In all cases except the Coombs method, plurality plus run-off and truncated point, no single winner is returned. However alternative a is ranked the winner by two procedures and the arbitrary nature of the truncated point method, in selecting an arbitrary number, does not augur too well for b. The criteria of monotonocity, anonymity and neutrality which were identified by May (1952) do remain an integral part of a fair or representative voting procedure. However the assumption of neutrality is violated by the sequence binary procedure in so much as the location of an alternative in the agenda may predetermine its defeat. The criteria outlined by Dummett, particularly that of majority preference considered in this chapter, does uphold the majority vote. That apart, Dummett did not rank it above his preference score method which is a variant of the Borda count method. He explained his position as follows: 'I am not very strongly disposed to advocate use of the majority number procedure, not having that belief in the rights of majorities needed to make it appear an improvement on the preference score procedure' (p. 296). In the particular circumstances introduced in this chapter with the addition of a sixth voter, the Dummett method only produced a unanimous winner when the additional voter's top preference was either of the Borda winners. While echoes of the tyranny of the majority which haunted Madison in his framing of a constitution unfold in Dummett's explanation, it would appear that there is an inherent unreliability with the Borda method as the number of voters increase beyond three.

Table 3.5: Preference profile: Outcomes of voting procedures

Procedure	Outcome
Majority Number	a,b
Preference Score	a,b
Truncated Point	b
Plurality	a,b
Plurality Plus Runoff	a
Coombs Method	a

In the absence of unanimity, majority rule is a well-defended alternative, either a simple majority rule or a two-third majority for certain constitutional issues. But it appears that satisfaction of the majority rule, along with anonymity and neutrality does not guarantee the absence of a cycle. The Condorcet cycle need not materialise if an individual voter, for example a chairperson, initiates the pairwise vote. We had earlier looked at the role played by agenda setters in this regard. Consider the following:

Table 3.6: Preference profile: Path dependent

A	B	C
x	y	z
y	z	x
z	x	y

In this preference profile with three individual voters A, B and C there is a possible cyclical outcome: xPy by the pair (AC), yPz by the pair (AB) and finally zPx by the pair (BC). However, if the chairperson started with xPz, x is defeated and the pairwise choice is between (zy) with A and B securing y as the majority winner. However had the committee started with yPz, z would have been defeated, and the pairwise choice would be between the pair (xy) with x the winner. The outcome is not path (the order in which x, y and z are selected) independent and this is open to manipulation by a chairperson, or any agenda controller. If voter C changed his order of preferences, for example if C votes insincerely with zPyPx, then y emerges as the winner and the outcome cannot be manipulated. Honest sincere voting not only generates cyclical majorities but is also open to manipulation. It is ironic that insincere voting which may be rational may in fact overcome these twin problems.

The attitudes of many individuals have been analysed as egoistic. The rational individual acts from prudence, defined by Beauchamp and Bowie (1983) as 'self-interest'; therefore our individual voter is out to promote his or her own interest. Hobbes assumed that human beings were sufficiently rational to recognise their own interests. For example in order to avoid anarchy they formed a state. The public choice theory emanating from Buchanan's (1993) interpretation of constitutional rules could argue that individuals would not vote for a decision that bestowed no individual benefits. The social choice paradox suggests that each individual would obey the social choice rule (no insincere voting) and trust that the outcome from the social choice is beneficial. However, such obedience and trust exist only because they are (implicitly) assumed; however one can only make such assumptions for as long as the social choice outcome coincides with individual egoistic outcome. Rationality as introduced by Hobbes, set up a Leviathan; public choice ought to argue that rational man would see that the social choice outcome would not be individually beneficial.

The social choice mechanism may not be the only method of allocating resources or making decisions. As Downs (1957) once commented: 'rationality thus defined refers to the process of action, not to their ends or even to their success at reaching desired ends' (p. 6). The argument is advanced in the later chapters of his work, where he comments that 'men are not always selfish ...

they frequently do what appears to be individually irrational because they believe it is socially rational' (p. 27). This would recast the paradox of voting into a search as to whether or not there was popular support for the initial set of Arrovian conditions. If the rational individuals in society do not accept the Arrovian conditions the foundations on which the paradox of voting stands would crack. Furthermore, one could deduce that vote trading and insincere voting were rational responses in a competitive self-interested voting world. If the citizenry had to choose their set of acceptable criteria for a voting rule would they unanimously select the initial criteria defined by Arrow. This is an intriguing question to which public choice scholars should devote attention.

ECONOMIC CONDITIONS AND VOTING

A related and rather interesting question within the context of public choice is the extent to which economic conditions contribute to voting behaviour either of individuals in a committee subject to a collective choice rule or to the mass electorate who return political parties to office. A characteristic of democracy is that if the electorate do not like the government of the day they have at their disposal the liberal remedy of the next election. There is a growing literature on how political scientists have attempted to match economic conditions with changes in congressional voting as in Alesina 91988), Fiorina (1991) and Grier (1991). Our concern here is to identify some economic conditions which may account for the relative success of government at elections. They may have some bearing on the relative behaviour of committee members and voting rules, notwithstanding the voting paradox. In a sense, we are looking behind the veil of vote trading, attempting to uncover a possible link between individual behaviour as manifested by the order of vote preference and voting. The literature has adequately looked at how the structure of a committee affects an outcome Ordershook (1986). Our initial concern is how individual voters react to specific economic events beyond a threshold level, for example, too high a level of unemployment.

In most political systems, decisions are taken at committee level and each committee easily translates into the voting arena covered by the voting paradox. In other words, each committee must make a decision subject to some operational voting rule, either majority rule or unanimity or some compromise rule, which has the acceptable criteria outlined. The committee members are political in the sense that they hold office and are subject to a re-election constraint. In addition each committee can be interpreted as a proper subset of the larger superset, the UK Parliament, the Irish Dáil or the US Congress. As the superset members take cognisance of economic conditions, so do the individual committee members likewise. In other words, a committee outcome may reflect changes in economic conditions and the possibility of an outcome may depend on economic conditions.

But this observation is not as straightforward and sanguine as one might be led to believe of small committees. Firstly, the majority of committee members are more than likely to belong to the incumbent party, the government party. Each committee will be representative of all the parties in the parliament but as the decision making authority increases, eventually to cabinet level, the proportion of non-incumbent members decreases. Hence, within each committee, with the exception of the cabinet, there is an unequal distribution of political committee members, whose vote will respond differently to changes in economic conditions. With n committees, all (n-1) committees bar the cabinet committee will respond differently to economic conditions and each committee voting outcome will differ according to the political representation of the committee between incumbent and non-incumbent members. This differs from vote trading or log-rolling where individual committee members trade with each other. In this situation, as argued earlier, the order of preference does not change but rather the individual committee member votes insincerely. This strategic mis-representation of preference proffered the public choice scholars an escape route from the voting paradox. However, when individual committee members respond to changes in economic conditions the order of preference does change and the voter behaves sincerely in revealing *a re-order of preferences* which takes account of the fluctuations in economic conditions. We are therefore suggesting that re-ordering of preferences is the sincere equivalent to vote-trading and may offer a further escape route from the voting paradox. The difference in the two escape routes, however, is in the possibility of a transitive sincere social preference with a re-ordering of preferences.

Theorem 3.4: With a re-order function f^{-1}, that is, if individual voting preferences are re-ordered and if a Condorcet winner exists, sincere voting will return the winner (See Chapter 8).

The interesting dimension to this is in asking how committee members learn of changes in economic conditions. In other words, how are economic events mapped into the voting arena? Futhermore, do individual committee members react to changes in all economic conditions or only to some specific conditions? If the level of unemployment increases, do committee members respond more than if interest rates increase. One obvious reply relates to the type of committee: for example, the social welfare committee members may respond to changes in unemployment figures more than (say) a transport committee. While the type of committee is arguably important in discounting committee member reactions to economic conditions, whether a committee member belongs to the incumbent administration likewise plays a decisive role in deciding how that individual committee member responds to the economic conditions and re-orders his or her vote accordingly. While these questions have been adequately covered in the context of legislatures *per se*, they have not been answered with respect to the many small committees which are subsets of the superset legislature.

The relevant economic conditions to which committee members respond is equivalent to the economic conditions to which political parties respond. In many respects we are trespassing on the political business cycle literature which has allowed economists and political scientists to endogenise economic conditions through different business cycle models. The traditional Nordhaus cycle had pre-election fast growth followed by a period of low unemployment; inflation increases as the election date draws near to be followed by a post-election recession. Alesina (1991) has questioned this cycle, supporting evidence for a new approach, the rational expectations business cycle. Once a right wing government gets elected it instinctively fights inflation which causes either a recession or a slowdown in growth. Eventually the economy returns to a natural growth rate as inflation remains low in the election cycle. Alternatively, when a left wing government assumes office, it expands the economy initially and succeeds until inflation expectations adjust and the economy returns to its natural rate of growth. Eventually the government is trapped in an inflation bias, entering the next election with a reduction in inflation as its main economic variable.

The fallout from this Nordhaus-Alesina type business cycle theory is that for committee members of the left, the relevant variables might include unemployment and other quantity variables such as accommodation shortages, hospital waiting lists, while the relevant variables for committee members of the right might include inflation, interest rates and other nominal variables, even stock prices. While not disputing the link between the relevance of particular variables and party affiliation at the national level, our main thrust of enquiry at the committee level is in identifying the acknowledged source of information on economic conditions, that is, the opinion polls primarily, which record the reactions of voters to changes in their specific economic circumstances. How this source maps into the committee decision making process remains to be answered.

The literature on elections and the economy looks at the relationship between the electorate, economic conditions and party support as enunciated by Fiorina (1991): 'the economy continues to influence the underlying balance of party affiliations just as it did during the New Deal and as it will undoubtedly continue to do in the future'. The political business cycle literature is part of this scene in political science. Our objective in briefly recounting the story in this section is to focus attention on the response of committee members *per se* to economic aggregates in arriving at (transitive) committee decisions. Albeit, economic developments have had an impact on electoral politics, but at the micro level of committee decision making, economic developments may have had a short term impact on voting outcomes. Committee members as local constituency politicians identify with this reporting of economic events. In particular, if individual committee members re-order their preferences in reaction to economic conditions, and if such a re-ordering leads to a transitive collective choice, one would like to conclude with the heroic assumption that economic conditions, through a re-ordering of preferences, contribute to a resolution of the voting paradox.

The issue is how to endogenise economic conditions in the committee voting process; it requires either (i) a new property or (ii) an assumption. The latter is more straightforward if we simply assume that voting behaviour in committees in endogenous. But this is precisely how vote trading arises in committees and as argued earlier, vote trading violates an Arrovian property. The alternative is to introduce a new property which complements the existing set of properties and accounts for the committee members' reaction to changes in economic conditions. One possible suggestion is a property of altruism. In other words, an altruistic committee member re-orders his or her preference ordering to enable a majority outcome; in so doing the altruistic committee member unwittingly allows a transitive social choice to evolve. The probability that a re-order of votes by an altruistic voter leads to a transitive outcome would have to be computed. A re-order mapping is noted in McNutt (1992).

A related property in political science, is sociotropy, where the individual committee member's voting behaviour is based more on individual perceptions of collective economic circumstances and less on individual economic circumstances (Powell 1981, Self 1993). But how would the property of altruism-sociotropy manifest itself in a voting rule? If we replace the binary vote (yes:no) with a binary vote (S:D), where the set, S, includes sociotropic decisions and the set, D, all other decisions, including vote trading and Pareto decisions, we could define a voter preference as: $aPb => a \varepsilon S \& b \varepsilon D$ and the voters choice set C, as: $C = (a \mid a \varepsilon S => aPb$ and $\sim bPa)$.

The choice sets are different in a social context than they are in an individual context. Consequently it would follow that the choice sets are ill-specified in social choice theory. By definition the social preference ordering bPa indicates that alternative b is a transitive insincere vote-trading outcome. Alternatively, the social preference ordering aPb indicates that alternative a is a transitive sincere social preference. Alternative b may emerge as the social preference by the Pareto criterion. The challenge for public choice scholars is to integrate the individual choice set with the real world of democratic politics, wherein voter choice sets and government policies diverge. The credibility literature in macroeconomics, Persson and Tabellini (1990, 1994) has now to be integrated with the microeconomics of choice sets.

4. The Growth of Government

The past three decades have seen the emergence, in countries of the OECD, of a phenomenon which has been termed 'the growth of government'. This refers to the increasing importance that government activities have come to play in the economic affairs of the industrialised democracies. Many economic and political commentators regard this with some alarm. Indeed, since about 1980, most government thinking in the OECD countries has reflected the view that the economic frontiers of the state should be rolled back. Mrs Thatcher on becoming prime minister in 1979, signalled the start of the 'Conservative Revolution' in economic policy which, with the subsequent election of President Reagan and Chancellor Kohl, quickly spread beyond Britain, and one of the ideological pillars of this revolution was that there was a need for less, not more, government.

Table 4.1 shows total government expenditure as a percentage of GDP in twenty OECD countries for selected years of the period 1960-90. A number of features of the information contained in this table deserve highlighting.

First, for every country in the sample the percentage of GDP preempted by government expenditure was higher in 1985 than it was in 1960; however by 1990 several countries had recorded falls in their government expenditure to GDP ratio. In particular, between 1985 and 1990 all the larger countries of the OECD (except the USA) experienced such a decline; among the smaller countries Ireland and the Netherlands showed sharp reductions in this ratio and, conversely, Greece, Norway and Spain showed sharp increases. Of the twenty countries shown in Table 4.1 only five - Greece, Iceland, Norway, Spain and Switzerland - had a higher ratio of government expenditure to GDP in 1990 than they did in 1985; however for all the countries in the sample this ratio was greater in 1990 than it was in 1970 and considerably greater than it was in 1960.

Second, between 1960 and 1985 for every country - except Germany and Norway - this percentage of GDP taken up by government expenditure grew steadily over time; for Germany and Norway this percentage grew over 1960-80 though it recorded a small fall between 1980 and 1985. Since 1985, as noted above, this percentage has fallen for fifteen of the twenty countries in the sample of OECD countries. Third, between 1960 and 1985, the mean percentage recorded a sharper rise for the smaller countries of the sample than it did for the larger countries; the overall mean for the sample rose from 27.2

per cent to 47.1 per cent in 1985 while the mean for the smaller countries rose from 26.2 per cent to 47.6 per cent. Since 1985 the fall in this percentage has been greatest for the larger countries: the overall mean fell, between 1985 and 1990, by 1.2 percentage points while the mean for the larger countries fell by 2.3 percentage points. The fourth feature of note is that, over the past thirty years, the variability of this percentage - across the countries in the sample - has also increased; a standard deviation of 5.6 points around a mean of 27.2 per cent in 1960 became, in 1990, a standard deviation of 9.7 points around a mean of 43.7 per cent; the fall in the mean percentage, between 1985 and 1990, has been accompanied by a slight reduction in variability.

Table 4.1: Total outlays of government as a percentage of GDP in OECD countries (selected years)

	1960	1970	1980	1985	1990
United States	27.6	31.6	33.7	36.7	33.3
Japan	18.3	19.4	32.6	32.7	31.7
Germany	32.5	38.6	48.3	47.2	45.2
France	34.6	38.9	46.4	52.4	49.8
United Kingdom	32.6	39.8	45.1	47.8	39.9
Italy	30.1	34.2	46.1	58.4	43.2
Canada	28.9	34.8	40.5	47.0	45.9
Unweighted Average Large Countries	29.2	33.9	41.8	46.0	42.7
Australia	22.1	25.1	32.1	36.6	34.3
Austria	32.1	39.2	48.9	50.7	48.7
Belgium	30.3	36.5	50.8	54.4	49.1
Denmark	24.8	40.2	56.2	59.5	58.3
Finland	26.7	30.5	36.5	41.5	39.7
Greece	17.4	22.4	30.5	43.2	52.5
Iceland	28.2	30.7	31.4	35.6	38.0
Ireland	28.0	39.6	50.9	54.6	42.4
Netherlands	33.7	43.9	57.5	60.2	54.1
Norway	29.9	41.0	50.7	48.1	53.7
Spain	18.8	22.2	32.9	39.3	41.8
Sweden	31.1	43.3	61.6	64.5	59.1
Switzerland	17.2	21.3	29.3	30.9	34.1
Unweighted Average Smaller Countries	26.2	33.5	43.8	47.6	46.6
Unweighted Average all Countries	27.2	33.7	43.1	47.1	45.24
Standard Deviation all Countries	5.62	7.85	10.11	9.83	8.3

Source: OECD Reports, World Bank and United Nations Reports

It is on the basis of the kind of evidence presented in Table 4.1 that many economic and political commentators spoke, in the 1980s, of the 'growth of government'. However, whether such growth should, as it did over the 1980s, excite alarm or whether it should be viewed in a more benign light requires a careful answer to several questions. Firstly, what is the nature of the animal called 'government'? Second, what is the nature of its spending activities? It is on the basis of past trends in such activities that the allegation has emerged that governments have grown 'too big'; in particular it is important to examine the details of government spending with a view to seeing the extent to which such spending is subject to ideological and political control and the extent to which it is determined by exogenous factors to which any government, regardless of its ideological persuasions, would have to respond. Lastly, what is the nature of the process that determines government expenditure? In Britain and Canada for example, the expenditure determining process is essentially an adversarial one with spending departments confronting the controlling department (the Finance Ministry or the Treasury); as a consequence the final outcome for government expenditure may reflect more a failure to control, than a failure to plan, spending. It is to answering such questions that the remainder of this chapter turns.

Public Expenditure: Definitions and Concepts

A common source of confusion in matters of public policy is the distinction between 'the public sector' and 'the government'. The United Nation's Standard National Accounts (SNA) defines the public sector as consisting of general government (ie. central government and local government), public financial institutions and public non-financial enterprises. There are relatively few problems about the definition of either general government (hereafter referred to simply as 'government') or public financial institutions. The definition of non-financial institutions is however more ambiguous. Pathirane and Blades (1982) point out that the basic criteria of public ownership is often supplemented by considerations of permanency of public involvement (Britain and Australia), of whether the market share of the enterprise gives it a near monopoly position (France), of whether the involvement is at the level of central government (Egypt and Canada), and finally whether the enterprise is of a sufficiently large size (India). At the same time in other countries like Spain, Portugal and Austria, the basic criterion of public ownership is sometimes diluted by considering as public enterprises those in which there is less than 50 per cent public ownership. The OECD, in defining public enterprises, adopts the basic criteria of public ownership and control, though it recognises that, since different countries often supplement this basic criteria with other considerations, its data refers to what each country perceives to be a useful public enterprise concept for its own purposes.

Expenditure by a country's public sector is referred to as 'public expenditure' while 'government expenditure' refers more narrowly to that undertaken by its government. In this context it is interesting to note that much of contemporary political rhetoric about the undesirability of big government is largely dissatisfaction about the degree of involvement of public enterprises in the economy and the concomitant policy of privatising such enterprises is not directed towards reducing the size of government *per se* but directed rather towards reducing the number of public sector enterprises.

Against this background there is no unique definition of public expenditure, with different definitions being required for different purposes. For example, in the context of Britain, at least three definitions may be distinguished:

(i)   Public expenditure as a planning total.
(ii) General government expenditure as defined in the National Income Accounts (NIA).
(iii) Supply expenditure as defined in the Exchequer Accounts.

Every year, in Britain, Her Majesty's Treasury publishes a White Paper setting out the government's expenditure plans for the coming few years. These plans are presented in four different ways. Firstly, they are presented in terms of the relevant spending authority. There are three main spending authorities in the public sector, *viz.* central government, local authorities and public corporations. Then they are presented in terms of the relevant spending departments. Thirdly, since public spending is intended to provide services to the public, the expenditure plans are also shown in terms of the nature of those services - defence, health, education, social services etc. Finally, although public expenditure is planned in terms of departmental spending, to be disbursed by the relevant authorities on specific services, an economic classification is also needed to assess the effects of such expenditure on the economy. A major economic distinction is between public sector pay, direct expenditure on goods and services and transfer payments to the private sector.

The total of public expenditure plans as published in the annual White Paper represents a control item. In other words, it represents the sum of all the items of expenditure over which the government has control and *ipso facto* excludes those over which the government has little influence. The planning expenditure total therefore differs from general government expenditure as defined in the NIA in two fundamental respects. First, the coverage of expenditure items by the NIA is wider than that of the planning total and includes items outside the government's control. Most notable of such items is debt interest. Second, the NIA restricts itself to general government (central government and local authorities) expenditure. This is the concept that is favoured for international comparisons because it is less affected by institutional differences between countries since, as was argued earlier, it is the public enterprise component of the public sector that reduces the consistency of inter-country comparisons.

Finally, Supply Expenditure is expenditure by central government that is submitted to Parliament in Supply Estimates for its approval. Such expenditure, which forms an integral part of the central government 'Exchequer Accounts', includes virtually all central government spending on goods and services, but less than half the transfers to the private sector and abroad. The major omissions among the transfers are National Insurance Fund benefits and debt interest payments; supply expenditure also includes grants to local authorities, which are excluded from NIA general government expenditure and also some transactions which do not count as central government expenditure in the NIA. Stibbard (1985) provides a detailed analysis of the concept of supply expenditure. The remainder of the discussion in this chapter will, however, be conducted in terms of the more familiar concepts of 'general government expenditure' and the 'public expenditure planning total'.

Government Expenditure and the Relative Price Effect

The introductory section to this chapter argued, on the basis of the data in Table 4.1, that the trend in government expenditure, in the countries of the OECD, has over the past thirty years been an upward one. In this section we flesh out this contention by examining, in this regard, the British experience. Government expenditure as a percentage of GDP, rose, in Britain, from 35 per cent in 1960 to a peak of 48 per cent in 1975; after the cuts imposed as a consequence of the 1976 financial crisis it fell to 42 per cent in 1977; thereafter it rose, reaching a peak of 47.6 per cent in 1985, before falling to 43 per cent in 1990. The post-1980 rise in this percentage for Britain highlights one pitfall of judging the growth of government by the percentage of GDP preempted by government expenditure, namely that the numerator and denominator of the ratio are not independent. Over this period government expenditure went up mainly through increased payments associated with unemployment and other social security benefits and this, in turn, was the result of the fall in GDP associated with the recession of that period.

However, the impression that government expenditure in the UK has, since 1960, been on an upward path remains even when such expenditure is considered independently of GDP. In 1960 the real value of government expenditure (at 1985 GDP prices) was £70 billion; by 1991 it had more than doubled to reach £162 billion. Over 1960-91 government expenditure (measured in constant 1985 prices) grew, on average, at an annual rate of 2.8 per cent; the corresponding growth rate for GDP (at constant prices) was 2.4 per cent. Although, over this period, the annual growth rates for both real government expenditure and real GDP varied, for every year in 1960-91 the former growth rate was greater than the latter.

This differential growth rate in real government expenditure and in real GDP was one reason why the percentage of nominal government expenditure to nominal GDP rose over 1960-91; a rise in this percentage reflected a 'growth of government'. The other reason for the rise in this percentage had to do with prices. Even if real government expenditure and real GDP grew at the same rate, differential productivity growth between the public and private sectors of the economy would ensure that, in nominal terms, government expenditure as a percentage of GDP would rise. This 'relative price effect' or 'Baumol Effect' (cf. Baumol 1967) occurs because while rising productivity gains, to some extent, offset the rising cost of labour in the private sector, it is conventionally assumed that there are no such gains associated with the public provision of goods and services. Consequently, if workers in the public and private sectors of the economy enjoy the same rates of wage increase, government expenditure as a proportion of GDP will rise. There is, of course, nothing inevitable about such a rise: the 'Baumol effect' relies on wage growth parity between public and private sector workers; the effect can be frustrated by a government deciding to hold public sector pay claims below public sector levels. Neither is there anything inevitable about the fact that productivity growth in the public provision of goods and services must always be zero; in the absence of reliable measures of government output this is simply a conventional assumption of national income accounting.

Mueller (1989) noted that there was a fair consensus among studies of government productivity that, in point of fact, its growth rate was less than that for private sector productivity and that this (former) rate could even be zero or negative. This consensus was however arrived at on the basis of studies conducted in the 1960s and 1970s. It is not clear that such a consensus would survive in the changed economic climate of the past decade. There is considerable evidence that, in Britain at least, there have been dramatic changes in the public sector in the 1980s both in terms of public sector pay and in terms of public sector efficiency.

On the face of it very little changed in the British public sector over the 1980s: the public sector employed 5.4 million persons at the beginning of the decade and about 5.2 million at its end. However, as Adonis (1991) notes, underlying this unchanged role of the public sector being an employer to 20 per cent of the British work force lay a considerable change in attitude to work practices whereby 'choice, standards and quality (were now) the catchwords; flexibility, performance and local management the tools; the private sector the model'. These changes have been marked in four areas: pay determination, performance incentives, flexible working practices and local management.[1]

In terms of pay determination the major change has been the breakdown of the monolith of public sector wage negotiations, both in terms of occupations and in terms of regions. By 1991, about 1.4 million employees - covering teachers, dentists, doctors, nurses, paramedics, senior civil servants - had independent pay review bodies; senior health service and local authority staff were on individually negotiated contracts; and local authorities in the South-East of England had broken away from national negotiations. In terms of performance incentives, the practice of performance-related pay was beginning to spread downwards from senior management. The increase in female and part-time workers, particularly in local government and the civil service, meant that the culture of the 9 am-5 pm working day was coming under attack. Lastly, the setting of objectives targets and the devolution of management responsibilities was now widespread in the public sector. Taken together, these changes implied that the assumption that the 'Baumol effect' - operating through higher public sector relative prices, engendered, in turn, by lower public sector productivity growth - would always serve to raise the percentage of GDP due to public expenditure, must be treated with some caution.

Oxley (1991) calculated the 'relative price effect', over 1907-91, for the OECD countries. The conclusion was that between 1970 and 1974 the relative price effect - which was defined as the deflator of government expenditure relative to the GDP deflator - grew at an annual rate of 1.7 per cent; over the second part of the 1970s this rate fell to 0.5 per cent and by the latter half of the 1980s this effect had virtually disappeared. This trend they ascribed partly to the decline in private sector productivity and partly to the growing resistance of governments to public sector wage increases. However, such an analysis is subject to caveats.

First, an implicit assumption made by those who point to the 'dramatic' changes in public sector attitudes (noted above) that took place in the 1980s, is that the quality of output remained unchanged while the efficiency with which output was produced improved. There is some reason to be sceptical of this assumption. An important property of many publicly provided services (particularly related to the provision of health, education and social services) is that they are highly labour intensive. Moreover, the 'quality' of provision for many of these services depends on a case-by-case examination of client needs. Thus increases in class sizes might improve the productivity of teachers but at the cost of lower quality teaching; increasing doctors' patient lists improves hospital throughput but arguably, since each patient gets less of a doctor's time, reduces the quality of health care. Of course one could argue that the earlier standards of quality were excessively high but that is a different argument from claiming that productivity improvements in the public sector do not entail quality deterioration.

Second, while it is true that governments in OECD countries, as the single largest employer in their respective countries, have increasingly adopted a policy to limit wage increases in the public sector, it is not clear whether this policy can be sustained over the longer run. The UK has seen the evolution of a 'two-tier' pay system with powerful public sector groups (police, firemen, doctors, dentists, armed services) being able to secure for its members pay formulas linked to comparable private sector awards while weaker groups, such as local government manual workers, have got much smaller increases. Thus the burden of controlling public sector pay has largely been borne, in the UK, by groups that lack industrial muscle.

However, the size of the Public Sector Borrowing Requirement (PSBR) in the UK - £50 billion in 1993 - means that a more drastic approach to controlling public expenditure and, ipso facto, public sector pay has needed to be taken. In the 12-month wage round beginning in November 1992 pay increases for all public sector workers were limited to 1.5 per cent and 'special' arrangements with respect to different groups were all suspended. Although public sector workers, albeit with much grumbling, have appeared to accept this situation for 1992/93 it is going to be much more difficult to impose a second overall public sector pay limit without provoking a damaging conflict with the powerful public sector groups who see in this uniformity an erosion of their relative position both *vis-a-vis* their other public sector colleagues and *vis-a-vis* their private sector counterparts.

The Composition of Government Expenditure

To understand why public expenditure in the OECD countries has risen so dramatically one must examine on what functions it is spent and, within the context of these functions, the economic categories on which it is spent. A prior question is, of course, one of spending authority, that is, who spends the money. Taking Britain as an example, in terms of the spending authority, 75 per cent of the planning total for 1992-93 was to be spent by the central government, 22 per cent by local authorities leaving less than 1 per cent for spending by nationalised industries and public corporations. Of central government expenditure about 40 per cent was to be on social security with the two other large central government expenditure items being defence and health. Local authorities were to spend over a third of their budget on education, with most of the remainder to be spent on law and order, housing and other environmental services, personal social services and transport.

Table 4.2 shows the shares, in GDP, of the main economic categories of government expenditure for five countries (USA, Japan, Germany, France and the UK) of the OECD for the years 1979 and 1990. It is quite obvious from Table 4.2 that two items dominate government expenditure: (i) cash transfers to the personal sector mainly in the form of pensions and other social

Table 4.2: *Structure of government outlays by economic category*

Percent of GDP

	United States			Japan			Germany			France			United Kingdom		
	1979	1990	Change	1979	1990	Change	1979	1990	Change	1979	1990	Change	1979	1990	Change
Total current disbursements	30.4	35.2	4.8	23.9	24.7	0.8	42.4	42.3	0.0	41.4	46.6	5.2	39.2	38.1	-1.1
Government consumption	17.0	18.3	1.2	9.7	9.0	-0.7	19.6	18.5	-1.1	17.6	18.3	0.7	19.7	20.0	0.3
Subsidies	0.4	0.2	-0.2	1.3	0.7	-0.6	2.2	1.9	-0.3	2.0	1.6	-0.3	2.4	1.1	-1.3
Social security and other transfers	10.2	11.5	1.3	10.3	11.2	1.0	19.8	19.3	0.4	20.4	23.5	3.1	12.8	13.7	0.9
Debt interest payments	2.8	5.2	2.4	2.6	3.8	1.1	1.7	2.6	1.0	1.4	3.1	1.7	4.4	3.4	-1.0
Government investment	1.7	1.6	-0.1	6.3	5.0	-1.3	3.2	2.3	-1.0	3.1	3.3	0.2	2.6	2.1	-0.5
Capital transfers	-0.4	-0.2	0.1	0.5	0.0	-0.4	1.8	1.1	-0.6	0.4	0.2	-0.2	0.7	-2.9	-3.6
Other transfers	-0.1	0.4	0.5	0.9	1.0	0.1	0.2	0.1	-0.1	0.1	0.1	0.0	0.0	0.0	0.0
Total	31.7	37.0	5.2	31.6	30.7	-0.9	47.6	45.8	-1.8	45.0	50.2	5.2	42.5	42.9	0.3

Source: OECD Reports, World Bank and United Nations Reports

security benefits, and (ii) government consumption of goods and services expenditure on which is dominated by the government's wage bill. For example public expenditure on goods, services and assets in the UK totalled £38.2 billion in 1988-89 and comprised 24 per cent of total public expenditure, of which £6.2 billion represented the gross domestic capital formation of general government and £4.2 billion represented spending on assets by public corporations; in the same year public sector pay accounted for 24 per cent of total public sector expenditure.

Table 4.3 shows trends in government employment for the same five countries of the OECD. This clearly shows that the rate of growth in such employment - which was highest in 1970-74 - declined sharply over the 1980s; this, however, was not reflected in a declining share of government employment in total employment since the slowdown in private sector employment was even greater. Thus in Britain the share of government employment in total employment rose from 18 per cent in 1970 to 19.6 per cent in 1990 in spite of the fact that levels of government employment were falling since 1979. Most countries of the OECD have also seen, since 1984, sharp falls in government wage levels relative to those in the private sector. In Britain, for example, relative wages fell at an annual rate of 3.1 per cent over 1984-90 while the corresponding fall for Germany and France was, respectively, 1.8 and 1.0 per cent; among the OECD countries it was only in the USA and Japan that government employees experienced increases (albeit modest) in their relative wage. The fall in the relative wage of government employees has been accompanied, over 1984-90, in some OECD countries (notably Germany and Canada), by a fall in their real wage; where the real wage has increased the annual rate of growth in most countries has been extremely modest.

Table 4.4 shows the composition of government expenditure (as a percentage of GNP/GDP), for the USA, Japan, Germany and the UK, by function of expenditure for the years 1979 and 1989. Four functions are distinguished: the provision of 'pure' public goods; the provision of 'merit goods' like education, health and housing; transfers; and general economic services. Table 4.4 shows that the share in government expenditure of expenditure on public goods has been very stable over the past decade: for the UK, for example, such expenditure accounted for 20 per cent of total government expenditure. However there are strong variations across the countries and this has a great deal to do with defence expenditure: the Japanese government spent, in 1989, only 11 per cent of its total expenditure on public goods while in the USA this percentage was 25 per cent; it is no coincidence that defence expenditure played a major role in the US budget while, in Japan, it was relatively unimportant.

All four countries, between 1979 and 1989, showed declining shares for expenditure on merit goods when such shares were expressed as percentages

Table 4.3: Government sector employment

Annual average growth rate

	1970-75	**1975-79**	**1979-84**	**1984-90**
United States	3.2	2.1	0.1	2.3
Japan	2.8	1.7	0.7	0.2
Germany	3.8	1.9	1.0	1.5
France	2.0	1.7	1.8	1.0
United Kingdom	3.1	0.8	-0.3	-0.2
Unweighted average	4.1	3.2	2.0	1.5

Share in total employment

	1970	**1975**	**1979**	**1984**	**1990**
United States	16.0	17.1	16.1	15.3	15.5
Japan	7.7	8.7	8.8	8.7	8.1
Germany	11.1	13.8	14.7	15.5	15.6
France	17.6	19.0	19.9	22.1	22.8
United Kingdom	18.1	20.9	21.2	21.8	19.6
Unweighted average	12.9	15.2	16.5	18.0	18.2

Source: OECD Economic Studies (Annual)

of GDP; however since the ratio of total government expenditure to GDP itself declined over this period the share of expenditure on merit goods in total government expenditure was very stable: in the UK, in 1979 and 1989, about 32 per cent of total government expenditure was on such goods. The exception was the USA: here the share of expenditure on merit goods in total government expenditure fell from 19 per cent in 1979 to 17 per cent in 1989.

The largest item in the government budget of all the countries was expenditure on income transfers: this varied from 32 per cent of total government expenditure in the USA and the UK to nearly 40 per cent in Germany. Income transfers were, in turn, dominated by transfers undertaken for income maintenance purposes and here, in turn, the dominant item was retirement pensions: in 1989 in the UK three-fourths of all income transfers were towards income maintenance, and retirement pensions constituted almost two-thirds of total income maintenance payments; however, since 1979, the fastest growing components of social benefits have been supplementary and family benefits which increased by 252 per cent between 1979 and 1985 closely

Table 4.4: Structure of general government outlays by function

	United States			Japan			Germany			United Kingdom		
	1979	1989	Change	1979	1989	Change	1979	1989	Change	1979	1989	Change
I Total Expenditure	32.1	36.3	4.2	31.1	31.6	0.5	48.0	46.8	-1.2	42.8	41.2	-1.6
TRADITIONAL DOMAIN												
II Public Goods	7.7	9.1	1.4	3.9	3.7	-0.2	8.3	8.2	-0.1	8.4	8.3	-0.1
1. Defence	4.9	5.9	1.0	0.8	0.9	0.1	2.8	2.6	-0.2	4.5	4.1	-0.4
2. General Public Service	2.1	2.5	0.4	3.1	2.8	-0.3	5.5	5.6	0.1	3.3	3.6	0.3
3. Other Functions	0.7	0.7	0.0	-0.0	0.0	0.0	0.0	0.0	0.0	0.6	0.6	0.0
THE WELFARE STATE												
III Merit Goods	6.2	6.1	-0.1	11.3	10.9	-0.4	13.3	12.7	-0.6	13.6	12.8	-0.8
1. Education	4.5	4.6	0.1	4.6	3.5	-1.1	5.0	4.3	-0.7	5.2	4.8	-0.4
2. Health	0.9	0.9	0.0	4.5	4.9	0.4	6.1	6.5	0.4	4.6	5.0	0.4
3. Housing and other	0.8	0.6	-0.2	2.2	2.5	0.3	2.2	1.9	-0.3	3.8	3.0	-0.8
IV Income transfers	10.8	11.7	0.9	-	-	-	19.4	18.5	-0.9	11.9	12.9	1.0
(a) Income maintenance	7.6	7.8	0.2	6.3	7.2	0.9	16.5	15.8	-0.7	9.2	9.6	0.4
1. Pensions	6.6	7.0	0.4	4.1	5.7	1.6	12.3	11.3	-1.0	6.4	6.2	-0.2
2. Sickness benefits	0.1	0.2	0.1	0.2	0.1	-0.1	0.8	0.7	-0.1	0.4	0.3	-0.1
3. Family allowances	0.4	0.4	0.0	1.6	1.2	-0.4	1.2	0.8	-0.4	1.6	1.6	0.0
4. Unemployment compensation	0.4	0.3	-0.1	0.4	0.2	-0.2	0.9	1.5	0.6	0.7	0.7	0.0
5. Other income supports	0.0	0.0	0.0	0.0	0.0	0.0	1.3	1.5	0.2	0.1	0.8	0.7
(b) Administration and other spending	2.5	2.2	-0.3	-	-	-	2.5	2.4	-0.1	1.3	1.5	0.2
(c) Other transfers (non-profit institutions and r.o.w.)	0.6	1.1	1.1	-	-	-	0.4	-.4	0.0	1.4	1.8	0.4
THE MIXED ECONOMY												
V Economic services	4.5	4.5	0.0	6.6	5.5	-1.1	5.4	4.6	-0.8	3.7	3.0	-0.7
1. Capital formation and capital transfers	1.6	1.7	0.1	4.4	3.9	-0.5	2.3	1.5	-0.8	1.1	1.0	-0.1
2. Subsidies	0.4	0.6	0.2	1.2	0.7	-0.5	1.9	1.9	0.0	1.1	0.5	-0.6
3. Other	2.5	2.2	-0.3	1.0	0.9	-0.1	1.2	1.2	0.0	1.5	1.5	0.0
VI Public debt interest	2.8	5.0	2.2	2.6	4.0	1.4	1.7	2.8	1.1	4.4	3.6	0.8
VII Balancing item	0.1	-0.1	-0.2	0.4	0.3	-0.1	-0.1	0.0	0.1	0.8	0.6	-0.2
VIII Net lending	0.2	-3.1	-3.3	-4.7	2.5	7.2	-2.6	-2.1	-4.7	-3.2	-0.1	-3.3

Source: World Bank Development Reports (Annual), OECD

followed by unemployment benefits which increased by 250 per cent. Over the same period pensions increased by 188 per cent.

The Demand for Public Expenditure

Several explanations have been put forward to explain the growth of government expenditure. The great mistake, as will constantly be emphasised in this chapter, is to believe that there is one single explanation for the growth of public expenditure and public choice theory is particularly prone to making mistakes of this kind. Instead, we argue that there are a multiplicity of factors that generate demand for the goods and services that government expenditure provides; equally there are several reasons - even within the ambit of 'political reasons' - why government may choose (either wholly, or in part) to meet these demands. Even after exhausting these demand and supply factors there still remains a residual reason for the growth of government expenditure and this has to do with problems connected with the formulation and implementation of expenditure plans. In other words the outturn for public expenditure, for reasons connected with government organisation, may be different from the expenditure that was planned.

One way of organising the different hypotheses purporting to explain the growth of public expenditure into a coherent framework is to think in terms of the demand for, and the supply of, public expenditure. Thus, a number of factors - demographic, social and economic - combine to generate demand for publicly provided goods and services. The nature of these 'demand-side' factors are discussed in this section. Governments then decide the extent to which they are prepared to meet this demand. This is the supply-side aspect of public expenditure and it is discussed in the subsequent section.

The 'Baumol' effect, discussed earlier, was designed to explain why there was likely to be a rise, over time, in the ratio of government expenditure to GDP. It did not, however, explain why government expenditure *per se* should increase over time. To understand this, one needs to examine the determinants of government expenditure. The idea that there was a long run tendency for government expenditure to grow can be traced to the writings of Alfred Wagner (1890) and is the basis of 'Wagner's Law'. Wagner ascribed three main reasons to the increase in government expenditure over time. Firstly, industrialisation and modernisation would lead public activity to grow at the expense of private activity since, in an increasingly complex society, the need for expenditure on regulatory activities would grow. Second, the demand for collective and quasi-collective goods - in particular for education and culture - was regarded by Wagner to be relatively income elastic. Lastly, Wagner asserted that because of 'the fundamental inefficiency of private enterprise' economic growth would require the state to take over the operation and management of natural monopolies. Consequently, expenditure on administrative services (for the first of the above reasons) and on health, education and social services (for the second and third reasons) would, relative to private expenditure, grow over time.

Consistent with Wagner's Law, there is, at least in Britain, considerable public support for state-provided services. Some evidence for this assertion is provided in a survey carried out by National Opinion Poll (NOP)[2] which asked a sample of 1,551 electors in Britain (in the period 23-25 November 1991) whether, if extra money became available as a result of economic growth, they preferred (as best for the country): (i) a policy which cut taxes while maintaining public expenditure at the present level; or (ii) a policy which increased public expenditure while maintaining the present level of taxation. Only 25 per cent of the sample favoured lower taxes, while higher public expenditure won the support of 71 per cent.[3] When respondents were asked which of the two options they preferred as 'best for you and your family', again a majority (by a margin of 55-36 per cent) favoured increased expenditure to reduced taxes and again this majority was maintained across supporters of the different political parties.

A variant on Wagner's Law was provided by George Stigler (1970), who argued that it was the middle and upper income groups that were the major beneficiaries of public expenditure programmes, and hence, it was from these sources that the demand for public services would be relatively strong. This was because upper/middle income groups were both major users, and major suppliers, of some public services. Le Grand and Winter (1987) corroborated this for Britain: they showed that families of the professional and managerial class were, proportionate to the rest of the population, high users of health and educational services[4] and also major suppliers (through being doctors, teachers etc.) of such services. It is not surprising, therefore, that in the NOP survey cited above, the largest support for a policy of increasing public expenditure came from the middle and professional classes (ABC1 electors): 78 per cent of the respondents in these classes favoured more expenditure to less taxation.

Another argument, one that has a great deal of plausibility, is that there are broad demographic and social factors that tend continually to raise the level of public expenditure. Glennerster (1979) argued that, since the late 1950s, Britain had seen a growing political demand for social services arising from the increasing numbers in the different client groups (and indeed of the groups) and society's greater knowledge about their needs. In turn, these needs themselves had grown enormously in the postwar period. On a related view, the decline of kinship and neighbourhood groups - as a supportive socio-economic system - had been particularly severe since 1945. The high employment levels and high labour force participation rates of the postwar years, combined with increased personal mobility and spending power, reduced the claims of community and family life to levels that could be regarded as minimal. According to this view, therefore, the relationship between the social structure, the economic system and public expenditure were fundamental to understanding the 'growth of government': a large part of public expenditure has been absorbed in coping with the effects of social and economic change; in many cases the effort was to prevent a fall in welfare by setting up alternative social structures (see Self, 1980).

Demographic pressures have perhaps been most strongly felt in expenditure on Health and Social Services. This is a combination of two effects. First, the dependency ratio[5] for the elderly went up in most countries of the OECD in the 1970s and 1980s and furthermore, demographic projections indicate that this ratio will continue to increase. Second, the needs of the very young and the elderly, in respect of health care, are considerably greater than the remainder of the population: it has been estimated that, compared to a person of working age, health care costs for the over-75s are nine times as great, for the 65-75 age group about four times as great and for the 0-4 age group about twice as great (H.M. Treasury, 1984). On one estimate,[6] average real spending[7] per head of population, across the OECD countries covered by the public insurance health system, grew at an annual rate of 5.3 per cent over the 1970s and at an annual rate of 1.9 per cent over the 1980s. The lower growth rates for the 1980s can be explained by attempts made by governments to control, during this period, the upward spiral of public expenditure in general and of expenditure on health in particular.

The other area in which demography plays an important role in determining expenditure is in the area of education. Here demographic changes have worked so as to reduce the pressure for public expenditure increases: falling fertility rates have ensured that, in most OECD countries, the dependency ratio of the young fell over the 1970s and the 1980s. The demographic factor has, however, been largely offset by increased participation rates in post-compulsory education, and a characteristic of the past three decades in the OECD countries has been a rise in the numbers of men and women in adult education as well as a rise in the number of children in extended schooling. One consequence of this trend has been a rise in the level of formal educational qualifications of the population: between 1984 and 1992 the percentage of males without any educational qualifications fell from 34 to 23 per cent and that for women fell from 45 to 32 per cent.[8] To a large extent, this emphasis on education has been due to a realisation on the part of governments that greater education and training are essential for maintaining industrial competitiveness. Falling numbers in compulsory education, due to demographic factors, but increasing numbers in post-compulsory education has meant that real spending per student continued to grow over the past twenty years - the OECD average annual growth rate for real spending per student was 1.8 per cent for 1975-80 and 1.6 per cent for 1980-88.[9]

The third important component of public expenditure heavily influenced by demographic changes is retirement pensions. Unlike expenditure on health and on education - which are payments for final goods and services - expenditure on pensions constitutes a transfer payment from the working age population to the retired population. For most countries of the OECD, payments of retirement pensions are a dominant part of total general government expenditure - in Britain for example, in 1989, they constituted 23 per cent of total expenditure.

Labour market trends, particularly relating to higher participation by women, have also had profound consequences for payments of retirement pensions. Although the number of elderly people in Britain - between now and the turn of the century - will not increase by very much, the total number of pensioners will increase by 600,000, largely because more women will be entitled to pensions in their own right. Lastly, the state of the economy has also a major influence in determining the level of social security payments. Typically, the loss of employment entails the payment of both insurance-related (but not means-tested), and means-tested (but not insurance-related) benefits. It was estimated by H.M. Treasury (1984), that every increase of 100,000 in the numbers registered as unemployed, led to a rise (over the year) of £185 million in total benefits paid to the unemployed.

The Supply of Public Expenditure

The previous section argued that demographic, social and economic factors combined together to generate demand for publicly provided goods and services. Governments then decide the extent to which they are prepared to meet this demand. In taking this supply decision, governments may be influenced by considerations of social welfare. In terms of the analytical framework developed by Sen (1981), a collapse of the 'entitlements' of a particular group of persons[10] may trigger public action because the consequences of such a collapse offend one's norms of how society should properly function. An extreme example of such action is public expenditure for famine relief;[11] another example might be government action to help the homeless who 'sleep rough' on the streets of cities.

Of course public action may arise as the consequence of the call for public action (for example through the media) since, under certain circumstances, inaction would threaten the very existence of a particular government. Thus Sen (1982) noted that an achievement of democracy in India (with all its accompaniments like a free press, vocal opposition parties, pressure groups etc.) was that large scale famines were no longer possible since, long before things reached such a state, public pressure would force governments to act. By way of contrast, around 20 million died in the Chinese famine of 1958-61 and remarkably, the famine - which was the largest ever, in terms of total excess mortality, in recorded history - continued over a number of years without public recognition and without any change in public policy.

One might, however, in assessing the motivation for decisions on government expenditure, take a narrower view of self-interest. This view relates to expenditure on activities where there is no obvious public perception of 'social welfare'; nevertheless these activities are funded because, in some well defined sense, it is in a government's self-interest to do so. Such expenditure decisions may be termed 'political' and it is such decisions - motivated by narrower considerations of self-interest - that form the basis of 'public choice' explanations for the growth of public expenditure.

Such politically motivated expenditure decisions may arise in a variety of ways.[12] First, the government may act as a redistributor of income and wealth. For example, the expansion of suffrage has meant that less well-off persons (with incomes below the median level) have been given the vote and, in turn, they have exercised their electoral power by voting for more egalitarian policies. Such explanations appeal to the median voter theorem. Second, the rise of interest groups (for example, the 'poverty lobby') has exerted pressure on governments to expand spending and this has not been helped by the fact that interest groups can be mutually re-enforcing in exerting such pressure.[13] Thirdly, the pressure for more expenditure may emanate from within government as ministers and bureaucrats attempt to expand their influence.[14] Since the last two of these explanations discussed later in this book,[15] it is to evaluating the first of the above 'public choice' explanations that this section now turns.

The 'redistributive' explanation for the growth of public expenditure, first put forward by Meltzer and Richard (1981), argues that circumstances could cause the preferences of the median voter to alter over time so that, at this voter's preferred outcome, he (or she) demands more expenditure by the government than before. Since this voter is the median voter, the survival of the government depends on supplying this demand[16] and hence public expenditure rises. The model is essentially a labour supply model in which an individual maximises a utility function, $U(c,l)$, whose arguments are consumption (c) and leisure (l). In turn, an individual's consumption is his (or her) total income which is the sum of transfer income, g, received from the government and after tax employment income, $(1-t)y$, where y is pre-tax employment income and t is a proportional tax rate; leisure is simply the total availability of hours less n, the hours worked. Thus:

$$c = g + (1-t)y \text{ and } l = 1-n \tag{4.1}$$

Employment income depends upon a productivity-related wage rate, w, and hours worked, n so that:

$$y = w*n \tag{4.2}$$

Substituting (4.1) and (4.2) into U(c,l) and maximising the function with respect to n yields n*, the optimum number of hours supplied, as a function of the model parameters: t, g and w.

$$n* = f(t,g,w) \tag{4.3}$$

Substituting (4.3) into U(.), yields the maximum level of utility the individual can obtain for a particular configuration of parameters as:

$$V = U(n*) = V(t,g,w) \tag{4.4}$$

where V(.) is the indirect utility function such that $dV/dt < = 0$ (with the equality holding if the individual is unemployed, i.e. y=0) and dV/dg and dV/dw > 0. The difference now (as compared to the usual indirect utility function of microeconomic textbooks) is that the individual, in his (or her) role as voter, can choose the preferred combination of t and g. This task is made relatively simple by the government's balanced budget rule which equates revenue (as calculated on average income, $\bar{y}$) to expenditure:

$$t* \bar{y} = g \tag{4.5}$$

so that:

$$g = g(t) \tag{4.6}$$

where $dg/dt = \bar{y} + (d\bar{y}/dt)*t$. Now $(d\bar{y}/dt) < 0$ (because of incentive effects) and hence $dg/dt > = < 0$ depending on whether $\bar{y}/t > = < -(dy/dt)$.

The task before the individual is to choose t so as to maximise (4.4) subject to (10). This is illustrated in Figure 4.1 in which for the employed person (whose indifference curves derived from (4.4) are upward sloping since $dV/dt < 0$) the optimum tax rate and level of transfer income are t_e and g_e respectively; for the unemployed person (whose indifference curves, since $dV/dt = 0$, are horizontal) the corresponding optimum yields a higher tax rate, tu and a higher level of transfer income, g_u. Thus, in this stylised example, depending on whether the median voter is employed or unemployed, government expenditure and taxes will, in the context of a balanced budget, be lower or higher. The final thread in the argument is to note that, if over time, the indifference curves of the median voter become flatter (say because the extension of suffrage draws more marginal[17] groups into the political process) the desired mix of fiscal policy would change, in Figure 4.1, from t_e and g_e to $t*$ and $g*$.

Peltzam (1980) also developed a model, based on political support, to explain the growth of government expenditure. Like Meltzer and Richard (1981), Peltzam treated government spending and taxation as a pure transfer - public good aspects of government spending were thus ignored. Also like Meltzer and Richard (1981), the Peltzam model was based on political support - the

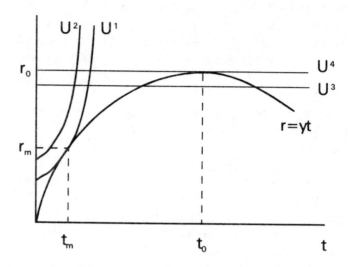

Figure 4.1: The optimal choice of tax rate

amount of spending was determined entirely by majority voting. The last point
of similarity between the models was that Peltzam too drew a connection
between public and private incomes - the higher rates of taxation required to
generate higher transfers would lead, through a reduction in the demand for
labour, to a diminution of private incomes.

The point of departure was that, in the Peltzam (1980) model there was a
clear distinction between the gainers and losers. The gainers (whose number
was, say, P) were those receiving the transfers - they did not have to pay for
this transfer income through taxes. The losers (whose number was, say, Q)
were those who were taxed in order to generate these transfers - they did not
receive any benefits from transfer income.[18] The only cost that the gainers
bore for increased transfers (which acted as a brake against a majority voting
for large transfers for itself at the expense of a minority of tax payers) was the
(inverse) link between public and private incomes discussed above.

Central to Peltzam's analysis was the notion of a 'politically dominant'
redistributive program. Each beneficiary would arrive at a judgement as to
whether a particular program (offering him, or her, an income of say, £g) was,
of the realistic alternatives available, the best program. Thus if there were P
beneficiaries to a policy, of whom a fraction, F, regarded it as the best policy,
then the political support for the policy (in numerical terms) would be P*F.
By converse argument, if there were Q losers from a policy which a fraction

E, of the losers, regarded as the worst policy [19] then the political opposition to the policy would be Q*E. The object of a government would be to choose the politically dominant policy, i.e. the policy that would maximise net numerical support:

$$M = P*F - Q*E \tag{4.7}$$

The fraction, F, of beneficiaries who regarded a policy as the best available would vary positively with the per-capita benefits, g, and inversely with the tax rate R levied to generate the transfers.[20] Moreover, F would vary inversely with Y, the per-capita (private) income of the P beneficiaries, for two reasons. Firstly, because of diminishing marginal utility of income, the perceived benefits of any level of g are lower for higher Y. Secondly, the losses in private income (due to labour market effects) from a given R are likely to be greater for higher Y. Thus a fall in Y would be equivalent to a rise in g or a fall in R. Hence:

$$F = F(g,R,Y) \tag{4.8}$$

where:

$Fg > 0; F_R < 0; F_Y < 0.$

Now a given g can be raised, for the lowest tax rate (R) and numerically smallest opposition (Q), by taxing the richest; also the benefits from raising g would be maximised by transferring this sum to the poorest P in the population. Hence, as the number of beneficiaries P increases, the per-capita income of the beneficiaries, Y, also increases: from the above argument, the marginal beneficiary is richer than the average beneficiary. Hence:

$$Y = Y(P) \tag{4.9}$$

where:

$YP_P < 0.$

In the context of the model defined by equations (4.7)-(4.9) above, Peltzam (1980) asked two questions. First, what happens when inequality *between* the gainer and loser groups changes, within-group inequality remaining unchanged. Second, what happens when inequality *within* the groups changes, between-group inequality remaining unchanged. The first question is easy to answer. When between-group inequality decreases, the mean income of the beneficiaries increases and hence, from equation (4.8), the forces for redistribution weaken: the wealthier beneficiaries now have a greater stake in labour market outcomes (as measured by per-capita private income) and these are adversely affected through redistribution.

The second question also admits of an unambiguous answer but now the reasoning is more complex. Specifically, suppose the per capita transfer to the P beneficiaries is fixed at g_0; the higher the per-capita income, Y, a smaller fraction, F, of the P beneficiaries will support this policy. And since, from equation (4.9), increasing P involves increasing Y, there is a trade-off between

increasing the number of beneficiaries (P) and reducing the fraction (F) that
would support the policy. Thus any redistributive policy (associated with which
is a per-capita transfer of g) traces a downward sloping locus of (P,F) values
(see Figure 4.2, first quadrant). The task before the government is to choose,
on this political transformation locus, the (P,F) point that maximises political
support - given by the product of P and F (see equation (4.7)). On Figure 4.2,
these iso-support curves are given by the rectangular hyperbolas S1, S2. The
optimal combination, (P* F*), associated with the policy which gives per capita
transfers of g_0, is given by the point E_1.

Any attempt to increase the number of beneficiaries from P* would mean
that the gain to the additional beneficiary would be less than the indirect cost
(through labour market outcomes) that the beneficiary would have to bear for
the additional taxes needed for this extension in numbers. Now suppose the
income distribution among the beneficiaries becomes more equal. Then the
P*+1 beneficiary would now have a lower income than before and thus be
faced with a smaller indirect cost: he (or she) would be more likely to support
the distribution policy. Hence the central result of the Peltzam model is that
reduction in within-beneficiary-group inequality stimulates the growth of
government while a reduction in between-beneficiary-group inequality retards
such growth.

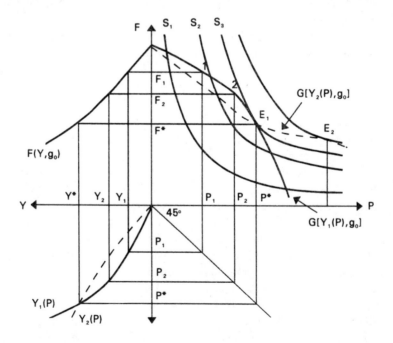

Figure 4.2: The Peltzam model

Conclusions

The preceding sections have painted a picture of growth in the demand for, and supply of, public expenditure on a large canvas in which issues relating to demography, society, politics and the economy have all competed for the viewers attention. Juxtaposed against a rich and varied picture of expenditure demand is the government which is responsible for meeting all (or part) of this demand. The public expenditure outcome is determined by the 'short' side of the market, that is by the extent to which government is prepared to meet demand. This supply-side decision is, as we have emphasised, no less complex than the discussion of demand side influences. In summary, a considerable part of the growth in government expenditure in the OECD countries might be explained by demographic and social factors. These factors generate a 'demand' for certain types of expenditure (both final and transfer). The sources of this demand are a larger number of claimants and also a desire for higher standards of per-capita provision; overlaying this trend in government expenditure are counter-cyclical movements in such expenditure generated by the income shortfall of those adversely affected by the state of the economy. In democratic societies, public expenditure decisions, no matter how well motivated, cannot be separated from be separated from what the public wants for, in its own interest, the government cannot ignore vociferous calls for action. Thus, governments choose to meet the demand for public expenditure because, in large part, it is in their political interest to do so.

NOTES

1. These changes have been detailed by Andrew Adonis in a series of articles in the *Financial Times*, July-August, 1991.
2. Reported in *The Independent*, 7 January 1991.
3. Interestingly 65% of Conservative supporters favoured higher public expenditure.
4. Both because they are more aware of the importance of such services and also because they live longer than working class families.
5. The dependency ratio is the ratio of the total number of dependents (i.e., both young and old) to the size of the working-age population.
6. OECD Economic Studies, Paris: Organisation for Economic Co-operation and Development, 1991.
7. Nominal spending deflated by health care price indicies.
8. Social Trends, London: CSO, 1994.
9. OECD Economic Studies, op cit.
10. A person's entitlements is the 'bundle' of commodities (e.g., food, shelter, health care, personal security) to which he (or she) has legitimate access.
11. See Dreze and Sen (1989).
12. See Mueller (1989).
13. See North and Wallis (1982).
14. See Niskanen (1971).
15. See Chapter 5.
16. Under the assumptions of the median voter theorem.

17. Marginal, that is, to the labour force. This was the argument used by Meltzer and Richards. This argument is slightly forced since, over the last three decades, when government expenditure ballooned in countries of the OECD, there was not any significant change in suffrage in these countries. The growth of government result would obtain, under the model, from a secular rise in unemployment rates with unchanged suffrage.
18. This was unlike the Meltzer and Richards (1991) model in which each person both received transfer income and also paid taxes.
19. Again from the set of realistic alternatives.
20. This negative relation between F and R flows from the fact that higher R would, through labour market effects, lead to lower private incomes for the P gainers.
21. Counter, that is, to the state of the business cycle.

5. Bureaucracy and Government Output

An economic analysis of the supply of public goods is couched within the economics of the public sector where, in essence, the market provision of goods and services is replaced by the political process. It is this replacement in the provision of the service which gives rise to the many public bureaucracies that distribute the public goods to the citizenry, both at regional and national level. Economic theory can easily support the view that by maximising the amount of funds available, the bureaucrat will not only overstate benefits but also induce an inefficient appropriation. Bureaucrats represent the third group in the collective determination of the public budget, the other two being the voter and the politician. One of the principal functions of elected government in a modern democracy is to supply public goods and redistribute real resources. The government, however, seeks re-election and in its efforts to relax the re-election constraint is wont to react to interest group demands and factional interests, each demanding their respective share of public funds.

The bureaucrat is an important linchpin in this entangled web of public decision making. In many respects, the humble bureaucrat or civil servant, that is, an individual who aids government decisions and administers government policies, does not really belong to the family of public choice. However, the bureaucrat as a self-interested budget maximiser most certainly does. These public bureaucracies (also referred to as agencies or bureaus) play an important role in most European economies. For example, the role of the government in administering and collecting taxes and in awarding tenders for capital projects is supplemented by fiscal authorities and local government institutions. Earlier studies on bureaus were conducted by sociologists inspired by the pioneering work of Weber (1947) who had intended his ideal set of characteristics to apply to all large organisations even the profit maximising firm. Likewise, the economic theory of bureaucracy, initiated by Tullock (1965), Downs (1967) and Niskanen (1971), henceforth the TDN model, looks at behaviour and relations between people within an organisation in receipt of a recurrent block of funds. The organisations in both models have an exogenously imposed hierarchical structure within which people are grouped into superiors and sub-ordinates. Referred to as the line management approach, it is best analysed as a principal-agent problem.

In this chapter we address the limitations of the TDN public choice model, evaluate the bureau-shaping models *a la* Dunleavy (1991) and offer some different insights into the behaviour of bureaus. The bureaus are generally defined as 'non-profit organisations which are financed at least in part by a periodic appropriation or grant' (Niskanen, p. 15). The participants in government, the public representatives composed of politicians and bureaucrats, are ascribed selfish utility functions to account for their behaviour as actors in a competitive political game. The game played between these public representatives and the citizenry has the hallmarks of a principal-agent problem. Furthermore, intra-bureau relationships easily translate into a principal-agent problem with a subordinate bureaucrat (the agent) and his principal superior, the politician as minister. Ministers in particular and politicans in general have what we label a *Janus complex*, that is, as the politician she is the principal in the bureaucrat-politician game reverting to the role of an agent in the voter-politician game. While public finance (Musgrave and Musgrave,1980), may question how fiscal institutions can be evaluated and proceed to determine an optimal public provision of social goods, public choice would be inclined to evaluate the intricacies of the Janus complex in the supply of public goods.

The literature on bureaucracy is replete with theories which tend to concentrate on either the oversupply hypothesis of Niskanen or on the divergence between a bureau supplied and an optimal supply of output. There is a dearth of analysis with respect to the optimal size of a bureaucracy. However, if one were to adopt the premise in this chapter that the bureaucracy was already beyond capacity size before decentralisation, what we observe is the following: as the size of government shrinks, the size of the bureaucracy in terms of numbers employed and total budget remain intact. The government and the bureaucracy are (net) complements. In other words, while both increase in size as government expands, a decline in the size of the bureaucracy lags any reduction in the size of government. That central bureaucracy has been divided into decentralised fiefdoms with the total central budget allocated accordingly, may have an important bearing on this net complementary behaviour. The interpretation of government and bureaucracy as net complements may proffer an alternative explanation to the bureau-shaping account of modern public sector bureaucracies adapting to decentralisation. However it may undermine the Niskanenesque tendency for bureaucracies to be self-perpetuating. At this juncture, we should re-evaluate the von Mises suggestion of minimising bureaucracy in order to reduce the size of government.

AGENTS IN THE PUBLIC SECTOR

Musgrave and Musgrave (1980) identify two roles for the typical public servant. The first we shall refer to as Niskanen's budget maximiser, and the second as the civil servant akin to Downs' statesman. The latter play a constructive role in the efficient operation of government, and the general public's perception of the civil service is one which characterises the service as the administrative wing of government. Although the composition of governments do change at each general election the core of civil servants remain intact. The tradition in post-election Europe is one where the civil service largely remains in place in sharp contrast to the American presidential system which does implant a partisan element into the administrative arm of the government. The former view as outlined by Niskanen is the more popular interpretation of the role of bureaucracies, where the bureaucrat's main objective is to maximise the size of the bureau budget. One important dimension to the interpretation of the bureaucrat as a self-interested agent, is the nature of the organisations and institutions that enable this self-interested behaviour to proceed.

Brown and Jackson (1990) proceed to look at the incentives and rewards and indeed the organisational slack that may perpetuate the role of the budget maximising bureaucrat. The inter-relationship between elected politician and bureaucrats is one angle which is considered, whereby the bureaucrat is presented as an agenda manipulator. Alternatively, the bureaucrat may be interpreted as a typical budget maximiser, a rather limiting interpretation, particularly when we realise that the behaviour of bureaucrats extends through the entire domain of the public sector decision making process. The possible creation of bureaucratic elites within the system of bureaucracies remains largely an unexplored area in the public choice literature. However, an analysis of the institutional structures within which budget maximisers can persist is a step in the right direction.

In particular, if the civil servant acts as an *agent provocateur* for the pressure group (principal), X-inefficiencies could arise in the public budget as additional wasteful expenditures are raised to meet the pressure group demands. This is an askewed version of the paradigmal case of rent-seeking outlined in Chapter 6 wherein the pressure group expends real resources to bribe the civil servant. Here we suggest that the civil servant of his own volition, grounded in whatever criterion of allegiance to the professional group, either redirects resources to that particular group or is responsible for the direction of resources to a particular interest group. The bureaucrat makes a decision or recommends a decision to the appropriate government minister using criteria of efficiency and effectiveness. The criteria are shrouded in mystery. In unravelling the mystery we can at least count on some guidelines. For example, the economic concept of allocative efficiency translates into the following set of questions:

(i) does the public sector produce the expenditures which the electorate demands? (ii) which voter preferences count? (iii) are the public services produced at a minimum cost? Arguably, the amount of public good determined by whatever efficiency criteria are employed by humble civil servants in general and by public representatives in particular, may not be immune from the median-voter preferences. Median-voter preferences must be satisfied for political survival but any alternative level of public output or range of service will represent an initial response to pressure group demands. In analysing public sector inefficiency we complement the comment made in Brown and Jackson (1990) that 'the business of politics is balancing up these different signals' (p. 196), with the belief that the humble civil servant introduced earlier, has a more incisive role to play in bringing pressure group demands (the signals) to the sponsor's attention. The civil servant either as an agenda setter, as alluded to by Brown and Jackson (1990), or as an *agent provocateur* as suggested in this chapter, can impinge rather effectively on budget decisions.

Undoubtedly the bureaucrat as adviser to government on the optimal provision of the public goods is a prominent actor in this game of government supply and demand played within the rigors of an exogenous line management structure. The relationship between the government and the bureaucracy, in particular the relationship between a sponsor and a subordinate, is the main theme of this chapter. How this relationship impacts on the supply of government output is the subject of intense interest in the public choice and public finance literatures. The size of government, measured as the ratio of central government expenditure to gross domestic product, is an important signal in analysing the redistributive role of government; it measures the level of government activity and the extent of government commitment to the provision of goods and services. Current trends in public policy across Europe are characterised by decentralisation and consumer choice in the provision of public goods. If by some norm the public sector behaves inefficiently, the solution is either to reduce the size of the offending bureaucracy or abandon a public provision of the good in favour of a market provision. In the wake of new right arguments to reduce public sector inefficiencies, any continued existence of large bureaucracies in a particular country may simply reflect its political ideology. In other words, we would expect to find larger bureaucracies in those countries where the government could be defined as more left-wing. In this chapter we shall examine the bureau-shaping model of bureaucracy which may shed some light on the apparent bureaucratic acquiescence in decentralisation. There may be a hidden factor embedded in this willingness to decentralise.

The empirical relationship between bureaucracy and size of government is unclear. As noted by Mueller (1989) 'bureaucrats and interest groups stand equally high on all lists of the causes of the growth of government ... but more systematic support for the bureaucracy-size of government relationship is sparse and contradictory' (p. 339). Bureaucracy and government are complementary and have been throughout history. In many respects this complementary relationship is best interpreted as a net complement, that is, bureaucracy is a net complement to government rather than a gross complement as assumed in the literature. With a net complementary relationship we can argue either (i) that as government expands less bureaucracy is required as existing X-inefficiencies within the organisation of the bureau are minimised or; (ii) as the government sector shrinks, the bureaucracy remains uniquely intact since it is already beyond capacity size. The latter is a characteristic of bureaus across all the models on bureaucracy in the literature. Public choice scholars are keenly interested in the determinants of the growth of government size. Many hypotheses have been put forward to account for the growth in government. For example, Wagner's (1890) Law asserts that government expands as the economy becomes more urbanised and modernised at which point the income elasticity of demand for public goods exceeds the income elasticity of demand for private goods. Meltzer and Richard's (1981) use the median voter theorem to argue that more redistribution takes place the lower the income of the median voter relative to average income. In their account of the growth of government attention is paid to the voter enfranchisement of lower income groups. The Peacock and Wiseman (1961) displacement effect states that government spending tends to evolve in a step like pattern coinciding with social upheavals.

They observed that expenditures over time outlined a series of plateau separated by peaks. As a theory about secular behaviour of government spending, it has been compared to Wagner's Law. For Kau and Robin (1981) it is technological change 'which had led to a reduction in the cost of collecting tax revenues and hence in the supply of services offered by the government'. Baumol (1967) implies an exponential growth of public expenditure on account of price due to systematic public-private productivity growth disparity. For example, a more rapid rate for inflation in the price of inputs or goods purchased by the public sector results in an increase in the ratio of nominal expenditure to gross domestic product. The hypothesis is also known as Baumol's Disease. In the spirit of this chapter, Peltzman (1980), with whom we concur, claims that the entire growth can be attributed to the interplay between vote-maximising politicians and the citizenry who demand and pressure government for their share of the income redistribution.

The Role of Interest Groups

The quintessential public choice hypothesis, Buchanan and Tullock (1962), advance the central idea that strong interest groups determine the size of the government while Niskanen (1971) argued that the bureaucracy contributed to the size of government. In the Buchanan-Tullock world each group attempts to win favour with the government by offering a supply of votes and in return the government takes cognisance of the interest group's demand for (say) low taxes and subsidies. Their hypothesis also represents the classic public choice interpretation of government and government output. The list of hypotheses explaining growth of government is by no means exhaustive, interested readers are referred to Mueller (1989) and Henrekson (1991). The absence of robust empirical findings does not distract from the central theme addressed by the these two latter hypotheses, in that the Pigovian interpretation of government is rather redundant. As alluded to in Musgrave and Musgrave (1980) a realistic interpretation of the fiscal system has individuals instinctively grouping into taxpayers lobbies and consumer lobbies.

Budget policy becomes more an instrument of interest groups accommodation and co-operation rather than a short term fiscal policy tool. The issue before us is whether or not lobbying indicated by the number of interest groups, generates excessive levels of government expenditure as identified in Lee (1985); if so, we have to add net (including benefits) lobbying costs to the production costs of government. The interest group theory of government translates into the positive theory of rent-seeking. Although the interest group theory was dominant in political science literature as 'pluralism', it was not until the publication of work by Olson (1965) and in particular by Stigler (1971) that public choice theorists adopted a basic theory. Stigler argued that regulation was in place for the benefit of special interest groups. Peltzman's (1976) generalisation of Stigler introduced the politician as the regulator who maximised votes by setting 'political' prices, that is the regulated prices over which the many interest groups lobbied government. McCormick and Tollison (1981) advance the original arguments and have helped to buttress the emerging theory.

They have built an Olson's (1965) theory of group formation. In general the interest-group theory is divided into the theory of economic regulation *a la* Posner (1974) and Peltzman (1976), and the economic theory of legislation *a la* Landes and Posner (1975), Crain (1977) and McCormick and Tollison (1978). The former attempts to explain existing government regulation while the latter seeks to explain the origin of government regulation. The central issue is to what extent the direction of government regulation is predetermined by vociferous industrial groups. How the direction is abated by self-interested agent-bureaucrats is of particular concern to public choice scholars. The interest group theory implies that political agents act in a self-interested way like economic agents. The behaviour of both agents will be different because of the different constraints in the political market. One can ascertain from the discussion on bureaucracy that the political market in which government and interest groups interact is imperfect. One hallmark of this market is the possibility of inter-bureau competition for limited central (sponsor) funds.

Consider the following situation: in a government-wide allocation G the ith bureaucracy's share depends ultimately on the share of the other bureaucracies, hence a linear equation of the form $Bi = (G - \Sigma Bi)$ represents an inter-group crowding-out constraint. If we were to include ΣBi as an argument in the bureaucrat's utility function, the derivative $\partial TU/\partial \Sigma Bi$ and its second derivative would generate the conditions for a maximum and a declining segment respectively of the bureaucrat's utility function. This would help to overcome the criticisms levelled at the arbitrariness of Niskanen's quadratic utility function. A utility function with ΣBi as an argument would elicit the necessary properties including that of a turning point.

The crowding-out effect appears in the bureau-shaping models as an external constraint. Stigler (1971) for example presented a model in terms of the costs and benefits to various groups of using government to increase their wealth. He showed that large producer groups like farmers and union members seek wealth transfers while smaller groups organise to resist negative regulation. He carries the idea across into Stigler (1976) wherein according to McCormick and Tollison, Stigler concludes that: 'the valuations that interest groups place on issues are perceived as a demand for legislation'. The interest group theory has since evolved to argue that politicians themselves are an interest group in their own right. They wish to secure re-election and hence curry favour with various groups.

A final observation relates the extent of interest group formation and consolidation of purpose in successfully influencing government and bureaucracy. The more successful the interest group becomes the greater the probability that it will be in a position to impact on the policy making process of successive governments. As Stigler (1976) pointed out many groups have similar interests and the possibility of realising economies of scale and of scope in lobbying is noted. But as society becomes more urbanised there does emerge a need for collective action whether it be for neighbourhood traffic regulation, water supplies, cleaner environment or better schools. Also increases in educational levels and socio-economic status contribute to political awareness which is further channelled through what van Winden (1983) has called the interest function approach, whereby individuals in the economy can be grouped, with each group having a coherent set of interests. In this discussion we are not explicitly concerned with a measure of the opportunity costs of government expenditures diverted to interest groups but acknowledge that the government can set up the scenario for individuals to secure a benefit or avoid a cost.

Aspiring monopolists will retain lobbyists to assure a favourable outcome and devote resources to the acquisition of the monopoly right. A government will more than likely grant monopoly privileges to various groups of politically influential people. Cartels and anti-competitive behaviour will be maintained and politicians will react to the demands of the more vociferous and well organised interest groups. It is government restrictions upon economic activity that gives rise to rents and the ensuing competition for those rents. The covert nature of the linkage between government and interest groups is addressed in discussion of the tenure cycle in McNutt (1995). What then are the implications for government and government output of the interest group theory? One important implication is that a government and the incumbent politicians are faced with a re-election constraint and that no policy will be introduced that could damage the possibility of re-election. The underlying question here is whether a government actually works in the public interest or operates conditional on a mandate that is pre-determined by powerful interest groups. This line of argument concludes that government is endogenous within the politico-economic system. Another implication is that the Pigovian interpretation of government as a benevolent dictator maximising social welfare, is redundant. As alluded to throughout this book, this leads a rational individual to conclude: why bother to vote? However the self-interest ego maximiser will both vote and take out membership of a vociferous interest group. Such strategic voters can have great influence, particularly if the rest of society behave as citizen free riders who regard the government as a public good and make no attempt to influence decisions or allocations. Their very existence is conducive to interest group success.

Models of Bureaucracy

Public choice models of bureaucracy appeared in the late nineteen sixties when the conventional public administration approach to understanding the behaviour of large government agencies came under attack. The principal works in the vanguard of this attack include Tullock (1965), Downs (1967) and Niskanen (1971). The most recognisable model is that of Niskanen whose name is synonymous with the economic analysis of bureaucracy. Although both political scientists and sociologists in particular have considered various theories of bureaucracy, it was not until the publication of Niskanen's (1971) work that a well defined economic analysis was undertaken. In public finance today no discussion on the supply of public goods is complete unless the role of bureaucracies is introduced. When Niskanen's work appeared it was the only comprehensive analysis of bureaucrats and bureaucracy from an economist's perspective. The Niskanen model is a static model of bureaucracy which may have overlooked some of the dynamic elements cocooned within the earlier Downs' (1967) model and alluded to later by Tullock (1974). In this chapter, we retrospectively resurrect Tullock's (1974) model on bureaucracy coupled with Downs' life cycle idea, in an attempt to derive the possible dynamics of a Niskanenesque bureaucracy.

Prior to the work of Niskanen, there was a dominance of sociologists in the study of bureaucracy. In the earlier pages of his work, Niskanen pointed out that most of the literature on bureaucracy, from the ancient writings of Confucius to the sociological theory of Weber, assumed that individual preferences were subordinate to the goals of the state. Niskanen in his economic method recognised the relevance of the preferences of individual bureaucrats. The bureaucrat, he commented is no longer a 'role player in some larger social drama' (p. 5), but rather like the consumer and the entrepreneur in classical economics, the bureaucrat is a central figure. Niskanen was rather circumspect in attacking the methodological foundations of welfare economics. There is a paradox in the history of economics in the general area of public policy and in the area of welfare economics specifically. The Benthamite legislator did not allow a preference function to have any role to play in shaping public policy under the auspices of the greatest happiness principle. The Benthamite legislator ascribed to the organic concept of the state where individual preferences were subordinate to the goal of the 'the greatest happiness of the greatest number'. Yet both Adam Smith and David Hume in their writings stressed the role of private self-interested behaviour. It is more than likely that economists before Niskanen who may have contemplated a theory of bureaucratic behaviour were saddled with an utilitarian calculus in public sector decision-making that presupposed the subordination of all individual self-interest.

It was becoming increasingly obvious across the literature that rational individuals were deciding against voting for a politician (with a probability of realising the objective), and opting instead for membership of a vociferous interest group who could best represent their objective, whether it be higher wages, better working conditions, reduced taxes, cleaner environment, or subsidies. A contemporary reading of the international evidence on voter turnout, Powell (1981), would re-affirm this position. If a government policy offers potential benefits to a group of individuals, they will attempt to acquire those benefits (rents). In other words the same group of individuals may form an interest group in order to lobby the government. Rent-seeking behaviour is generally associated with such interest group formation. The suggestion implicit in this argument is that government decisions can be influenced by interest groups who continually lobby government. Whether or not this is in the public interest is irrelevant to the interest group *per se* but should be of direct concern ultimately to the economist. For example, if an interest group is trying to avoid a cost like higher taxes, it is conceivable that their relative success may impinge upon the government's attempt to offer (say) increased tax allowances to another sector. A demand to increase expenditure in the direction of one sector will inevitably reverberate on other competing sectors in the economy.

In Chapter 6 we introduce the idea of induced rent-seeking which may be related to what appears to be an interest group crowding-out effect in the allocation of public funds. In this case it is of direct concern to the economist as it impacts on allocative efficiency. Questions have to be answered, *vis-a-vis* are the limited real resources being directed to the more productive individuals in the economy? If not, the observer may ask: does government realise the common good? That it does is very much the implicit assumption in Keynes' theory. Furthermore classical welfare economics which underpins modern public finance begins with the premise that government is a benevolent agent maximising social welfare and correcting market failures. Bureaucracies are a natural complement to government in the initial stages of the political process. Eventually they acquire a Niskanenesque independence as the mechanism for providing public goods integrates a general theory of supply by the bureaus concerned with a behavioural theory of representative government. Niskanen (p. 9) acknowledges the inspiration gained from the earlier insights of Weber (1947) and von Mises on the concept of bureaucracy and from the analysis outlined in both Tullock (1965) and Downs (1967). While Downs presented a more pluralist picture of the complicated workings of bureaucracies, Niskanen unwittingly offered a new right account of the their aggregate behaviour. His oversupply hypothesis, on which he has since retracted (Niskanen 1987), gave credence to the von Mises inspired reduction in size of government which has become the hallmark of new right governments in the nineteen eighties and nineties.

PUBLIC CHOICE PERSPECTIVE

The scene for a public choice analysis of bureaucracy was set by Tullock (1965) in focusing on the relations between individuals within a bureaucracy. There is a non-zero opportunity cost of withdrawing from these organisational relationships which maps into promotion or peer group pressures. Consequently one could apply a bilateral monopoly framework to the situation where the bureaucracy-monopolist supplier of the public good interfaces with the government-sponsor monopsonist. The indeterminate solution characteristic of such a model inevitably requires a non-economic bargaining outcome. Likewise, in a principal-agent characterisation of the relation an information asymmetry problem arises between the superior and the subordinate. The distinguishing feature of a public choice model is in interpreting the individual as a maximising individual, with which the model is able to predict the bureaucrat's wants. In a direct analogy with profit a maximising entrepreneur, the bureaucrat, wishes to maximise the bureau's budget. There is a remarkable similarity between the Niskanen bureaucrat and the manager in the Baumol-

Marris-Williamson type models of managerial behaviour. The budget is allocated to the bureau by the sponsor in return for an amount of public output. The sponsors expect to be presented with proposals for additional funding so that during the screening stage attention will focus on the marginal increases being sought. If no increase is sought the sponsor is confused.

The traditional Weberian relationship between superior and subordinate was somewhat reversed by the Niskanen-Tullock public choice model. Before that as captured by Machiavelli (1952), attention was paid to the behaviour of the superior-Prince *vis-a-vis* the subordinates while in a public choice model attention is paid to the behaviour of the subordinates *vis-a-vis* the superior. Niskanen (1987) comments that 'Machiavelli's *The Prince* was the closest model to Tullock's book on bureaucracy' (p. 136). Niskanen (1987) identifies a common mistake in both Machiavelli (1952) and in Tullock (1965). Niskanen (1987, p. 136) in defence of an economic marginal analysis indicates that both theses highlight incorrect advice, particularly if the benefit of additional information (ΔTB) exceeds the additional cost (ΔTC) in assimilating the new information. If it is the case that $\Delta TB > \Delta TC$ the new information may have led to an efficient outcome; the public administrator (the sponsor) cannot possibly make an efficient decision based on incomplete information. Machiavelli apparently dissuaded the Prince from accepting advice unless the Prince had specifically requested it, while Tullock came to the conclusion that subordinates support the decision of the superior if it is consistent with current information. The current information which a superior has, however, is dependent on the advice and information made available by the subordinates. Within a principal-agent framework as argued earlier, the self-interested agent has a survivalist incentive to misinform the principal. Most of the literature on bureaucracy assumes an organic concept of the state in which individual preferences are subordinate to the goals of the state. In contrast Niskanen's theory of bureaucracy assumes 'an instrumental concept of the state' (p. 4), where the state is regarded as an instrument of the citizenry.

The dominance of the sociological theories was evident in the mid-sixties which reflected the influence of Weber who had devoted little attention to the economic behaviour of bureaus. Economists were prepared to leave the analysis of bureaucracies to the sociologists; any concern they may have had on the supply of public goods was ameliorated by the assumption that public goods were supplied by a competitive industry. In other words, bureaus supplying public goods would behave like a competitive industry. That apart, von Mises (1944) had argued that there was no meaningful comparison to be made between the behaviour of profit maximising firms and the behaviour of bureaus. By this line of argument, von Mises concluded that bureaucracies were a necessary form of public administration, a view shared later by Downs. In his scholarly Weberian interpretation of bureaucracy as an important characteristic in the administration of the state, Downs had focused attention on the organisation of bureaus and on the behaviour within a bureau rather than on 'the economic behaviour of bureaus as it affects their performance in supplying public services' (Niskanen, p. 6).

On the economics side, von Mises provided a critical insight into bureaucracy in suggesting that the only way to minimise the problems in a bureaucracy was to reduce the size of the government. This assertion was echoed by Niskanen in his opening paragraph wherein he comments that 'those who want to restrict the role of government are quick to use the poor performance of the bureaucracy to support their position'. And here lies a dilemma for bureaucracies, namely, are they required to supply public goods, maintain public services, alleviate poverty, regulate the economy, clean up the environment without an appropriate budget? We could generalise and wonder whether or not the same is expected of politicians. If we could extract the marginal valuations of each citizen for one bureaucracy-supplied public good, an optimal size of budget could be determined. Tullock (1965), to whom Niskanen admits an intellectual debt in formulating his own theory of bureaucracy, used a model to explain advancement and promotion procedures within bureaus. Downs' (1967) model looked at behaviour within the bureau and developed a theory of management process within them. However, both authors fell short of a theory where the bureaucrats do impact on the supply of public goods.

As Niskanen pointed out both scholars did not address two fundamental questions *vis-a-vis* 'given demand and cost conditions how much output is produced at what total cost? (and) how do these output and cost levels change with changing conditions?' (p. 8). The answers to these questions remain in abeyance today. A compromise may be gleaned from Niskanen's comment, that Downs, contrary to von Mises assertion, argued that bureaus provide many goods and services that can be marketed. If so the sponsor could derive shadow prices with which to compute the total output gain from the input of government funds. In general the input of funds into the bureaucracy leads to a public good output. If the output/input ratio is less than 1, one could argue that X-inefficiency may exist in the bureaucracy. In other words the absence of a 1:1 translation from input of resources into a public output arises from internal inefficiencies within the bureaucracy, manifesting themselves either as organisational diseconomies, asymmetric information or redirection of public funds to ameliorate interest group demands.

Downs-Lindblom Model

Downs' (1967) contribution is important in understanding the motivation and behaviour of bureaucrats and in looking at the strategies of rational bureaucrats.

The personalities and characteristics of bureaucrats is very important in the strategic analysis of bureaucratic behaviour. Downs described the personality of different bureaucrats in a scale ranging from climbers who maximise their own self interest, to statesmen, the altruistic civil servant who does not abuse the power invested in him or her. The range of personalities generated a range of laws about how bureaucracies behave both internally and externally. Bureaucracies have a life cycle as new bureaus form and others are amalgamated to form larger bureaus. Although no formal analysis was presented by Downs, we contend that his life cycle model predates the bureau-shaping model. The bureau-shaping model, unlike the Niskanen budget maximising model, offers an explanation for the administrative trend, labelled by Dunleavy (1991) as de-institutionalisation (DE). Defined as the running down of an established bureau in favour of a new bureau, the DE process may be equivalent to the earlier Downs' life cycle. Downs' law of increasing conservatism asserts that as the bureaucrats get older they become more conservative by assumption. Likewise, as bureaus age they become less expansionist.

Downs very much adopts a Weberian picture of government agencies in that his self interest axiom suggests that rational actors will not co-operate unless compelled to do so by a command-like chain of authority. This picture is qualified by a more pluralist emphasis on the individual's self interested inclinations to resist the demands of a superior. While one is prepared to accept the point made in Musgrave and Musgrave (1980, p. 124) 'that knowledge is power', one may be rather reluctant to accept that bureaucrats in maximising self-interest may seek to maximise power. The line of argument developed by both Downs and Niskanen independently, acknowledges that the input of bureaucrats, even the inputs of Downsian statesmen, into policy making decisions catapults them into a position of power. In this Downs-Niskanen perception of the bureaucratic world, the implementation of a government decision ex-post by the bureaucrat likewise enhances power. Bureaucrats play the same game as entrepreneurs and managers in the modern theory of the firm according to Downs, who offers a pluralist account of bureaucracy. But surely, pluralism can only exist when no single elite dominates the bureaucratic decision making process. The promotion structure can screen the recruitment of subordinates from different socio-economic backgrounds to the rank of superior. Dahl (1961) in a different context but on a similar theme, comments that 'the poor man is not likely to gain high influence; but if he does, somehow on the way he is no longer a poor man' (p. 287). The acquisition of such power may be an important covert characteristic within bureaucracies. It is different to the (internal) administrative power of the Downs-Niskanen utility function. In this case the power extends beyond the bureaucracy in contributing to an unequal distribution of the public resources.

The pluralism arises because of the decentralised hierarchical decision making in which every individual interacts and mutually affects the policy result. At different levels there will be coordination superiors and any policy making delays are handled by the line of command. Downs' approach regards motivational diversity as central to the working of a bureaucracy. The Downs' model specifically proffers some interesting insights that are important in understanding the general behaviour of bureaucrats. He identified key aspects of motivation in all bureaus including the fact that subordinates distort information to superiors and that they respond to superiors in a discretionary way. Basically if two policies were indifferent, the bureaucrats would select that policy which maximised their self-interest. In advancing the Downsian position further we conjoin Downsian pluralism with the political interpretation of pluralism, and in particular with the pluralism or 'partial mutual adjustment' of Lindblom (1977).

We do so in order to develop a point that has been apparently overlooked in the management structure that characterises both the Downsian bureaucracy and the bureaucracy within a bureau-shaping model outlined later. The Niskanen bureaucrats are outside our remit since their *raison d'etre* is to maximise budgets. Quite simply, there may be a covert behavioural characteristic of bureaucrats that has been overlooked in the non-budget maximising models. With the line system of management in the Downsian bureaucracy different policies will be influenced by different individuals which is consistent with the principle of democratic equality. In any bureaucracy there are many different policies and different bureaucrats identified by rank. In the bureau-shaping model superiors handle the policy with prestige while subordinates handle the less important policy. In bureaucracies generally superiors handle different policies to the subordinates. It is an explicit characteristic of the bureau-shaping model and it may be implicit in a Downsian bureaucracy. If so a crack appears in the pluralist dimension to the model.

By extending the typology in Lindblom (1977) we divide the policies into two distinct groups namely, (i) policies which deal with 'ordinary issues' and (ii) policies which deal with 'grand issues'. The latter pertain to the structure of political economic life and include issues on income distribution, taxes and welfare programmes. On policies dealing with ordinary issues, routine tasks such as planning applications, tenders for government contracts and capitation grants, pluralism may apply, otherwise it is absent. In dealing with the grand issues the superiors dominate in the line of command with a tendency towards a corporativist outcome. It is more than likely that superiors within a bureaucracy belong to a homogenous socio-economic group with a common schooling and indoctrination. Policy making within a line management bureaucracy, particularly on grand issues, may not be consistent with the ideals of democratic equality.

This is more striking, *a la* Mueller (1989), the greater the number of professionals like doctors, lawyers, and teachers that make up the composition of the public service. Aligned either by professional trade union bonds, socio-economic class allegiance, old boy networks and various club memberships, the hithertofore humble civil servant may have been overlooked in the economic analysis of bureaucracies in preference to the budget maximiser. A major problem with the bureaucracy models is that they tend to concentrate on the internal and overt characteristics of the bureaucrat. This iceberg vision of the bureaucrat, and of the bureaucracy in general, counsels a neglect of possible covert ideological standpoints and class antagonisms within an organisation. In the budget allocation decision-making process within the bureaucracy such standpoints may eventually come to bear on the final outcome. Consequently the picture that emerges from these models, irrespective of the motives of the bureaucrats, is that agreement on policy thus becomes the only practicable test of the policy's correctness.

Niskanen's Model

The Niskanen model is rather straightforward, as illustrated in Figure 5.1. Looking at our illustration with a negatively sloped average revenue (AR) schedule equating with the MV (marginal valuation) curve and a constant marginal cost (LMC) equating with the average cost (LAC), we can identify three possible output levels as follows: (i) q1, where the private monopolist would produce at MC = M; (ii) q2, where a government (Pareto) social optimum output is reached; and (iii) q3, an arbitrary bureaucracy output that principally depends on the size of the budget; arbitrary in the sense that a smaller budget would have a bureaucratic output less than or equal to the social optimum. If a bureau is given a budget equal to the rectangle (fdh0), the bureau will supply public good output to q3 which is greater than the social optimum level of output at q2. This arises principally because of the self-interested behaviour of the bureaucrat in increasing the budget size. The Niskanen conclusion is very much in support of an output that exceeds the social optimum. Within a principal-agent framework we can return to our question and ask if this higher output is in the best interests of the principal government, as representing voters?

How does Niskanen arrive at his conclusion that a public sector bureau expands public sector output to a level twice the social optimum level? The answer is in the assumption that the bureaucrat is a monopoly supplier while the sponsor (the legislature) is assumed to be a monopsonist. The self-interested bureaucrat seeks to obtain as large a budget as possible while the voter simply wishes to maximise the total benefit from the public good. The bureaucrat is able to extract consumer surplus (abc) in Figure 5.1, and divert it into more output simply because in negotiating a budget the bureaucrats have superior information on the costs of public output than the sponsors.

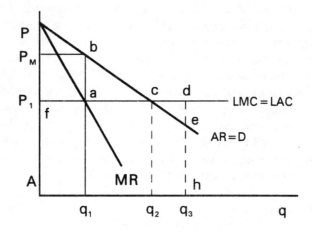

Figure 5.1: The Niskanen model

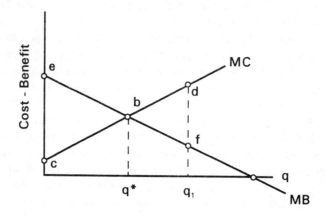

Figure 5.2: The Niskanen model

Figure 5.2 illustrates the argument quite well. The marginal benefit (MB) and marginal cost (MC) curves are illustrated and the output level q* corresponds to a social optimum. The bureaucrat will expand output to where total benefit (TB) = total cost (TC) at an output level q1. The triangular area (ebc) is a consumer surplus and represents the traditional benefit to society of having q* output. The triangular are a (bdf) however represents a social waste which offsets the consumer surplus. If this did occur the bureau is not contributing to social welfare. If the q1 output was at the point where the MB intersects the x-axis and if both triangles (ebc) and (bdf) are equal, the bureau would be unable to offset completely the value of the consumer surplus.

One reason why an output level like q1 occurs is due to weak sponsor controls which enable the bureaucrat to extract the (bdf) surplus. The information asymmetries however are not sufficient to explain the level of bureau output; one must also consider the institutional setting of the bureau. For example, the case of q1 which corresponds to a TB = TC point of intersection, could occur when new bureaus are established, particularly in a period of high public demand for their output. Niskanen does acknowledge that legislatures can impose limits on the bureau. In particular, legislatures can stop bureaus from reducing total social welfare. If the bureau contributes to the high costs, public complaints from voters and interest groups alike may force the legislature to cutback on the bureaus budget. This retraction of funds manifests itself as voters realise that public expenditures are no longer required, as with defence in the post-Cold War era.

The diagram that is usually represented in texts as an example of Niskanen does not do justice to a central argument in his original thesis on the difference between an efficient and an optimal bureau output. Figure 5.3 illustrates the original Niskanen diagram with two marginal valuation curves V_1 and V_2 for output demand and a linear cost represented by (C,C). This discussion is abstracted from the basic model in Niskanen (1971, pp. 46-8). In the screening process the sponsor will reduce the budget of the bureaucrat who will inevitably summit a budget 'which maximises the expected approved budget subject to the constraint that the approved budget must be sufficient to cover the cost of the output expected by the sponsor at that budget level' (p. 46). The equilibrium level of the expected output at the approved budget is determined by setting the first derivative of TB = 0. The constrained output level is found by solving TC = TB, which represents a reduced level of output.

The equilibrium level of the expected output at an agreed budget level is computed by maximising the quadratic TB curve:

$$TB = aQ - bQ^2$$

which yields $Q = a/2b$. Given the quadratic TC function defined as:

$$TC = cQ + dQ^2$$

by setting TC = TB an output level Q~ is attained such that:

$$Q\text{~} = (a - c)/(b + d)$$

both Q~ and the Q level of output are equal when $a = 2bc/(b-d)$. Hence as Niskanen pointed out the equilibrium level of output is:

$Q = a/2b$ if $a > 2bc/(b-d)$ and;

$Q = (a-c)/(b-d)$ if $a \leq 2bc/(b-d)$.

A bureau's output is *efficient* if it produces at the minimum cost whereas it is *optimal* if the level of output generates the largest net benefit. For the lower marginal valuation V_1 the equilibrium output is in the budget constrained area (ea_1gh) and since $(ea_1gh) = (ecfh)$ there is 'no bureaucratic fat' in this bureau as the total budget covers the minimum total costs. There is demand level V_2 which represents groups who have a higher demand and those who have interests in the factors used in producing the public output. This translates into legislatures being dominated by functional interests, the equilibrium level of output is in the demand constrained (MV = 0) region and total budget exceeds the total costs. There is 'bureaucratic fat' in this bureau and the bureau has no incentive to be efficient. In addition the output is above the optimal.

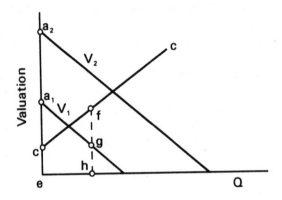

Figure 5.3: Niskanen's 'bureaucratic fat' model

In comparing both V-demands the central Niskanen conclusion that output exceeds the optimum obtains, but it overshadows one important economic fact. In the smaller budget-constrained equilibrium the bureau output is efficient but not optimal while in a larger demand-determined equilibrium the bureau output is inefficient and optimal. In both cases a cost-benefit analysis which looks at optimality conditions would conclude that both bureaus are large. The application would be erroneous as it completely underestimates the opportunity costs of resources used by the interest groups in ensuring the higher bureau output. The traditional representation of the Niskanen model is equivalent to the V_1 demand as witnessed in Mueller (1989) and in Brown and Jackson (1990). They both allude to the rent accruing to the interest groups at the higher bureau output and the abrogation of legislative and constitutional responsibility by the sponsor in allowing the bureau output to be determined by group interests rather than by the public interest.

This public choice insight has to be explored before a new right prescription can confidently assert that all bureaucracies be reduced in size. The simple economics of the Niskanen model suggests that the V_2 demand-determined output should be the first target of government retrenchment on expenditures. Niskanen's principal conclusion that 'all bureaus are too large' (p. 33), affirms the new right attitude to bureaucracy. However, in the real world the bureau which supplies a V_1 output becomes the first target of a new right attempt to reduce the 'bureaucratic fat'. One can notice this by the sequence of cutbacks in the public budget which began with cutbacks on health and education budgets to be followed later by cutbacks in the military and agricultural budgets. The significance of this argument assumes Orwellian proportions when we connect with our earlier argument on pluralism and the power of superior ranking bureaucrats in implementing bureau policy.

Tullock's Hypothesis

The Tullock hypothesis is referred to as a dynamic hypothesis on bureaucracy. Our interest in resurrecting it is to examine the possibility of applying an exponential growth function to bureaus. Tullock had concluded that through time a bureaucracy grows in size and did not remain at initial size (say) Bt. The rational budget maximising individual is faced with a problem in increasing bureaucracy size; the problem manifests itself in an attempt to increase the numbers employed, N. Tullock's dynamic hypothesis could possibly fall under the remit of the Downs' life cycle approach, particularly if one could apply an exponential growth function to account for bureaucracy growth. A function of the form $B_{t+1} = B_t \exp(rt)$, where B_{t+1} is the number (size) of the bureaucracy in time period (t+1) and B_t in time period t. A dynamic element in Tullock's model could be developed into a growth function of bureaucracy. If the application were possible a Gompertz type relationship would yield an upper asymptote on the size of bureaucracy, an issue raised in rather a different cloak in the bureau-shaping models. It may also be implicit in his mixed demand curve which offers support for a life cycle approach to bureaucracy growth, r.

In Tullock's model the bureaucrat has a higher utility (demand) for the growth of the bureaucracy because a salary is derived from the bureaucracy in addition to services provided. In time period t Tullock concludes that the legislature considers a mixed demand curve. This curve is a combination of what the citizens perceive as the optimal bureaucratic size and what the bureaucrat perceives as the optimal size. Given costs C, the legislature (sponsor) purchases an amount of bureaucracy. It is inevitably greater than that required by the citizens. Tullock further states that in (t+1) the process will lead to an additional expansion of bureaucracy size,which causes a dynamic shift in the mixed demand curve to the right.

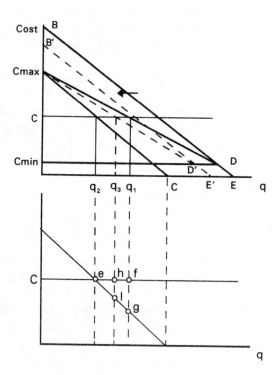

Figure 5.4: Tullock's model of bureaucracy

We have advanced the original Tullock diagram (not reproduced here) into our Figure 5.4 which offers a more robust method to the original method in Tullock (1974) of extracting the mixed demand curve. Costs are represented on the vertical axis while bureau output-supply is represented on the horizontal axis. At C_{max} the cost of bureaucracy is prohibitively high, that the citizens prefer to do without, while at C_{min} the citizen would demand a large bureaucracy size. As in Tullock's original characterisation the bureaucrats demand for bureau size is greater and represented by the higher positioned B line. The sponsor's mixed demand ($C_{max}DE$) may be interpreted as follows: if the sponsor knows both the citizen and the bureaucrat demand, the sponsor can determine the derived demand. One could interpret the derived demand as a compromise between both demands.

For a given cost, represented by the linear cost C, the sponsor demand is q_1 which is, as in the original Tullock model greater than the citizen demand q_2. The difference is translated into a dead-weight loss measured in the sub-panel of Figure 5.4 by the triangular area (efg). If the bureaucrats reduce their demand as illustrated by the dashed line B' a new mixed demand curve evolves, (C_{max}D'E'). The dead-weight loss falls to (ehl) and at the cost C an operational size of bureaucracy q3 will obtain. Likewise if the citizens increase their demand for bureau output the divergence decreases. What this illustrates is a choice between an operational size of bureau, between q2 and q1, which minimises the difference required by citizenry (q2) and sponsors (q1), in other words an efficient operational size of bureau with a minimum dead-weight loss obtains. In Figure 5.4 the monopoly bureau would produce q3 level of government output.

Breton-Brennan-Buchanan Model

Breton's (1974) theory of representative government is consistent with the model outlined by Downs. In a Breton-Downs' world the government is in complete control of the legislature and Breton further argues that the government takes advantage of its position as the monopoly supplier of the public goods. In his theory of monopoly government Breton lists the various strategies open to government to deter the entry of the opposition parties, including 'full line supply by combining policies in such a way as to elicit or maintain political support' (p. 143). Brennan and Buchanan (1980) extend the monopoly-government model one step further in assuming that the citizenry impose a constraint on government by limiting the tax base. The Brennan-Buchanan model of bureaucracy is fundamentally different from other public choice models and it has implications for the optimal theory of taxation. We have decided to advance the treatment of the model portrayed in Mueller (1989) and to examine the behaviour of the bureaucrat in this unique world. While they accept the Niskanen hypothesis that bureaucrats seek to maximise their budgets, Brennan and Buchanan shift emphasis away from the allocation of the budgets to a consideration of the constraint imposed on the bureaucracy by the tax laws in the particular country. In other words, they interpret tax laws as a constraint on bureau growth. In addition their model challenges the traditional public finance role of taxation when they suggest that tax laws are citizen-imposed constraints on bureaucracy. We conclude that such constraints may not be necessary if we look closely at the microeconomics underpinning the model.

An analysis is briefly outlined in Mueller (1989), where the conclusion is reached that the bureaucracy's capacity to tax the citizenry 'is weaker under a narrow definition of the tax base than under a broad one' (p. 169). If a citizen expected bureaucrats to maximise their budgets they would constrain their ability to do so by constitutionally restricting the kinds of income and wealth that could be taxed. In order to examine this further we amend Mueller's figure 6.3 into our Figure 5.5 and apply the following set of assumptions, namely, *Assumption (i)* the citizenry maximise utility subject to a budget constraint; *Assumption (ii)* there are two goods leisure and work both of which are normal; *Assumption (iii)* the only government expenditure is a lump sum transfer to mollify the high tax-payers; *Assumption (iv)* there is a balanced budget so that tax collected is distributed to bureaucracy and the transfer and *Assumption (v)* we have a linear marginal tax. The reinterpretation of the Mueller approach is to suggest that the income and substitution effects of a tax in a simple tax model may be more important than the tax base as predicted by Brennan and Buchanan. Indeed they may have underestimated the effects contrary to the spirit of Breton (1974).

The Mueller argument is as follows. The individual is initially at point E_0 with before tax income of AB. The ideal tax which by definition does not distort (that is, there is no substitution effect), the relative choice between work and leisure is represented by the budget line CD. The budget line CD is parallel to the budget line AB. Each budget line is an income constraint. The

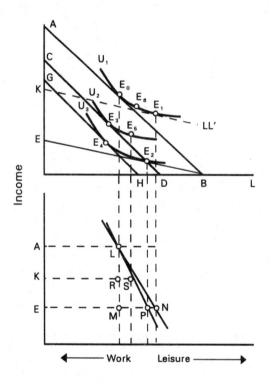

Figure 5.5: Constraints on bureau growth

higher marginal tax is represented by the budget line EB and equal to AE/A0. The optimal points for the citizenry are E_0, E_1 and E_2 for the marginal tax, and E_3, E_0 with the ideal tax. As U_2 is a higher indifference curve than U_3, the conclusion is reached that the citizenry would prefer the ideal tax on the more comprehensive (less distortionary) base. Alternatively if the citizenry were to tolerate a reduction in utility to U_3, the budget maximising bureaucrat would attempt to change taxes to level AG.

Let us re-examine this more closely. For the marginal tax rate AE/A0 the citizenry utility is reduced from U_1 to U_3 and the optimal point is E_2 and not E_0. Allow the government to offer a non-distortionary lump sum transfer to abate the higher taxes; this translates into a compensated budget line LL' as illustrated in Figure 5.5 which is tangent at an optimal point E_1. The distance (E_0E_1) represents the substitution effect and the distance (E_1E_2) is the income effect; since the substitution effect dominates the income effect the labour supply curve is negatively sloped with a negatively sloped price consumption curve (PCC) passing through points E_0 and E_2. Likewise there is a positively sloped income consumption curve (ICC) passing through points E_1 and E_2. This accords with the accredited literature on optimal taxes *a la* Atkinson and Stiglitz (1980).

The slope of the PCC line indicates an increase in work at the higher tax while the slope of the ICC curve indicates a reduction in work. The net effect of the higher tax on work effort is ambiguous in this naive case. However, with respect to the interpretation given to the ideal tax in Mueller (1989) there is no substitution effect hence a positively sloped ICC passes through E_1 and E_3 indicating a reduction in work. This would surely reduce the tax source for the bureaucracy. With such ambiguity in the Brennan-Buchanan model it is difficult to see how they can confidently make their assertions on tax. To advance this argument further consider a bureaucracy-imposed tax level less than AE/A0, for example AK/A0, with a corresponding tangency point with indifference curve U_2 at E_5. Neither the income constraint nor the compensated line are shown in Figure 5.5 in order to maintain clarity in the construction. The excess burden of the tax is less as indicated in the sub-panel to Figure 5.5 with (LMP) < (LMN). The distance (E_0E_6) represents the substitution effect and the distance (E_6E_5) represents a negligible income effect as E6 lies almost vertically above E_5. With this lower tax the negatively sloped PCC passing through E_0 and E_5 illustrates an increase in work effort.

With E_5 and E_3 on the same indifference curve U_2, the central question is whether or not the citizenry is still indifferent between an ideal tax and a distortionary tax. With the lump sum transfer and the reduced excess burden the citizenry may prefer the distortionary tax. The implication for the bureaucracy in this case is to seek a combination of taxes that neither decrease the work effort nor require the citizenry to impose constitutional constraints.

One way of arriving at this objective is for the bureaucracy to take cognisance of its own survival by nominating a tax which minimises the excess compensated tax burden. That tax can be selected from either a broad or narrow base.

ALTERNATIVE PERSPECTIVES

In this section we apply duality theory to decipher the impact of bureaucracy on public good supply. We have argued earlier that the bureaucrat has to determine a supply q of the public good. We assume that the citizen is a public good output taker but faces a set of political Peltzman (1976) prices p. The citizen spends an amount r on rent-seeking expenditures. We show that if there is no citizen welfare effect, substitution effects may exist which determine the comparative static behaviour of this system. The substitution effects are equivalent to the interest group crowding-out effect enunciated earlier in this chapter. Our simple result in this section now confirms, although under restrictive assumptions, the importance of the substitution effect. Essentially the bureaucrat determines the relative supply of public goods.

The citizen's indirect utility function may be defined as:

$$V(p,q,r) = \text{Max}_q \, (U[q] \mid pq = r)$$

The bureaucrat's expenditure function may be defined as:

$$E(p,q,u) = \text{Min}_q \, (pq \mid U[q] = u).$$

We assume that for any amount q the bureaucrat exhibits regular preferences ala Varian (1992). In particular, we assume that E(.) is differentiable with respect to the political prices, which yields the compensated demand functions:

$$c(p,q,u) = Ep(p,q,u).$$

Let us assume that q is a scalar. Then $Eq = \partial E / \partial q$ is the compensating variation associated with dq. It is the amount by which r must change to provide exact compensation for dq. This follows from the total differential:

$$Eq \, dq + Eu \, du = dr.$$

If exact compensation is provided, that is du = 0, then the necessary change in public goods supply is given by:

$$dq = dr / Eq$$

Turning to the compensated demand function, the parameters $\partial c_i / \partial q$ are the demand responses to changes in q at constant prices and utility. They are equivalent to the induced rent-seeking expenditures in Chapter 6. These responses satisfy:

$$p.cq = dpi \, \partial c_i / \partial q = Eq.$$

Apart from this we impose no restrictions on the terms $\partial c_i / \partial q$. Changes in q have two welfare implications for the citizen. First, there is the citizen welfare effect:

$$\partial V / \partial q = Vq = -Eq/Eu.$$

The second effect is compensated, that is, public good supply compensates r amount of rent-seeking funds. This we call the bureaucratic behaviour effect summed up by the vector of compensated responses as:

$$\partial c / \partial q = cq.$$

The total response by the citizen to a change in q ala Russell and Wilkinson (1979) is summed up by the Marshallian response:

$$dm/dq = mq = cq + Vq\ cq.$$

It is the citizen welfare effect, Vq, together with its implications for citizen behaviour that is the usual focus of interest in the welfare economics literature. The dm/dq equation shows very clearly that, even if Vq = 0, so that there is no citizen welfare effect, substitution effects may exist which determine the comparative static behaviour of this system. For the purposes of this section, the precise bureaucratic manner in which q is determined does not matter. Its important characteristic is that, though variable, it is unaffected by any action of the citizen, who acts as a quantity taker. The bureaucrat directly determines the supply of government output.

Dunleavey's Bureau-Shaping Model

In order to define an alternative to the budget maximising models of bureaucracy behaviour one has to uncover a more plausible set of objectives that can explain the observed behaviour of bureaucrats. The bureau-shaping model offers that alternative. The interested reader is referred to Dunleavey (1991) for a detailed account of the model. To understand the motives for bureau-shaping behaviour we need to consider a rather important assumption implicit in his model. The assumption is that pecuniary gains in the bureaucrats utility function do not influence behaviour. The reasons offered in support are compelling in so far as evidence shows that higher ranked bureaucrats place more emphasis on non-pecuniary utilities such as status and prestige and evidence also shows that work related utilities seem to influence the way in which individuals behave in the public sector. In particular, self-interested individuals have strong feelings about the quality of work assigned .

In addition, any attempt to pursue pecuniary gains in a public sector bureaucracy is limited by the tiered structure, the absence of perks as in the private sector, and a clearly defined career path. This confirms the non-pecuniary utility related to the intrinsic value of the work involved. Dunleavy (1991) sums up the position quite well: 'clearly, there is always a pecuniary parameter in bureaucrats' concerns - a level of income and of near-money benefits which they will seek to achieve as a condition of the pursuit of other utilities. But this is unlikely to be a constraint which is surmounted relatively easily and thereafter is not very influential positively or negatively in structuring individual behaviour especially when officials are making policy decisions' (p. 201). He continues to argue that rational bureaucrats orientated to work related utilities pursue a bureau-shaping strategy 'designed to bring their bureaus into a progressively closer approximation to staff (rather than line) function, a collegial atmosphere and central location' (p. 202).

This objective is maximised within a continuous bureau budget constraint. At each stage of budget allocation bureaucrats set out to achieve a satisfactory budget which is predetermined by their previous success in restructuring the tasks of the bureau. As the bureau is reshaped into either a control, transfer or contracts agency, the budget constraint is eased and bureaucrats' utility is increasingly unhinged from the bureau budget. The bureaucrats devote their energies to bureau-shaping rather than to budget maximising. Like budget maximisation the bureau-shaping strategy requires collective action and the behaviour of top level officials accords in reality to that of bureau shaping. In other words bureaucrats shape their particular bureaus 'into a high status organisational pattern' (p. 205). In pursuing this shaping strategy the bureaucrat has some contributory factors. The first concerns internal reorganisation where menial or low profile tasks are removed from the remit of senior officials. As a consequence policy officials improve their work tasks and are able to extend their discretionary control on policy. A final factor is more accountability for the routine menial tasks with an emphasis on collegial decision making and team effort. The hands-off approach is carried through to dealings with external bodies in order to cut down on the routine workload. Finally bureaus compete for the more prestigious policy-related government programs, moving into policy areas which suits their perceived image of the bureau.

Before we look at the type of bureaucracies or agencies it is helpful to consider the definition of budgets as used in this model. Simply the core budget is the smallest budget which includes salaries, personnel and administrative costs. The bureau's budget in addition to the core budget includes debt interest, variable cost and contract costs with private firms. The program budget includes the latter two and funds which are sent to other government agencies. Finally the largest budget is the super program budget which includes all three plus other funds raised by the agencies. The budgets interrelate like a series of Chinese boxes; the core budget is the bureaucracy's own budget and is close to the budget maximised in a Niskanen world of self interested bureaucrats. The bureaucracies are shaped (away) from the traditional line management structure that characterises every other model of bureaucracy to what inevitably becomes in agreement with Cawson (1982), a more corporativist model. There are five principal types of agency and the size of budgets differ across agencies.

The delivery agency is the classic representation of the Weberian theory and public choice analysis. The structure is a line management form, the subordinate to the superiors within the bureaus and then the sponsor. They produce public good output and their core budgets absorb a high proportion of their bureau and program budgets mostly on staffing costs. Regulatory agencies are responsible for controlling the behaviour of citizens and usually have a smaller budget than the delivery agencies and they have a smaller number of staff. Since they are inspection agencies their core budgets absorb a high proportion of their bureau and program budgets.

Other agencies include transfer agencies which handle transfer payments which tend to have a large staff and unlike the delivery or regulatory agencies their core budget does not expand with the program budget. Contract agencies deal with tenders for capital projects and their core budgets absorb only a small proportion of bureau budget. Control agencies channel funds to other public agencies in the form of grants and it is possible for large program budgets to increase without affecting the core budget. In arriving at the optimal budget level we make use of two curves which are central to the analysis of the bureau-shaping model.

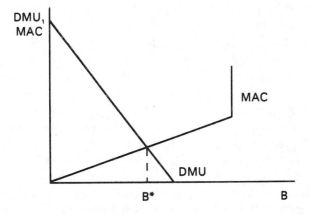

Figure 5.6: Bureau-shaping model: top rank

The two curves are defined as follows: (i) the discounted marginal utility (DMU) curve and (ii) the marginal advocacy cost (MAC) curve. The DMU curve is influenced by the probability of influence (the top level officials are on a higher DMU curve) and by the relation between the core, bureau and program budgets. The top bureaucrats in delivery, contract and regulatory agencies have elastic slopes while those in control and transfer agencies have steep slopes. The MAC is influenced by the size of the existing program budget

and the external objection to the agency getting the budget and by the rank
position of the bureaucrat. When the agency is at the point where it is unlikely
to get an increment, the MAC is vertical as illustrated in Figure 5.6. MAC
curves are higher (lower) the further up (down) in rank the individual is in the
agency as illustrated by the position of both MAC and DMU for bottom ranked
bureaucrats in Figure 5.7.

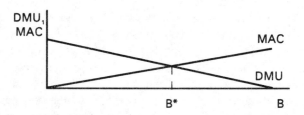

Figure 5.7: Bureau-shaping model: bottom rank

In Figure 5.6 the bureaucrat advocates expansion in the agencies activities
if the program budget is to the left of their equilibrium budget B*. If, however,
the current position is on the right, the bureaucrats do nothing, switching
attention instead to other individual or collective strategies for improving their
welfare. The importance of this is really that the alternative to budget
maximisation is inaction not advocacy of budgetary reductions. However there
is no unique equilibrium point for any bureaucracy. This arises we contend
because there are so many different shapes and positions for the DMU and
MAC curves. The claim is that the Niskanen model is inaccurate but the bureau-
shaping model replaces inaccuracy with indeterminacy. There appears to be
two subtle points worth noting. (i) Rank within the bureaucracy affects the
DMU curve. For a given reduction in the program budget the bottom ranked
bureaucrat discounts the reduction more than the high ranked individual. (ii)
The type of agency is important particularly if influencing the degree to which
an individual can pursue individual strategies to reap private benefits. For any
two high ranked bureaucrats different DMU arise with different agencies with
the control and transfer agencies having the steeper DMU curve. These
conditions factor into the determination of the bureaucrat's action and
behaviour.

Monopoly-Bureau Output

In this section we extend the traditional diagram that accompanies an economic
analysis of bureaucracy as illustrated in Brown and Jackson (1990) or Mueller

(1989). We allow the bureau to behave as a private monopolist in the supply of the public good. This characterisation of the bureau may be interpreted as either (i) local authority decentralisation or (ii) a bureau with incentives and rewards like a tax collecting bureau. We proffer (i) as our point of departure. Our purpose in doing so is to re-examine the divergence between a typical monopoly rule (MC = MR) provision of the public good and the social (MC = AR) optimum. We define the following set of criteria which determine the rule-guided bureau outputs: (i) MC = MR rule for a private monopolist, (ii) MV = MC for a social (government-induced) optimum, (iii) maximise TB and (iv) setting output TC = TB which is the bureaucracy output. For example,in Niskanen's model output (iv) is double the (ii) level of output while (iii) is the median voter output.

Figure 5.8 illustrates an alternative way of looking at the public good provision when the output provision is switched from a central government provision through a budget-maximising bureau to a decentralised provision through a bureau behaving as a private monopolist. This somewhat extends the Breton monopoly government argument to a private monopoly bureau provision.We have a passive sponsor and an active bureaucracy behaving as a private monopolist in the supply of the public good. The supply of output is tax dependent, that is, if the bureau can maximise the tax revenue, the supply of public good can be maximised. The transparent tax ensures that a private monopoly rule guided output level is attained.

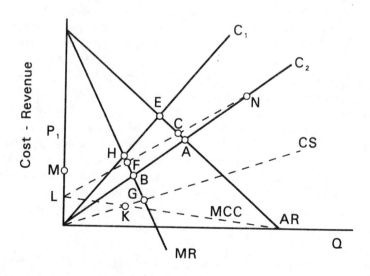

Figure 5.8: Monopoly bureau output

The AR and MR schedules are the regular curves in an imperfectly competitive market and we assume a linear cost curve AC = MC for convenience. The social optimum level of output in a Niskanen world is identified at point E while the output of the bureaucracy-monopolist is identified at the lower level of output B. The difference in costs, which is equivalent to different budget allocations from the sponsor, between the budget maximising bureau and the monopolist bureau is represented by the cost savings $(C_2 - C_1)$, illustrated by schedule CS. We introduce the concept of (marginal) control costs represented by the MCC schedule; the curve is read from right to left which implies that control costs increase as output falls. The concept of control costs which the monopoly bureau provider incurs is a direct consequence of the citizen adjustment to the re-organisation and rationalisation in the supply of the public good which follows in the wake of transfer from one bureaucracy to another. Once we identify these costs we can locate points such as K, F and C.

The intuitive reasoning behind control costs is that it is less costly to go from a large budget maximising bureau output to a lower level of output than it is to go from a lower bureau output to no bureau output. These costs are vertically added to the monopoly bureau AC curve, which yields the ΣC curve, illustrated by the segment (LNC_2). If the monopoly bureau follows a profit maximising rule output will be reduced to F which is lower than B. However if the monopolist bureau decided to trade-off the marginal control costs with the cost savings an output level K would be attained. This would be most unsatisfactory from a welfare point of view. Alternatively there is the point C where $\Sigma C = (MCC + AC) = AR$. This would occur if the monopolist bureau were a perfect price discriminator where the marginal consumer would be charged a price p1. In the provision of public goods there are costs of adjustment and a recognition that a less than optimal supply of the public good is provided by a monopolist rule. One can argue however that a monopolist bureau can minimise the control costs by rationalising costs, centralising the service and then developing the remaining service. However in rationalising the service a monopoly bureau through the control costs can mitigate the divergence from the budget-maximising output. In considering a monopoly bureau, a schedule like $\Sigma C = (MCC + AC)$ must be considered. The schedule ΣC is central in arriving at a conciliatory level of monopoly bureau output between the social optimum level E and the bureau optimum (either C or A); the divergence that is traditionally considered in the provision of a good between a monopolist and a perfectly competitive supplier does not obtain.

The level of output provided by the monopoly bureau is greater than the social optimum at outputs level C and A only. The price p1 could be charged to the marginal consumer with all other consumers paying a price greater than p1. The cost savings reflect the reduction in Niskanen's bureaucratic fat and in organisational X-inefficiencies as the provision of the public good is transferred to a monopoly bureau. All the criteria with the exception of setting $\Sigma C = (MCC + AC) = AR$, result in a level of public output that is less than the social optimum. The significance of these equilibria points (K, F, C, A) is that they force one to reconsider the divergence from the social optimum that characterises the Niskanen type models of bureaucracy. One must consider the criteria by which bureaus arrive at the supply of government output. The two criteria are as follows: (i) output is where (marginal) control costs (MCC) = cost savings (CS) which yields output level K, and (ii) output is where $\Sigma C = (MCC + AC) = AR$ which yields output level C. The level of output at C is greater than at the social optimum output level at E. It is conceivable that a bureaucracy could behave as a monopoly supplier of the public output. In particular if the bureaucracy were to behave as a perfect price discriminator a range of prices would exist for consumers. If the policy decision was to allow bureaucracies unilateral decision making and budget allocative decisions and if they were to behave as a price discriminating monopolist, a criterion on offer is the $(MCC + AC) = AR$. If they continue to follow a TC = TB rule the output would be somewhere between (EA) at a level of output that is greater than E, the social optimum, but unlikely to be twice as great as concluded by Niskanen.

The analysis illustrated in Figure 5.8 may facilitate the Niskanen response to how a bureau should behave if its costs fall over time. His answer, thought to be counter-intuitive by McGuire (1981), is that the bureau will expand the output. For the Niskanen bureau the cost reduction enables the waste to offset the consumer surplus. For a monopoly bureau engaged in perfect price discrimination, the higher output increases the consumer surplus transfer. This criterion may be more appropriate for a bureaucracy that has a budget partially determined by the income it generates. In particular, if the bureaucracy under consideration was a tax collecting agency its modus operandi would be entirely different to traditional bureaucracy whose budget size is related to an allocation of central government expenditure. If government expenditure is reduced as under a new right government the allocated bureau budget is reduced. The extent of the reduction depends on the negotiating skills of the bureaucrats. However, if the bureaucracy is a tax collecting authority its objective would be to maximise total tax revenue. This is the premise in both the Niskanen and in the Brennan-Buchanan world of bureaucracy. This alternative analysis suggests a lesser subordinate role for the bureau.

For example, in arriving at an optimal amount of tax to be collected, the bureau may be guided by a MC (of collecting extra taxes) = MR (of additional tax revenue) rule. Alternatively the bureau could adopt the criterion introduced earlier of setting $(MCC + AC) = AR$, where AR could represent the average tax yield and MCC would reflect the marginal control costs of policing the tax collection with its ever increasing AC of provision. In this case, the self-interested motivated behaviour of the bureaucracy is to be welcomed in that it translates into more tax revenue for the government. The bureaucracy in mind here would possibly be a sub-department within the Niskanen model rather than a variant of the Brennan-Buchanan model. The intuition of the bureaucracy behaving as a perfect price discriminator is in collecting the unpaid tax in accordance with ability to pay. This maximises the total tax revenue. In a naive bureaucracy model this extra revenue is redistributed as part of the allocated budget to the bureaucracies which affirms the monopoly-bureau's position in the government budgetary process.

CRITICAL OVERVIEW

Line Management

The main comparison between all the public choice models is the line management structure. Even though the Downs' model and the Niskanen model differ on methodology they both adhere to the line management structure and both apply a utility function to bureaucrats. In the Downs' utility function there were five arguments, in Niskanen's utility function there were eight arguments. The only variables common to both were a pecuniary variable and power, although the latter was not treated in any significant manner. Niskanen included the output of the bureau as an argument which generated the relationship between bureau output and utility of the bureaucrat. In addition Niskanen applied the utility analysis of managerial theories of the firm to an analysis of bureaucracy. We have earlier commented upon the use of a utility function in ascribing bureaucratic behaviour. The behaviour of the budget maximising bureaucrat is analogous to the behaviour of the profit maximising manager. Niskanen pays little attention to systems of bureaucracies a serious error identified by Dunleavy (1991, p. 172) and perpetuated by scholars like Auster and Silver (1979).

The latter treat the system of bureaucracies as a single firm. The historical analogy between Niskanen-type models and models of the firm no longer holds with the advances in the theory of the firm which may have escaped the attention of public choice scholars. The weaknesses in the public choice models are associated with the framework within which the models are developed. The absence of inter-bureau comparisons and inter-personal comparison within the bureau is surprisingly in line with the neo-classical welfare economic theory which does not make inter-personal comparisons. The persistent use of line management is a carryover from the Neo-Classical theory of the firm with its undifferentiated management team. Dunleavy (1991) advanced the bureau-shaping model as 'a restructured public choice model from a radically different standpoint' (p. 173). His model departed from the budget maximising hypothesis and from the line management structure. The delivery agency in his model, however, is the classic example of the line bureaucracy in the Downs-Niskanen world.

The Budget

The use of budget is ambiguous as noted by Dunleavy (1991) who distinguishes between four budget types, with bureaucrat utility associated with growth in the core budget and advocacy costs associated with the programme budget. The ambiguity is clear in his further comment 'when Niskanen argues that (top) bureaucrats budget maximise, what exactly does he mean? (p. 172)'. Very little is said about what the bureaucracies do with the maximised budget as witnessed by Bendor (1988) who comment 'we cannot say how excess budget is used' (p. 1047). One insight, referred to as Niskanen's dynamic hypothesis by Blais and Dion (1988), is that 'bureaucrats gain from increased budgets' (p. 7). One important underlying assumption in the public choice model is the assumption that the bureaucrat is a monopolist supplier of a public good and that the legislature represents the monopsonists in a model aligned with bilateral monopoly. The bargaining solution which rescues the indeterminacy result in a bilateral monopoly model is absent from the analysis of bureaucracy. Conflict resolution options such as Axelrod's (1984) voluntary co-operation or the kinship system of personnel relations used in Japanese firms outlined in Ouchi (1980), are not applicable to a Downs bureaucracy because of the adherence to what he referred to as the law of hierarchy, which states that 'co-ordination of large scale activity without markets requires a hierarchical authority structure' (p. 52).

Information about the production and cost functions in the supply of public goods is asymmetric across bureaucrats and sponsors. This arises not only as a consequence of the continuity of service with public servants irrespective of a change in government but also because of their expert knowledge about the provision of public goods. The principal-agent problem could be applied to this particular area of bureaucracy. Once the budget is allocated the sponsor has no accurate way of determining its use unless some monitoring system is established. And typically monitoring boards are composed of bureaucrats who are unlikely to welch on their peers. Niskanen assumes that the bureaucrat's utility function is monotonic in budget size and is quadratic. Jackson (1982) has argued otherwise. Niskanen's model has been criticised on many fronts. The criticisms are as much a fault of the perpetuation of the oversupply hypothesis as with the economic analysis underpinning the model. In this chapter we did address some possible oversights that recur in the approach to bureaucracy and proffered some new insights. The many models do have common characteristics. The quadratic utility function in Niskanen which has been widely criticised can be easily amended to include the crowding-out constraint introduced earlier. A maximum (turning point) requirement is acquired by adding a variable which captures the external interaction of bureaus.

Competing Bureaus

A new public choice model which generalises the Tullock-Downs-Niskanen model may be an interesting alternative to either of the three models independently. The addition of the term ΣBi from the crowding-out constraint, to the Niskanen utility function would extend this model to an economic analysis of competing bureaus. While Downs did allude to inter-bureau activity there is little economic analysis presented in order to support this activity. A standard critique of the Niskanen model is directed at two properties of the utility function, namely monotonicity and the quadratic functional form as alluded to earlier. The property of monotonicity, by which the bureaucrat's utility increases as the budget size increases, may be counteracted by the humble civil servant whose duty it is to simply serve the public interest. There are two properties, separability and independence, embedded within this characterisation of Niskanen's model which may allow us to buttress Niskanen's approach to bureaucracy. If bureaucrats are divided into at least two groups (say) the budget maximisers and the civil servants, the property of monotonicity would imply that the budget maximisers are in the majority in the bureau. Alternatively we could argue that the utility function ascribed to a representative bureaucrat in the Niskanen model is strongly separable and maximised subject to the crowding out constraint. In other words, the altruistically-minded civil servant is irrelevant to the budget process which translates into an independence of irrelevant civil servants assumption.

Brown and Jackson (1990) admit that there are bureaucrats who as civil servants are motivated by serving the public interest and not by their own aggrandisement. However this does not underestimate the outcome in the Niskanen model which draws attention to allocative inefficiency in the public sector bureaucracy. The level of public sector output generates a net loss to the citizenry which is a feature of large Niskanenesque bureaucracies. Bureaucrats cannot be dismissed; this is a feature of most democracies and was one of the contractual characteristics identified by Downs. Inability by the sponsor to dismiss bureaucrats contributes to the inefficiency in the system. The inefficiency in numbers can be partly mitigated by bureaucratic expansion as the average cost of inefficient bureaucrats decreases as more are employed. An opportunity cost defined in terms of lost output arises in the allocation of a central budget to different departments. This approach overlooks many inter-related issues which tend to characterise a modern public bureau. For example, bureaucrats can be re-deployed to routine task low budget departments and large bureaucracies have a monolithic survival instinct which supports a conciliatory response from a bureau under threat in an on-going process of decentralisation. In this situation the amount of public sector output generated is a minimal net loss to the citizenry.

Moreover the estimation of each departmental budget by the superior is based on information from the subordinates. One could argue that individual budget maximisers will lead to the situation where the central budget is misallocated. As a result the optimum amount of public good will not be provided efficiently from the allocated funds. The size of the budget is not an argument in the bureaucrat's utility function. If we assume the balanced equation that $G = T$ then the ith individual's utility function cannot be a monotonic transformation. There is a crowding-out affect in the allocation of the G budget which translates into an inter-departmental rivalry. As one department gets more of a budgetary allocation another department will get less. If the ith bureaucrat is in the latter department a disutility factor will enter the utility function. This may generate a downward sloping branch to the bureaucrat's utility function. Is it possible to re-organise the civil service bureaucracy and minimise costs or limit the X-inefficiency that exists? The answer from the bureau-shaping model is in the affirmative as senior officials willingly accept bureaucratic re-organisation. Dunleavy (1991) asserts that 'the bureau-shaping account can explain the two aspects of UK cutback management also consistent with the budget-maximising model, namely the tendency for central spending to be cut last and for budgets to be cut before staff' (p. 215). Whatever little empirical support there is for the bureau-shaping model it is encouraging in the area of cutback management. Dunsire and Hood's (1989) analysis of cutbacks in the UK when cross-checked by type of bureau indicates that none of the delivery agencies suffered while transfer and control agencies had a more mixed record. The delivery agencies include defence and law and order while welfare services are in the transfer and control agencies. This also confirms our earlier suspicions on the limitations of pluralism within bureaucracies.

An X-Theory

There are aspects of a general theory of bureaucracy embedded in the literature. Some of the aspects have been alluded to in this chapter. For example, the utility function should include different arguments to that of bureau size and properties such as separability and independence could be used to buttress the use of a bureaucratic utility function. A crowding-out constraint facilitates inter-bureau rivalry and offers a constraint against which the utility function is maximised. The recognition that bureaus and government are net complements coupled with the recognition of a power struggle within the bureau may allow us to explain a bureau acquiescence in the process of decentralisation. Finally, alternatives to the traditional monopoly and Pareto optimality criteria for deriving an optimal level of government output may direct attention toward conciliatory bureau output rather than at output levels diverging from some norm. In many respects the activity of bureaucrats in transferring consumer surplus to the bureau and the activity of interest groups are alike as each represent examples of rent-seeking behaviour.

Brennan and Buchanan (1980) take as their postulate the Niskanen position that government bureaus maximise their expenditures. In their model of citizen voter cum government bureaucracy they look at the constraints placed on governments by the tax laws of a nation. In this regard they differ from the traditional public finance interpretation of taxation as a means of raising revenue, to an interpretation of taxation as an explicit constraint on the size of government bureaucracy. As Mueller (1989) commented 'a citizen who expected bureaucrats to maximise their budgets would constrain their ability to do so, by constitutionally restricting the kinds of income and wealth that could be taxed' (p. 169). It remains unclear as to how this restriction evolves in the political system. For example, if citizens limit a governments right to engage in tax-price discrimination, then a policy of horizontal equity would emerge. This could occur with a policy of uniform tax rates which essentially constrain government revenue. But in Chapter 6 we shall argue that induced rent-seeking militates against uniform tax as a tax policy.

Breton and Wintrobe (1982) argued that Niskanen concentrated too much on the supply side to the neglect of demand conditions. He assumed that the bureaucrat faced a fixed demand schedule. The Tullock mixed demand schedule may be more appropriate. Miller (1977) using game theory introduced an interactive model of supply and demand, where the demanders of the public good or service (e.g. parliamentary committees) were able to bribe the bureaucrats. The result was a Prisoner's Dilemma result with a Pareto-inferior outcome, which essentially demonstrated that the bureaucrat would only moderately comply, if at all, with the demander's wishes. On the industrial economics side, Baumol (1959), Williamson (1963) and Marris (1964) had independently developed theories of the firm that deviated from the Neo-Classical profit maximisation hypothesis. Baumol suggested sales revenue maximisation as an alternative goal of the firm, and in Marris's model the goal was the maximisation of the rate of growth of demand for the products of the firm and of the growth of its capital supply. Williamson argued that managers had discretion in pursuing policies which maximised their own utility rather than attempting to maximise the profits of the firm. Profits however acted as a constraint on this level of behaviour, as shareholders required a minimum profit level.

One of the main assumptions on which the Niskanen model rested was that asymmetric information on production costs enabled the bureaucrats to pursue goals other than the maximisation of the demander's welfare. Here is the free rider problem that is so pervasive in any principal-agent characterisation of an issue, whether it be shareholder-manager or politician-bureaucrat. The assumption of maximisation of public sector output is akin to the Baumol-Marris-Williamson behavioural assumptions. Drawing on the literature pre-1970, one can easily see how Niskanen could have been influenced by the advances in industrial economics on the theory of the firm (which supplies a private good). The goals of either managers or bureaucrats can be treated in the context of a utility maximisation problem. The utility function has two arguments namely y which is the variable that the sponsors seek to maximise, and x which is the bureaucrat's goal. The key result in the (xy) opportunity set is that at a particular point utility is maximised, and that at another point y decreases as x increases. Hence the bureaucrat's goal and the sponsor's goal eventually conflict.

Niskanen (1971) lists as the goals of the bureaucrat to include the following: 'salary, requisites of the office, public reputation, power, patronage output of the bureau, ease of making changes, and ease in managing the bureau' (p. 38). As outlined earlier in this chapter, the monotonicity property asserts that these goals are positively related to the size of the budget. Williamson (1963) listed salary, security, power, status, prestige and professional excellence. The equilibrium of the Williamson firm is determined by a point of tangency of the profit (y-variable) - staff (x-variable) curve with the highest possible managerial indifference curve. Since the indifference curves have a negative slope, the equilibrium will always be on the falling section of the profit-staff curve. Hence the conflict of goals reappears. The conflict results in greater output levels; Mueller (1989) comments that 'one gets the impression from Niskanen's book that the net effect of supplying public output by public bureaus is a substantial expansion of the size of government' (p. 162). This accords with the view of von Mises addressed by Niskanen when he commented 'that a broader education in economics will reduce the popular support for large government and the consequent pervasive bureaucracy' (p. 7). Ironically, von Mises seriously underestimated the popular support that was to launch Keynesian deficit spending on an unsuspecting world. Bureaus increased in size and numbers with an ever increasing responsibility for the provision of government output.

Migue and Belanger (1974) had pointed to the fact that the pursuit of the X goals would be constrained by the use of budget funds to expand the bureau's output. Many additions were made to the X goals, which collectively were subsumed into Leibenstein's X-inefficiency theory. Within the economic analysis of public sector, X-inefficiency arose with the absence of a minimum cost output production. If the bureaucrat is maximising her goal, she could - as in the case of US defence contracts - be maximising costs in order to acquire the same budget outlay. The concept of government outlined in this chapter departs from the traditional interpretation of the benevolent dictator acting in the best interests of the government. Parallel to the concept of a monopoly government is a conceptualisation of the state as consisting of the elected and the non-elected interest groups, having possibly different and conflicting interests. From a Downsian perspective the incumbent party is faced with a re-election constraint which can be relaxed by reconciling interest group demands subject to the overall public finance constraint of the economy.

As Tollison (1982) commented 'rent-seeking theory generalises in positive economic terms to the interest-group theory of government and legislation'. Hence the more recent empirical estimates on rent-seeking costs have evolved from politico-economic models purporting to explain the size and growth of government. Bureaucracy growth and rent-seeking both reflect government failure; bureaucrats as *agent provocateurs* may induce rent-seeking while politicians aware of their re-election constraint, court interest groupings. Within this web of modern political life, the role of a bureaucracy is crucial and the relative position of bureaucrats, as argued in our presentation of a duality function, has yet to be fully accounted for in the literature.

While the impact of interest groups on the legislature is well developed and recognised in the literature, a secondary and more insidious role attributable to the bureaucrats is not. In many respects the principal-bureaucrat may respond to the wishes of the agent-interest group. This external dimension to bureaucracy could be a rewarding area for future research.

6. Classic Rent-Seeking

Rent-seeking, originally introduced by Tullock (1967), Krueger (1974) and Posner (1975) has come to represent and characterise many different interpretations of the original idea. No longer exclusively introduced in the context of public sector decisions, it is more than likely to persist in most transactions where individuals attempt to avoid a cost or reap some benefit. Rent-seeking is an intriguing concept. The conventional wisdom across the public choice literature, which we label the *classic* view, has two hallmarks, namely that rent-seeking is unequivocally socially undesirable and that rent-seeking activities are not confined to public sector decision making. We shall argue in this chapter that this classic view of rent-seeking is a special case of the rent-seeking insight, one which is essentially unresponsive to the contemporary developments in the political economy of property rights. Rent-seeking occurs in private markets as with advertising and patents and in political markets as witnessed by lobbying and campaign contributions. However, these contributions *per se* are not examples of social waste (Buchanan, 1980). So what is the rent-seeking insight?

Definition 6.1: Rent-seeking mirrors the implicit or hidden costs attributable to the creation of artificial scarcity initiated in many instances by government issued monopoly rights and includes the subsequent expenditure of real resources by aspiring monopolists and citizens alike through bribery and the lobbying of government.

In many respects one could argue that the public choice school of thought has acquired a dominance in the treatment and analysis of competitive rent-seeking, as an activity occurring primarily, although not exclusively, through the political process. This is not surprising as an allocation of resources through the political process generates a social waste while an allocation through the market generates a social surplus. However we do agree that to treat rent-seeking activities as characteristic of public sector economics is to ignore the fact that similar phenomena are to be found elsewhere. Within the past twenty years the rent-seeking insight has developed into a significant research programme which impinges upon the treatment of monopolies, externalities, public goods and trade restrictions. It proffers an analytical perspective on politician behaviour, the role of interest groups, on bureaucrats and on the size and growth of government. The domain of rent-seeking essentially looks at the cost, in terms of real resources expended, incurred by individuals in attempting to either avoid a cost or secure a benefit. More specifically it is the opportunity cost of resources devoted to rent-seeking that best represents social waste.

Rowley, Tollison and Tullock (1988) were able to collect the major writings into one accessible volume. The 1988 volume was in many respects an update on the Buchanan, Tollison and Tullock (1980) volume. The earlier volume contained a majority of articles on the theory and measurement of rent-seeking, with a particular emphasis on the social costs of monopoly. Cowling and Mueller in their reprinted contribution concluded that 'our results reveal that the costs of monopoly power, calculated on an individual firm basis, are, on average, large'. Their comment that 'the monopoly problem is broader than traditionally accepted', accords with the general theme of that volume. However no tractable estimates on the social costs of rent-seeking were delivered in that volume. The 1988 volume extended the area covered by the rent-seeking literature, from efficient rents to the broad application of the rent-seeking paradigm to the voting paradox, bureaucracy, the Coasian firm, the environment and the law. The volume almost exclusively concentrates on rent-seeking in the public market place and most of the authors according to Rowley and Tullock 'would concur that, *ceteris paribus*, rent-seeking behaviour should be minimised as imposing waste upon society'. The many applications of the rent-seeking insight challenge the established orthodoxy of Neo-Classical microeconomics, but the litmus test for any new approach in the 1990s must be the existence of tangible evidence.

Rowley, Tollison and Tullock (1988) made the remarkable comment that 'the exact measure of rent-seeking costs, however, turns out to be elusive, even at the level of pure theory'. This is not acceptable. It may be kosher to add Tullock costs to the Harberger losses and conclude that the traditional estimates of the social costs of monopoly are inaccurate. But it is an entirely different argument to suggest that rent-seeking activity, independently and exclusively, contributes to that inaccuracy. For example, a relaxation of one of Harberger's original assumptions, that the price elasticities of demand in all industries equals one, would have generated losses in excess of Harberger's original estimates. But if the monopoly problem is simply one of anti-competitive behaviour with prices deviating from long run marginal costs, coupled with unproductive (high opportunity costs) use of limited real resources, then the main proprietial claim of rent-seeking is simply its ideological base which extends its application to non-market decision making. By definition such applications are surely immeasurable; life among the triangles and trapezoids is more complicated and less tractable than Higgins and Tollison (1988) had anticipated. Their concluding remark that 'the impact of rent-seeking behaviour on the wealth of society becomes much less clear than the current literature makes it out to be', was prophetic.

THE DOMAIN OF RENT-SEEKING

Whither the Literature?

Buchanan (1980) noted that 'economists will sense the ambiguities' with respect to the use of rent in economic history. The concept of rent-seeking, is functionally different from the concept of economic rent that includes quasi-rents, monopoly rents and Ricardian rents. One important difference is that these rents are (a transfer reward for increasing output or improving quality) an incentive to increase production. More producers enter the competitive market, prices fall and the consumer benefits in the long run. Consequently we proffer a comprehensive definition of rent-seeking which embraces the ever expanding domain of rent-seeking activity. In this chapter rent-seeking is defined as expenditures of real resources undertaken by individuals or groups of individuals in order to either obtain an increase in their wealth by securing government franchises or to avoid a cost or reversal of an exclusive right. Rent-seeking theory is exclusively directed at contrived rents as distinct from the natural rents arising from profit seeking. The theory is also concerned with the use of interest group power to manipulate government. It is continually argued within the literature that the real resources used in rent-seeking are wasteful (not wealth creating). Although many of the complex issues raised by the rent-seeking literature have come under attack, few scholars with the exception of Bhagwati (1982) and Varian (1989), have considered the possibility of benefits arising to society from rent-seeking activity

Across the literature, with the notable exception of DUP theorists, the benefits of rent-seeking activity is generally overlooked. The DUP result is a second best outcome, that emanates from Bhagwati's (1982) general equilibrium analysis of wasteful expenditures. Other scholars such as Varian (1989), Sisk (1985) and Milgrom and Roberts (1990) allude to the benefits of lobbying in secondary markets, in abridging property rights, or in securing valuable information on projects, respectively. The absence of acceptable rent-seeking estimates necessitates that rent-seeking, as a measure of the social cost of a monopoly, ought not to be considered independently of these developments. We contend that the Tullock rectangle remains a measure of the social cost as long as nobody benefits. In categorising benefits we cannot overlook the possibility of economies of scale in lobbying. This chapter has suggested that there are economies in lobbying. By re-interpreting the lobbyist as a multi-issue firm representing many clients and lobbying on their behalf economies of scope may exist in the lobbying firm.

Corollary 6.1: With economies of scope in lobbying the efficiency gains may offset the rent-seeking costs. If the efficiency gains fully offset the rent-seeking costs then society is no worse off with lobbying than without lobbying.

Across the literature scholars despair of ever finding tractable estimates of rent-seeking. Tullock (1990) recently acknowledged the absence of a general definition of the term rent-seeking and agrees in principle that 'measuring the cost or even putting one's finger on it, is difficult'. Durden (1990) summed up a position in the literature: 'there is no way that I can think of which would separate rent-seeking from other negative influences associated with increasing government size'. Public choice scholars may have to broaden the intellectual depth of the rent-seeking concept rather than its range of application. Hartle (1983) writes that: 'the normative issues raised are fundamentally too conservative to be persuasive', while Nicolaides (1990) comments that 'modelling of rent-seeking activities ... has not led to any major empirical results'. In writing this chapter we have opted to examine critically the normative basis of rent-seeking.

Elsewhere, McNutt (1995) introduces an alternative econometric model to the size of government model within which positive estimates of rent-seeking are computed. The role of interest groups in contributing to the rather high levels of government expenditure is an important issue. The role as characterised by the persistent lobbying presupposes that within a political theory of government, politicians curry favour with interest groups, ranging from trade associations to local community action groups. This interpretation of government as responding to interest group demands contradicts the Pigovian interpretation of government, as a benevolent dictator maximising social welfare. The line of argument here concludes that government is endogenous within the politico-economic system, something to which political macro economists like Alesina (1991) are now turning their attention in the search for an explanation of the political business cycle.

Quite frankly, government is not elected primarily to solve market failures but rather to be manipulated. This tends to suggest that direct participation by individuals in the vote process is of secondary importance to the indirect participation via membership of an effective interest group. The unresolved issue however is the Downsian question: why bother to vote? At this juncture Schumpeter (1954) is rather appropriate in his definition of the new democratic method: 'that institutional arrangement for arriving at political decisions in which individuals acquire the power to decide by means of a competitive struggle for the people's vote'. 'Is there a place for good government.' Is there just popular government? There is within many interest groups the making of a political movement of populist dimension. By this we mean that appeals to 'the people' have an integrating and legitimising effect that can be useful to interest groups. This is particularly the case where both environmental and moral issues are concerned. The political observer would be concerned about the possibility of interest groupings supplanting government. Government does create the situation whereby individuals or groups can realise rents and in many ways the nature of the political system is one where government, in order to survive politically, is manipulable.

Alas, there is no great conspiracy theory. In a modern democracy government require information: Nicolaides comments that 'even if the government is civic-minded in a world of incomplete information it can take action only by considering whatever relevant information is available'. Alternatively, interest group lobbying has become a function of the governing process, in other words 'the incumbent party enjoys whatever the assets of incumbency are and the opposition hopes to profit from whatever liabilities governing brings' *a la* Rose and Mackie (1980). While scholars may concur on a possible positive role for lobbying and for interest groups in informing government they are less forthcoming in appraising the potential benefits accruing from rent-seeking behaviour. A related issue is to what extent there is rent-seeking in society given the absence of a perfectly competitive political market. Surely a recognition of the fact that if groups compete in the economic market they will attempt to acquire vantage points for competition in the political market should assuade scholars of the existence of rent-seeking. Consequently if rent-seeking behaviour is continuous from one state of nature to another, the emphasis should be on the benefits of rent-seeking behaviour.

There are many issues to be addressed in any re-examination of the normative theory of competitive rent-seeking literature. One particular issue is the basic welfare trade-off diagram - as used to discuss the social cost of monopoly - and the level of monopoly price (denoted in all Figures by Pm), that is central to the calculation of geometric areas. The idea of a consumer lobby depressing the level of monopoly price is introduced in Figure 6.4; this Baysinger-Tollison measure of rent-seeking identifies a lower than expected monopoly rent. Once the monopoly is established the level of monopoly price, independent of rival reaction, is very much at the discretion of the monopolist. Should he decide to deter entry by price manipulation, the regulator may be faced with incomplete information on the level of monopoly price. Hence errors arise in the estimation of the social costs of rent-seeking. We define these errors later as type-2 errors and examine their implications for the computation of reliable rent-seeking estimates. Predatory behaviour and entry deterrent strategies require the monopolist to expend real resources which have to be factored into the social costs of rent-seeking. The inability to exactly determine the monopoly price compounds this problem; Leibenstein (1980) in a different context commented that 'monopoly prices, according to estimates, appear to be only 8 per cent on the average above competitive prices'.

The Rent-Seeking Insight

The competition for monopoly franchises in which aspiring monopolists expend real resources in order to obtain the monopoly represents competitive rent-seeking. The paradigmal example of competitive rent-seeking, a potential monopolist expending exactly the monopoly rent in order to acquire a monopoly franchise, was independently treated by Tullock (1967) and Krueger (1974) who coined the expression 'rent-seeking', although Sraffa (1926), Leibenstein (1966) and Stigler (1971) may have unwittingly alluded to the concept, in their respective work on competitive conditions, X-inefficiency and regulation. Sraffa (1926) in particular may indeed be the earliest contributor to the rent-seeking debate. In his classic article he looked at how individuals attempt to escape from competition, through monopolisation and cartelisation. In many respects this is the essence of rent-seeking behaviour as introduced by Krueger (1974). He concluded that individual firms would not opt for competition if at the margin the gains from maintaining perfect competition were less than the potential rents from cartelisation.

In this chapter we have decided to revisit the classic view of rent-seeking from two different perspectives, namely, the rehabilitation of the basic trade-off diagram and the development of a property rights approach. At issue for public choice scholars is the extent to which rent-seeking should be defined as an undesirable activity not to be condoned by society. The extreme position of scholars like Benson (1984) who argue that rent-seeking *per se* is undesirable cannot be sustained, we contend, within a wider interpretation of the rent-seeking paradigm on offer in this chapter. While public finance scholars are content to acknowledge rent-seeking as a consequence of government failure, public choice scholars are adamant that rent-seeking is both undesirable and wasteful. We contend that in order to characterise rent-seeking as an undesirable and wasteful activity two simple preconditions must hold, namely, (i) whether or not output has changed, and (ii) whether or not the transfer of resources initiated by rent-seeking was unwilling or not. Quite simply, if output is not altered then rent-seeking is not wasteful. Likewise, if individuals are compensated for the transfer rent-seeking is not undesirable. Consequently the Tullock definition of classic rent-seeking as an undesirable and wasteful activity only holds if neither the citizenry nor the individual benefit.

With the endogeneity of government behaviour now established, public finance scholars have recognised that a uniform tax may be unlikely (Brown and Jackson, 1990), as the special treatment of one group induces the special treatment of another group. What we call induced rent-seeking may be a special case of Tullock's undesirable and wasteful rent-seeking, particularly if it contributes to a larger public budget and begins to undermine the very essence of representative democracy. Stigler's (1965) definition of Director's Law as implying that success in the markets translates into success in politics is rather appropriate in the particular context under discussion. A lack of well defined property rights is at the heart of many public policy debates. The control of world pollution is an obvious example which would benefit from a well established system of property rights. While rent-seeking will ensure different alignments of resources (for example, permissible pollution levels), the actual process of establishing and protecting property rights is a productive activity. A more fundamental question addressed by Samuels and Mercuro (1984) is a distributive one: where do rents go and who gets the rents? Public choice is found wanting in supplying answers.

The rent-seeking insight challenged the orthodox analysis on the social costs of monopoly, by adding rent-seeking costs (Tullock costs), to the dead-weight loss of the Harberger triangles. In our re-examination of X-inefficiency and rent-seeking we hope to show that Tullock costs play an ambivalent role in the normative theory of the social costs of monopoly. From a public policy perspective, Tullock costs challenge the complacency of the Chicago position on the insistent use of Harberger losses in the regulatory environment (Stigler 1966, Posner 1980 and Becker 1983). The absence of a common approach contributes to the intractable empirical estimates on the social cost of monopoly. We revisit the basic theory of monopoly and suggest some key indicators of a common approach. For example, a general equilibrium approach, Varian (1989), allows for the calculation of the cost of (say) minimising crime to include the indirect costs of changes in the supply and demand for burglar alarms, locks and insurance. Likewise, when taxes are imposed on individuals or corporations, real resources used to avoid taxes are expended on the demand for lawyers.

Tullock-Krueger Axis

Figure 6.1 illustrates the demand curve for a monopolised product with a monopoly price at Pm which is in excess of the long run competitive price Pc. If the monopolist charges the price Pm, rents of an amount R accrue in addition to the net consumer surplus loss of an amount L. In the traditional theory of monopoly, L is treated as a measure of the efficiency loss due to monopoly with producers securing a transfer of resources from the consumers who pay the higher monopoly price for a fixed supply. Tullock's initial insight was that a monopolist would be prepared to expend resources of an amount R in order to secure the monopoly franchise. There is no dispute about the analytical content of the competitive model. Albeit the resulting dead-weight loss, the Harberger triangle L in Figure 6.1, was deemed to be insignificant, Mundell (1962) noted a complacency amongst economists on monopoly positions in the economy. The insights of both Tullock and Krueger indicated that the monopoly producers may have to expend real resources in order to secure the monopoly rent. This is the most useful way to think of rent-seeking, in terms of the opportunity cost of the resources used to acquire the monopoly position. Additional resources are spent but no additional output is produced; indeed the consumer is further denied the output of the alternative use of the resources.

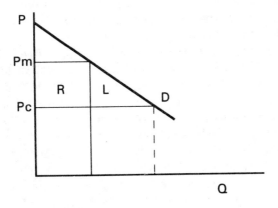

Figure 6.1: Classic rent-seeking model

The implication of the rent-seeking insight on the Neo-Classical analysis of monopoly was obvious; the traditional measure of the social cost of monopoly was inaccurate, the measure was at best an under-estimate of the true social cost of monopoly. That was the position in the mid-seventies but an adherence to this line of argument now is more difficult to sustain in the light of developments in the pricing strategies of modern firms. We briefly develop an argument later that introduces an asymmetry in information on actual monopoly price between the monopolist and the regulator, which may result in inaccurate (geometric) estimates of the social costs of monopoly. Rent-seeking is generally illustrated in the context of government regulation of the economy. The establishment of a monopoly fixed supply or the restriction on supply imposed by licences and quotas proffers the opportunity for aspiring monopolists to engage in rent-seeking. For example, ten bidders for a government issued monopoly right with a value of £10, would each expend £1 for a one in ten chance of securing the bid. Likewise with a monopoly profit of £10, a monopolist would be prepared to spend exactly £10 to secure or maintain the monopoly position. The exact expenditure is now defined as the rent-dissipation theorem; scholars have found evidence of both under- and over-dissipation of rents under particular circumstances.

Stigler (1971) in his contribution to regulation alluded to the interaction between monopoly rents and the regulated price. It therefore behoved monopolists to put pressure on regulators for a higher price. One important economic characteristic is that output is restricted and because of that rent-seeking does occur. So if there is a case of output restriction that is, where competition cannot expand output, will rent-seeking always occur? Tollison (1987) alludes to this point and to the recurrent dispute in the public choice literature when he asks whether 'the mafia, competitive advertising by oligopolists and the competition among siblings for inheritances are possible examples of rent-seeking in a private context'. The latter point is addressed in the next section. Tollison's concern is an example of the extended application of the rent-seeking paradigm, immune to continued criticisms levelled at public choice on the absence of tractable empirical estimates. We note this concern but respectfully suggest that public choice theorists should spend more time deliberating upon the appropriate economic analysis of rent-seeking activity. More mainstream economists like Varian (1989), have addressed the issue of rent-seeking within a greater micro-economic brief looking at the impact of a general equilibrium model interpretation on the costs of rent-seeking. The extent to which the impact of rent-seeking expenditures on a secondary market is significant, like the market for lawyers, depends on the elasticity of supply in that market. This and other factors contribute to a rather unclear picture as to how to extract a normative measure the costs of rent-seeking. It raises the question on just how accurate the Tullock measure really is. A full answer to this question requires a re-assessment of the micro-economic basis behind the normative theory of rent-seeking. We shall address this specific issue later.

Bhagwati-Buchanan Axis

Bhagwati's (1982) classification of 'directly unproductive profit seeking (DUP) activities', has widened the domain of rent-seeking to include instances in private non-government regulated markets which include the examples of rent-seeking mentioned earlier and the Bhagwati and Srinivason (1980) 'revenue-seeking' activities designed to acquire revenues generated by price intervention. The clash between DUP and rent-seeking could be interpreted as a clash between a general equilibrium and a partial equilibrium analysis respectively. The key insight in the combined DUP and rent-seeking literature is that if government policies or policies in general create an economic environment where benefits will accrue or costs will occur, individuals will expend real resources to either avoid the cost or to acquire the benefit. This rent-seeking behaviour will impinge on the equilibrium conditions of a secondary market. The implications for rent-seeking costs are ominous; the rent-seeking expenditures undertaken to enact even a simple transfer from one individual to another may be deemed wasteful. An example of such expenditures is the lobbying of government in order to obtain a monopoly franchise.

Buchanan (1980) identified three types of rent-seeking expenditures. His concept of 'third-party distortions' as applied to campaign funds would refer specifically to the transaction costs in making such contributions. In other words, the social waste attributable is embodied in the fees that may have been paid to lobbyists, in the interest groups competitive lobbying of particular politicians and in the time (opportunity costs) invested by politicians in seeking interest-group support. All of this is characteristic of rent-seeking activity but it remains unclear whether or not the expenditures and costs incurred are socially wasteful. Rent-seeking activity may have a positive contribution to make to everyday life as the rent sector in general remains omnipresent. However, it is the long-term commitment and allocation of real resources by rent-seekers in order to sustain their activity and the complementary redistribute flow of government resources by politicians, that is wasteful as argued in our opening remarks. It is the existence of this flow and how one could measure it that provoked the econometric analysis adopted by McNutt (1995). Mueller (1989) captured the idea when he commented that 'the iron law of rent-seeking is that wherever a rent is to be found, a rent-seeker will be there trying to get it'.

Frozen Market Perspective

Apart from the conditions of perfect information and minimum transaction costs, the existence of property rights is a requirement for the definition of a market. Traditional economic theory has always assumed that property rights were exogenous. The traditional complacency on the relationship between a market and property rights can no longer be sustained. Quite frankly, if property rights did not exist there would be no market; each individual could take what others possess. With property rights and the attendant punitive legal system, the taking of possessions is theft, punishable by law. A property rights dispute creates an environment conducive to rent-seeking. The resolution of the dispute in an Alchian-Demsetz type world requires individual cooperation while at an institutional or government level an alternative superior method of assigning property rights has to evolve. Rent-seeking, like theft or the market, is a method of assigning property rights. We define individuals who perceive the government as a public good as citizen free riders *a la* McCormick and Tollison (1981). Citizen free riders by not participating in the political process enable other individuals, the rent-seekers, to exploit government.

We would like to introduce two further preconditions which reflect the growing literature on property rights. Firstly, rent-seeking could supplant government as a rights allocating mechanism and secondly if lobbying costs are recognised as inevitable in order to secure government decisions then a positive amount of rent-seeking may be necessary. With respect to the former precondition, rent-seeking as an allocating mechanism is surely preferable to either theft or indeed revolution as allocating mechanisms. The second fundamental theorem of welfare economics assures us that, under certain strict conditions if a Pareto optimum allocation exists, a perfectly competitive market mechanism will realise that allocation. Embedded in that theorem is an assumption in principle that if the citizenry do not like the Pareto allocation, a perfectly competitive revolution, as a method of re-allocating resources, will realise the alternative allocation. And with respect to the latter precondition on lobbying costs it is becoming increasingly obvious from the direction and content of the research agenda in political science (Laver and Schofield 1990), that government behaviour is no longer regarded as endogenous in the political system.

In situations where initial resources are unassigned, rent-seeking, in contributing to the institutional arrangements on property rights, is efficiency-increasing. Rent-seeking is omnipresent as a political phenomenon and a preferred method of allocating resources. If the market is suspect the inevitable temptation is to resort to more or greater intervention which increases the amount of real resources devoted to rent-seeking. A liberal reading of the fundamental theorems of welfare economics would suggest that with no market restrictions, entrepreneurs will seek to achieve profits by using new technology, developing new products, pricing competitively and by anticipating market trends. If allowed to function within a set of laws and institutions that protect property rights, markets should allocate resources in an efficient manner. To deny this is to adhere to what we call a frozen market perspective. Ironically the proponents of the frozen market perspective set up artificially controlled advantageous positions that are exploited by the better informed and well organised groups in society. Markets are then replaced by politics.

NORMATIVE THEORIES OF RENT-SEEKING

Let us turn our attention initially to the fundamental trade-off diagram which underpins the partial equilibrium analysis of rent-seeking. Before the arrival of the rent-seeking insight the welfare analysis of monopoly was rather straightforward. Figure 6.2 represents a basic trade-off diagram, where aspiring monopolists secure a price Pm and output is regulated to qm. As with neo-classical microeconomics the monopoly price is higher than the perfectly competitive price Pc and the monopoly output is lower than the perfectly competitive output level at qc. An amount equal to rectangle (PmCAPc) is transferred from the consumer surplus (EPcB) to the producer monopolist.

The dead-weight loss, or Harberger triangle (CAB) is transferred to no-one and its rather insignificant area contributed to a complacency about the social cost of monopoly.

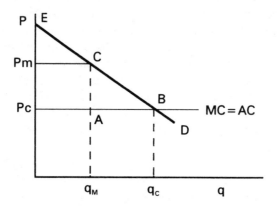

Figure 6.2: Basic trade-offs: constant costs

Tullock (1967) responded in a sense to Mundell's (1962) earlier questioning of the complacency within the profession on the role of the monopolist. Tullock hinted that aspiring monopolists were prepared to spend real resources of an amount equal to their expected monopoly profit (PmCAPc) in order to acquire the monopoly position. His insight laid the foundation for the classical normative treatment of rent-seeking as an economic concept. The social costs of monopoly include the Harberger triangle and the Tullock rectangle, yielding a much higher social cost of monopoly captured in the trapezoidal area (PmCBPc). There are many ambiguities and complexities attached to this rather simple partial equilibrium analysis. The fact that it is a partial equilibrium framework is in itself a source of criticism. There is the explicit absence of the marginal revenue curve in many of the diagrams in the literature, justified by many authors including Tollison (1987) on the grounds that 'the marginal revenue curve is *omitted* to avoid *cluttering* the diagram (our italics)'. But we contend that a cluttering of the diagram as Tollison hinted, should be the norm not the exception in order to uniquely distinguish the rent-seeking concept within the growing literature on the social cost of monopoly.

In Figure 6.2 the assumption of a constant marginal cost is employed, and the intercept E on the price-axis assumes a linear demand schedule. The location of the monopoly price Pm well above the competitive price is a carryover from the traditional model illustrated in Figure 6.1 which Tullock had intended to criticise, with respect to its measure of the social cost of monopoly. Any deviation from this rather basic analytical framework, which is the basis of the competitive rent-seeking theory, leads only to complications. Fisher (1985) commented on this very point by showing that any other normative theory would introduce problems in deriving the Harberger reduced-form equation and hence in deriving estimates of rent-seeking. The essence of the normative approach to rent-seeking include the rectangular area introduced earlier in Figure 6.2 and the principal argument that the amount of real resources spent (PmCAPc), by aspiring monopolists will exactly dissipate the rent. This is referred to as competitive rent-seeking and it is the rent-seeking addressed by Tullock (1967), Krueger (1974) and Posner (1975). It remains popular in the literature because of the exact dissipation result and the exact geometric areas.

Consider Figure 6.3 where monopoly profit (producer surplus) is the trapezoid (PmEBA), and the existence of this potential profit is conducive to rent-seeking behaviour. The Tullock trapezoid from this diagram is the area (PmECBA) which represents the social cost of the monopoly position to society. Again we notice that the Harberger triangle is included with the monopoly profit. The only difference between Figures 6.2 and 6.3 is an increasing linear marginal cost curve; the same analysis applies in both cases.

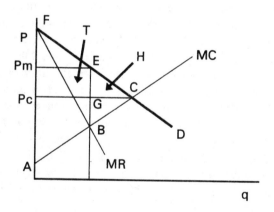

Figure 6.3: Basic trade-offs: increasing costs

The higher monopoly price is retained; it is not the midpoint in Figure 6.3 between the intercept F and Pc, the perfectly competitive price. The uncompensated transfer identified earlier would be equivalent to the area of (PmECPc) and this area depends crucially on the level of monopoly price. Since (PmECPc) is a loss in consumer surplus terms, which at the competitive level equalled triangular area (FPcC), one would expect consumers to lobby against a price Pm. Baysinger and Tollison (1980) noted this shortcoming in both Tullock and Posner's original work, commenting 'on the implicit assumption that the monopoly profit maximising price always prevails in the end'. Their eventual conclusion was that the rent-seeking costs were much smaller than hithertofore. These authors by their observations, have contributed to the introduction of uncertainty into the discussion of normative (competitive) rent-seeking. The competitive rent-seeking model, as illustrated, is analysed in a certain world with a zero-profit free-entry condition. The possibility of multiple rent-seekers, of consumers lobbying against the monopoly price, and regulators trying to eliminate the rents, opened the discussion on non-competitive rent-seeking. It is often referred to as efficient rents after the Tullock (1980) paper in which he changed his original position on rent dissipation. In so doing he changed the way that rent seeking was to be further analysed.

Many of the fundamental issues addressed in both the normative and positive issues of rent-seeking are interrelated. We need to expand the basic micro-economic model used to consider the theory of rent-seeking. The model must take on board the fact that consumers could lobby to reduce monopoly price below Pm, which would translate into a lower measure of the Tullock trapezoid. We look at a variation of this issue in a later section of this chapter. Lobbying of interest groups may secure a net benefit to society. The positive size of government type models within which rent-seeking estimates are computed may require the addition of new variables or modifications of existing ones. It would be worthwhile to include if possible an explicit measure of the benefit to society arising from the award of monopoly franchises and from lobbying. Such a measure remains elusive although McNutt (1995) proffers an economies of scale measure. The positive theory of public choice in a breakaway from the size of government models could introduce variables to account for the benefits arising with rent-seeking behaviour. To achieve this he developed a measure of benefit which is equivalent to an economies of scale in lobbying measure. On the normative side the opportunity costs of resources used in rent-seeking as suggested by Congleton (1988) must be identified in the partial model.

Efficient Rents and Social Waste

It is only quite recently that public choice scholars have argued that the full monopoly profit should be added to the Harberger costs, particularly if the whole rent is dissipated in the competitive process. In assessing whether rents are under or over dissipated two models have been introduced into the analysis of rent-seeking, namely the lottery model of Tullock (1980) and the perfectly discriminating contest model of Hirschleifer and Riley (1978) and Hillman and Samet (1987). Ellingsen (1991) explains the difference between the models as follows: 'in the lottery model the probability that a given player wins is proportional to the relative size of his expenditures, whereas in the perfectly discriminating contest the player who spends most resources always wins'. The chapter does not present an exhaustive review of the emerging literature on rent-seeking games. The reader is referred to Mueller (1989) and the interesting papers by Hirschleifer (1989) and Applebaum and Katz (1987). A Tullock lottery model with the assumption that the probability of winning is increasing in own expenditure but that the highest bid does not win with certainty is analysed in detail by Hillman and Riley (1989).

The following equation which summarises the relation between rent-seeking expenditures (Sn+1) and the number of contesting sellers (n), is adapted from Ellingsen (1991). The amounts T, monopoly profit and H, the dead-weight loss associated with non-competitive pricing are as illustrated in Figure 6.3.

$$Sn+1 = T(n[T+]/n[T+H] +T).$$

There are two points worth noting, namely, (i) the rent-seeking expenditures are monotonically increasing in n and (ii) are never less than half of T and never exceeding T. According to Ellingsen 'only in the limit, as the number of potential monopolists goes to infinity, is there full rent dissipation'. This is similar to the result derived as equation 13.3 in Mueller (1989, p. 232), who comments that 'entry continues to the point where the number of rent-seekers is such that the total amount invested in rent seeking fully dissipates the rents to be received'.

Tullock's lottery model introduced risk into his calculations and developed a model of spending on lottery tickets (rent-seeking expenditures) in order to win the lottery (the right to create a monopoly). He showed that the optimal expenditure would be guided by marginal analysis rather than by the average analysis implicit in existing work. An individual's spending on lottery tickets would influence the probability of success in winning the lottery. The risk, was the risk of not winning the lottery. Tullock concluded that rent-seeking expenditures could either underestimate or overestimate the amount of rent. The underestimate result was of particular interest to public choice scholars. Several possible explanations have been advanced to explain the underbidding result including risk aversion (Hillman and Katz 1984), comparative advantage among monopolising inputs (Rogerson 1982) and game theoretic as outlined by Tullock (1980, 1985). Fisher (1985) argued that the advances to explain underbidding equilibrium make the problem of analysing rent-seeking more difficult, and less tractable.

The rent dissipation result depends upon the assumption of risk neutrality across the rent sectors. In a competitive rent-seeking model with risk neutrality the funds invested by the rent-seekers will completely dissipate the expected rents. Hillman and Katz (1984) arrived at a dissipation result with risk-aversion which was introduced into their model by assuming a logarithmic utility function for rent-seekers. Mueller (1989) in reference to their work commented that 'rent-seeking can be expected to result in nearly a full dissipation of the rents even when the rent-seekers are risk-averse'. The Hillman and Katz (1984) result however depends on the ratio of rents to be gained to the rent-seekers, initial wealth. The smaller the ratio the more dissipated the rents. A small ratio can be arrived at in two different ways. For example, in the case of farmers receiving a higher price for milk, the initial wealth is the total wealth of all farmers. By definition the ratio is small because of the larger denominator, that is, a higher total farm wealth. For a given initial wealth calculated as either the individual rent-seeker wealth or a total interest group wealth, the ratio declines as the numerator (expected rents) declines.

Hence smaller than expected rents, as one would expect, generate less rent-seeking expenditure, but a higher total farm wealth would suggest more rent-seeking. This ambiguity over how the ratio falls would appear to contradict the direction of the argument in Hillman and Katz. Mueller (1989) somewhat compounds the problem of wealth by considering a principal-agent perspective. An interest group representing a multinational, or the manager investing firm revenue to acquire a franchise (each are rent-seeking agents investing the principal's money), all are risk-takers. With this assumption Mueller arrives at an over-dissipation result. When rent-seekers are agents expending the resources of principals, over-dissipation results. This raises an interesting question; if rent-seekers were principals would an under-dissipation of rent be expected? In particular we could recognise a principal-agent problem in political lobbying; in the decision to lobby government by lobbyist-principals one would expect under-dissipation.

This line of argument would undermine the implicit assumption that all rent-seeking expenditures are socially wasteful. Later in this chapter we shall argue against the accepted interpretation of undesirable rent-seeking as uncompensated and unwilling transfers. We had argued for a compensation criterion by suggesting that product quality and differentiation was a direct compensation for higher monopoly price. Tirole (1988) considered the case of airlines competing for customers by offering quality services; and he continued 'this type of rent-seeking behaviour was not entirely wasteful, because customers enjoyed the services'. Ellingsen (1991) in recognising the lobbying ability of buyers in order to reduce the monopoly price, concluded that 'buyer lobbying strictly reduces the expected payoff for the potential producers ... (e)xpensive buyer lobbying may well increase welfare'. But it was the under-estimate of rent-seeking, rather than the extent or relevance of a compensation criterion, that paved the way for non-competitive theories of experimental games. A Brennan-type game of a sealed bid for a prize requires the assumptions of (i) no collusion amongst bidders, (ii) no refund on bids, (iii) highest bidder wins, and (iv) the lottery pockets the profit (loss) of the game. Tullock (1980) added a fifth assumption (v) that if there is a correct strategy in the game, all players will discover it. In a Brennan game two individuals would invest £5 for a £10 prize, whereas in the Tullock game each would only invest £2.50 each. The underestimate result obtained.

The DUP Angle

An alternative normative theory *a la* Bhagwati and Srinivasan (1980) and Bhagwati (1980) is now well established in the literature. There is some disquiet about the difference between Bhagwati's (1982) directly unproductive profit-seeking activities (DUP), and rent-seeking. Their analyses are within the general equilibrium framework, which immediately contrasts with the partial equilibrium approach of the public choice school of thought. In their application of the theory of the second best to rent-seeking, they conclude that the diversion of resources into lobbying can be welfare-improving. Their proof hinges on two points, namely, that the shadow price of the resources used for lobbying is negative and that part of the rent-seeking gains are lump-sum transfers. Bhagwati (1983) attempts to expose the differences and concludes in agreement with both trade theorists and public choice scholars that a DUP or rent-seeking activity is wasteful if scarce resources are used for the redistribution of income. Bhagwati (1982) showed that a reallocation of resources could improve social welfare; for example, what emerges in the government issue of licences is simply that the economic effects of rent-seeking activity depends on how the activity occurred. Licences could be evaluated on the basis of a need for the licensed good or service, which encourages potential licensees to justify the licence. Producers, for example, may install excess capacity to justify requests for imports - this distortion, due to rent-seeking activity, is rather similar in nature to X-inefficiency.

Nicolaides (1990) comments on this point in arguing that the producer who is successful initially in the allocation of quotas has an advantage over his competitors and hence has greater political power. The group which first acquired the monopoly right has, according to Nicolaides, a strong incentive to *change the rules* to influence subsequent stages of the competition for political favours' (our italics). Within the property rights approach the rules of the game determine the positive (or negative) contribution of rent-seeking to society. There are two rather important implications arising from this. Firstly, any empirical analysis of the social costs of rent-seeking must factor in the benefits of rent-seeking arising from the economies of scale in lobbying. With economies of scale there is less waste of resources. Secondly the assumption of a competitive political market may be redundant in the size of government models. If the political market is imperfectly competitive, it can best be characterised by the following set of assumptions: (i) the existence of barriers to entry especially for smaller parties and represented by political hegemony (ii) the absence of perfect information for the government in policy issues, and (iii) policy homogeneity which has both the government party and the opposition with similar policy agendas, differing only with respect to the details rather than the substance of a policy.

McKee-West Axis

In a McKee and West (1981, 1984) type world it is assumed that governments actually induce distortions by extending privileges to special interest groups. Ng (1987) has challenged their model in arguing that it does not account for natural distortions in the market. McKee and West (1987) in response to Ng, have argued that governments can decide not to correct natural distortions; this could be interpreted as the consequence of political bargaining. This covert activity represents the hidden costs of rent-seeking alluded to by Tullock (1990) and may account for the absence of tractable rent-seeking estimates. McKee and West have argued that lobbying does not reduce welfare by suggesting that those who lose as a consequence of the lobbied policy would incur greater losses if they tried to oppose the policy. It is the natural distortion of incomplete information which would be too costly to improve upon, that accounts for this result. Sugden (1986) reassures us that special interest groups will not monopolise all markets. This would suggest that interest groups and in particular professional lobbyists opt to concentrate on one issue. In addition, if the electorate remain politically inactive and citizen free riders abound, the problem of lobbying induced policy making is exacerbated. When one argues that DUP or rent-seeking is wasteful, one is comparing the status quo and the final allocation point, assuming in particular that the relatively unknown final point is not Pareto superior to the status quo.

   The explanation for rent-seeking expenditures in terms of incomplete information and other imperfections, both political and non-political, raises the question of the identification of a society free from rent-seeking. Suppose real resources of an amount E are used by a monopolist to acquire the legal services of a lobby group in order to maintain the monopoly position. The expenditure of these real resources accrue to the private sector and within the private sector they will accrue to one particular group. Hence the income of this group is increased by Y and the monopolist retains (E - Y) of resources. The increased Y will impact on other product and factor markets by a ß multiplier factor, so the private sector enjoys an increase in real resources of $Y/(1-ß)$. One has to compare this with the opportunity cost of Y real resources,

C. If it is the case that $C \leq Y/(1-\text{ß})$ then the result of Bhagwati and Srinivasan obtains and there may be benefits accruing to society from rent-seeking.

Tullock's Trapezoid

The areas traditionally identified as Tullock's trapezoid, both (PmCBPc) in Figure 6.2 and (PmECPc) in Figure 6.3, represent a public choice estimate of the social cost of monopoly. The area is noticeably greater than the original Harberger triangle in each case. One of the key insights of the rent-seeking literature is that economists had underestimated the true social cost of a monopoly position. The true estimate, one must remember, was defined relative to the original (low) Harberger (1954) estimate of less than one percentage point of gross domestic product rather than with respect to a norm which emanates from a correctly specified descriptive model of monopoly behaviour. Notwithstanding, the exact dissipation result generated a measure of the amount of real resources a monopolist would be prepared to spend. However the trapezoidal area really belongs to a world of certainty with a simple monopoly diagram characterised by the condition that $q_m = 1/2.q_c$, and by the use of linear demand and cost schedules. Figure 6.4 replicates the exact construction.

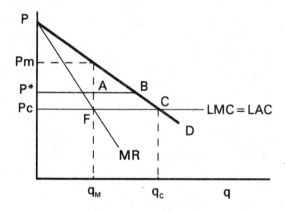

Figure 6.4: Rent-seeking and monopoly price

We illustrate in Figure 6.4 a monopoly price P* that may arise from consumer lobbying or indeed from a lower than expected price set by the regulator. As Tirole (1988) commented 'one cannot a priori measure rent dissipation without going into the micro foundations of the particular situation'. The higher the price set by the regulator, the larger the rent accruing to the monopolist. Stigler (1971) focused attention on how lobbying determined the regulated price and away from setting a regulated price in order to minimise a consumer surplus loss. Peltzman (1976) integrated Stigler's model with a vote maximising politician who reacts to the lobbying from both producer and consumer interests in setting price. Hirshleifer (1976) contended that some of the expected rent was dissipated by the producer and consumer, and since each group lobby for 'opposite changes in price, at least one side's expenditure is wasted' according to Mueller (1989). This accords with our earlier argument in reviewing a property rights dimension to rent-seeking. The final regulated price is a compromise and lies somewhere between a monopoly price and a competitive price.

   Tollison (1982) pointed to the fact that if producers expected that price would be set at the perfectly competitive price, the rent-seeking expenditures would be zero. If consumers expected the monopoly price to always prevail, their expenditures on lobbying to reduce the price would likewise be zero. We convert these two statements into two heroic assumptions: *Assumption 6.1:* consumers expect Pm to prevail, and *Assumption 6.2:* producers expect Pc not to prevail. With these two assumptions the Tullock dissipation result will always obtain. The geometric areas (P*AFPc) and (P*BCPc) in Figure 6.4 represent the maximum rent-seeking expenditures and social cost of monopoly respectively. The former area (P*AFPc), we shall label a Baysinger-Tollison (1980) measure of rent-seeking. It is generated by a breakdown in either of the two assumptions above, a breakdown which contributes to the inaccuracies in the normative geometric areas of rent-seeking. There is one particular point of interest to the theme of this chapter that tends to be overlooked in the public choice literature on the partial equilibrium model. It arises with the introduction of P*. Do we unintentionally abandon the profit maximisation (MC = MR) pricing rule in the use of P*? The location of P* is random and it is seldom a profit-maximising price for the potential monopolist. It would appear that arguing against the Pm and nominating a P*, such that Pm > P* > Pc, legitimises an abandonment of the profit maximising rule. Tollison's (1987) explanation for the omission of the marginal revenue schedule, sits rather uncomfortably with this observation and buttresses a complacency within the public choice school about the position of the marginal revenue curve.

Varian's Fishtail

Varian's (1989) economic analysis of rent-seeking activities represents a general equilibrium (secondary markets effect) attempt to reconsider whether we can use the area of a rectangle or trapezoid in a single market as a proxy for dead-weight loss. The model used by Varian replicates a consumer surplus analysis; on the producer side two goods q1 and q2 are produced and a third good X which is the numeraire. On the consumer side the representative consumer has an additively separable quasi linear utility function. The additive utility function with constant marginal utility of income enables Varian to establish the demand function in terms of own price. And as he comments 'each market can be treated in isolation ... the general equilibrium analysis of this economy is simply a sequence of partial equilibrium analyses'. This sentiment was echoed by Tirole (1988), who later commented that 'the rent-seeking games vary considerably in practice, we are obliged to analyse the issue case by case'.

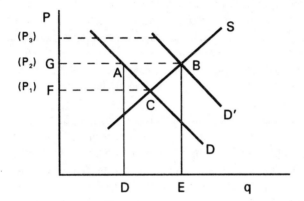

Figure 6.5: Varian's fishtail

Important is the consideration of a secondary market and in particular the impact that rent-seeking expenditures in the first market have on this secondary market. The dead-weight loss due to the expenditures on rent-seeking are offset by the net gain in producer surplus in the secondary market. For example, he argues that if the demand for restaurant meals goes up due to the demand of lobbyists, then the owners of restaurants will earn producer surplus. This requires that secondary market supply curve be inelastic. Figure 6.5 represents the dead-weight loss in the secondary market due to rent-seeking; Varian comments that 'it is neither a rectangle nor a triangle but a fishtail'. The price of the good in market 2 goes from P_1 to P_2, and the loss in consumer surplus is (GACF). The producer surplus gain is the area (GBCF), so triangle (ABC) is the net change in both consumer and producer surplus, as deduced from the welfare economy analysis in his paper. The total dead-weight loss in the secondary market is the fishtail area (ACBED). Therefore, the true measure of the rent-seeking costs in market 2 would be the rectangle (ABDE), but these expenditures are offset by the net gain (ABC), which yields the net area (ACBED).

The total amount that the beneficiaries of the government decision in setting a subsidy would be prepared to expend on lobbying is the sum of the consumer and producer surpluses. This extra expenditure could increase the price in the secondary market to (say) P_3 in Figure 6.5. The Tullock trapezoid as a measure of the total social costs of monopoly may not be an accurate measure except in special circumstances. We take up this point in a later section on type-2 errors. A contributory factor is the economics of the secondary market where prices change, supply and demand conditions change and existing distortions in the secondary market may be either mitigated or amplified by rent-seeking activity. The main ingredient in Varian's paper was the use of a general equilibrium consumer surplus model in order to arrive at his geometric areas. The net deadweight loss due to rent-seeking in secondary market, area (ACBED,) is added to the net deadweight loss in the first market. But the area (ACBED) clearly depends on the shift in demand from D to D_1: the smaller the shift, the smaller the area (ACBED); consequently the increase in price is lower.

If the increased demand for restaurant meals is a complement to the increased demand for lobbyists, then the demand for lobbyists as a derived service complements rent-seeking behaviour. For any two complementary goods a decrease in the price (increase in quantity) of one good shifts the demand for the complement to the right. Hence an increase in the demand for lobbyists complements rent-seeking activity, and the extent of the shift in the demand schedule for lobbyists clearly depends on rent-seeking activity. We could capture this in a ratio C, of lobbyists income, L, to rent-seeking expenditure E, which reaches a maximum value of $C = 1$ when rent-seeking expenditures are completely spent on lobbying. A value $C = 1$ is the rent dissipation argument where we have a unique expenditure on lobbying. The ratio, C, is essentially a cost ratio relating to the opportunity cost of the real resources spent on lobbying. The smaller the cost ratio the smaller is the shift in demand in the secondary market. Tirole's (1988) strategic and administrative costs would translate into $C \leq 1$. Varian's conclusion however is that the partial equilibrium measures are an overestimate of the true social cost of rent-seeking. In support of this claim he refers to the need to compute supply elasticities in the secondary markets, to examine free riding amongst lobbyists, to look for existing distortions in the secondary market that may be either mitigated or amplified by rent-seeking, and whether bribes were used, and to deduce whether they were just direct transfers with no dead-weight loss attached.

In addition to economies derived from the scale of the lobbying firms' operations there is also the possible cost savings arising from a simultaneous production of several different information amounts, that is, output by a single multi-issue lobbying firm. For example a lobbying firm on behalf of group A would be specialised and thus reap economies of scale in the supply of A-related issues, but this same level of expertise could be acquired by a multi-issue lobbyist representing different groups A, B and C. Denoting L as lobbying costs, one could define the cost-savings obtainable by economies of scope *a la* Baumol, Panzer and Willig (1982), that arise from the scope of the lobbying firms activities by:

$$L(A + B) < L(A, O) + L(O, B)$$

The presence of such economies creates an incentive for lobbying firms to merge. Smaller firms could, as Varian (1989) hinted, free ride on the information amounts made available in the lobbying process by the multi-issue firm. If lobbying can generate cost savings in the lobbying activity, then less expenditure of real resources by rent-seekers is incurred with economies of scope than otherwise. Third best outcomes and economies of scope create the situation therefore wherein lobbying may have positive benefits and be efficiency-increasing. The distortionary effects on the secondary markets are significant in the context of third best outcomes. However, with uncertainty and a lack of complete information, we really do not know what will happen in a secondary market once a tax or a subsidy is imposed. Suppose, as in the example in Ng (1979), that good X justifies a Pigovian tax of £t per unit. If good X is highly complementary to good Y and Y has external economies, the reduction in demand or use of Y as a consequence of tax on good X, has additional secondary effects to the lobbying costs incurred in attempting to avoid tax £t in first instance. A subsidy for good X would have beneficial consequences for society through the extra use of good Y, and the lobbying activity would likewise be efficiency-increasing.

A PROPERTY RIGHTS DIMENSION

In this section we endorse a property rights perspective on rent-seeking. In many respects a property rights allocation could be characterised as a zero-sum game. In any economic transaction there are non-zero costs and property rights can reduce the costs of transactions. Neither the consumer nor the producer gain all the benefits involved in the transactions; there are externalities and misinformation. An important issue is whether the allocation of property rights can reduce the externality. Lobbying can be interpreted as a rights allocation mechanism, a general self-interested process for ensuring the transfer of rights and of rents. Within the domain of neo-institutional economics it is the rules of the game that determine the extent of the negative contribution. Eggertsson (1990) comments that 'the rules of the game (are) in part controlled by the state'. In other words, a theory of property rights requires a complete theory of the state. In the absence of a clear definition of what the state is, except an aggregate of competing interest groups, it is not surprising that both

Benson (1984) and Eggertsson (1990) dissociate the rent-seeking paradigm from a full theory of property rights.

We have already alluded to the possibility that rent-seeking may be necessary and desirable in an economy. One example which springs to mind is that of an unused commons acreage that has been transformed into a multi-storey car park by a firm who was awarded the contract by lobbying. Rent-seeking in this case is socially desirable, the party (community) who surrenders the resource receives a local public good in return. The community has been compensated; here we suggest that undesirable rent-seeking may involve an uncompensated transfer of wealth. Sisk (1985), in applying a property rights perspective to rent-seeking, commented that 'producers might wish to obtain uncompensated transfers by excluding competitors and limiting the right of consumers to purchase where they choose'. The right to produce in this case conflicts with the right of competitors to compete and the right of consumers to purchase. Hence 'rent-seeking emerges when rights are challengeable' and lobbying for clearer legislative definitions of property rights will occur. We contend that there may be benefits accruing to society from this challenge.

The relationship between rent-seeking and the economics of property rights has been addressed by Buchanan (1980) and Benson (1984), the latter having demonstrated that the two approaches yield identical conclusions. The rent-seeking approach as argued recently by Eggertsson (1990) 'is conceptually the same as the interest-group theory of property rights'. This theory seeks to explain the structure of property rights in terms of interaction between competing interest groups. Property rights in this context address the interests of a particular interest group, which as argued in the classic rent-seeking literature, make a negative contribution to the economy. The conclusion is that the government can affect the net wealth of the economy by allocating property rights. This conclusion, however, should be independent of the allocating mechanism.

Sisk continued to argue that the rent-seeking literature does not explicitly mention property rights although undesirable rent-seeking is associated 'with the abridgement of someone's property rights in an unwilling transfer'. One reason for this, surely, is the presentation of the paradigmal case of rent-seeking as the acquisition of government issued monopoly franchises with a consumer surplus (unwilling) transfer. He resurrects Tullock's example of theft as a classic rent-seeking case where real resources are expended to obtain 'uncompensated transfers of wealth from the unwilling'. This is likened to the loss of consumers of purchasing power in the face of barriers to entry. Sisk identifies the unwilling uncompensated transfers as the essence of the undesirable rent-seeking literature generated by Tullock (1967) but disagrees with Buchanan's (1983b) attempt to show that undesirable rent-seeking occurs in the case of willing uncompensated transfers. The Sisk-Buchanan argument centres on the treatment of rent-seeking within a property rights dimension. The resolution of this argument really belongs with the neo-institutional economics school of thought.

What is at issue really is the identification of the traditional concept of rent-seeking with either a willing uncompensated or an unwilling uncompensated transfer. It would appear that the writings of both Sisk and Buchanan concur on transfers being uncompensated. We would disagree by suggesting that an agreement between scholars on uncompensated transfers side-steps an important issue on whether or not the initial resource is unassigned as in the example of the commons acreage. Earlier Posner (1975) had advanced the idea that property rights will be more clearly defined as the resources become more valuable. If we couple this idea with the existence of (marginal) theft as a free rider response to collective respect for individual property rights, the issue of compensation would need to be examined further in any normative re-appraisal of rent-seeking.

Theorem 6.1: On the existence of marginal theft.

Proof: The following is a simple inductive proof that marginal theft will always exist in a barter society based on mutual trust. Let there be three individuals A, B and C. Each individual has a Q production amount of a commodity (say) potatoes. Each individual steals q amount of potatoes from his neighbours. Consider individual A's output, the difference between what he produces and what the other two individuals steal. We define this difference as $QA - (qB + qC)$. Individual A steals in order to compensate for the loss $(qB + qC)$ of potatoes. By extension both B and C steal; hence no potatoes are produced. If no potatoes are produced there is no production. So individuals agree not to steal. With this agreement there is the incentive for one individual to steal given that everybody else will not steal. Hence marginal theft exists.

Therefore, rather than allow anarchy to persist unimpeded in a society wherein everybody is a thief a consensus forms within a society based on mutual respect and trust, signalling that there is a thief. The implication of Theorem 6.1 is that society recognises that some rights to resources will not be fully enforced. Other members of society take cognisance of this, become more vigilant and take precautions and establish institutions in order to protect their possessions. As a consequence society is better protected, better insured and for any possession lost or property stolen, a compensatory amount is paid. With the existence of theft and crime, institutions are established in this society by rent-seeking activity which enable individuals to receive compensation. In this regard the theft is a compensated transfer.

When the initial resources are unassigned, however, rent-seeking expenditures are used to obtain the property right, but there is no unwilling transfer of resources. There is a dilemma here in using a property rights dimension to characterise rent-seeking. The dilemma arises in the following way: if the only thing on which to agree is that Tullock's original concept of rent-seeking is an uncompensated and unwilling transfer, then one can only conclude with a tautology that rent-seeking is wasteful, unless the transfer is compensated. If, however, at the other extreme there is a willing and compensated transfer of resources as in the case of the commons acreage, desirable rent-seeking would occur. In this instance the assignment of the resource through rent-seeking activity was of direct benefit to society. Accepting that resources are assigned by rent-seeking activity, the description of the activity as wasteful really does depend on whether the individual or society is compensated or not. Undesirable rent-seeking arises when the individual or society is not compensated for a (willing or unwilling) transfer of resources.

If rent-seeking activity assigns a property right, and society does not benefit (that is, no compensation) from such an assignment, then rent-seeking is undesirable. In our earlier example, a once unkempt acreage is transformed into a needed multi-storey car park. In this case the benefit to society in having such a car park should be factored into the costs of rent-seeking. If as argued elsewhere by other authors, Musgrave and Musgrave (1980), that the role of government is to abridge property rights then an argument in favour of government arises that would be anathema to many right-wing public choice theorists. One must not forget that market equilibrium requires an assignment of property rights, in addition to zero transactions costs and perfect information. Zero transactions costs as defined by DeAlessi (1983) 'means that the costs of obtaining information about alternatives and of negotiating policing and enforcing contracts are zero'. Rent-seeking activity as exemplified by lobbying not only assigns property rights but conveys information. This debate switches the interpretation of rent-seeking away from the traditional one of monopoly and franchise rights acquisition in the context of industrial organisation, where ironically the application of rent-seeking has been noticeably absent, to a more open forum in the context of interest group behaviour.

But one could argue from a traditional economics perspective that a price above the long run marginal cost of production is an unwilling transfer. Chamberlin (1933) however, may have acknowledged compensation for the consumer for the higher monopoly price by the availability of many differentiated products. Interpreting product differentiation as compensation to the consumer is equivalent to interpreting insurance as compensation to the victim of theft. While undesirable rent-seeking is associated with an unwilling transfer not all unwilling transfers are regarded as undesirable. The reason for this, according to Sisk, is that some unwilling transfers are compensated; for example, taxation for national defence is a classical example, or indeed the compulsory purchase of land by a city council. We would push the Sisk argument one step further in suggesting a role for Hicksian compensation, whereby the transferee is made no worse off but certainly not better off unless in the case of speculative buying of land before rezoning. The undesirability of rent-seeking in this instance is captured by DeAlessi (1983) quoting Alchian concluding that 'different systems of property rights present decision makers with different structures of incentives, resulting in different alignments of resources'. This raises a different issue on the initial assignment of rights to the use of resources.

But can the issue of property rights be reconciled with the classic position on rent-seeking as an undesirable socially wasteful activity? The key to answering this question is the definition of compensation. One can insure against theft, and both product quality and design do compensate the consumer for the higher monopoly price. This does not deflect from the expenditure of real resources in acquiring the monopoly position but it does suggest that undesirable rent-seeking in the spirit of Tullock, contrary to Sisk, may occur with a compensated unwilling transfer of resources. The unwillingness criteria may be further weakened by Corollary 6.2 which asserts that the issue of property rights is a pairwise issue with alternative outcomes which are not mutually exclusive.

Corollary 6.2: Define ri as the ith individual's right. The set of rights, defined as $R = \{ri ... rn\}$ is connected, hence $ri \cap rj \neq 0$.

In other words a property rights dispute involves a pair of rights and the solution will inevitably involve a compromise. A support group for this position may be found in Sen's (1976) nihilism where a debate over relative rights relegates the importance of rights, or in Rae's (1975) assertion that some rights issues drift into the resolution of public goods. By contrast Hart's (1973) example of the farmer (right to exclude) and the hiker (right to movement) exhibits the pairwise dispute where one right is constrained for the advancement of another right. Likewise, priority across rights in Rawls' (1973) original position is not possible because of an absence of sufficient information about rights. In a Hart-Rawlsian type world $ri \cap rj \neq 0$. The solution of a rights dispute requires an expenditure of real resources in order to enforce a mutual contract. Each individual will take into account the benefits accruing from any transfer of rights. Rent-seeking expenditures can resolve the issue of priority across rights whether it be between producer or consumer, farmer or hiker. And a manifestation of this is through successful lobbying.

More information as contended by Mueller (1989) enables the rights issue to be resolved. The farmer may allow limited access. Here we generally have a compromised though unwilling transfer of a right and the transfer is generally institutionalised. A 'no trespassers' sign would suffice in (say) Hart's example. However in a wider context if a property right issue was resolved by lobbying, the resulting rent-seeking expenditures are not wasteful. The move from a society with marginal theft to a state of (say) anarchy is not Pareto improving;

here is a normative requirement for a third party intervention to abridge property rights. If this arises due to lobbying, the outcome is not wasteful but rather efficiency-increasing. Milgrom and Roberts (1990) in their paper on organisational decision processes enunciated the positive attributes of rent-seeking: 'the very elements that make a process open to rent seeking may also add flexibility and responsibleness, helping to ensure that important ideas and proposals are fully considered'. The costs of rent-seeking are balanced against the value of information obtained in the decision process. If the net benefit of rent-seeking expenditure is equated with the social cost, and an optimal level of rent-seeking expenditures could be determined.

McLean (1987) also considers the benefits of lobbying citing as he does the miners eight hour day as one example. In this case the law changed property rights 'without forcing the gainers to pay the losers (coalminers)'. The prevention of a risk of nuclear war or the introduction of a public inoculation programme arising from lobbying is beneficial; hence expenditure on lobbying is not representative, in this instance, of the social costs of rent-seeking. The outcome of lobbying is therefore a public good. We should recall that economic issues which fundamentally are property rights issues are resolved in the Pigovian-Hicksian welfare economics by recourse to either bribery (for example, increased taxation on cigarettes) or compensation (for example, subsidisation of housing near a nuclear plant). Notice that in the case of traditional welfare economics there is an implicit acceptance or toleration of the denial or loss of a right as alluded to by Kaldor (1939) 'if all those who suffer as a result are fully compensated for their loss the rest of the community will still be better off than before'. Our discussion here has been to introduce the property rights dimension to reconsider the concept of rent-seeking. Unwillingness as a criterion can be weakened but compensation as a criterion needs to be further examined, before undesirable rent-seeking can be exclusively identified as the spending of resources to obtain uncompensated transfers.

If rent-seeking activity is to be interpreted as an abridgement of property rights, then traditional rent-seeking is desirable if the individual or society is adequately compensated for the transfer of resources that takes place. In the transfer of resources from the government to the monopolist all that is required in order to render rent-seeking behaviour as desirable is that the transfer-recipients compensate the transferee. Compensation such as product quality, innovation, product reliability, acceptable market price, green-space, are all quantifiable as positive gains from rent-seeking which may reverse the undesirable status of the rent-seeking activity which had initiated the transfer of resources. Whether the transfer is willing or unwilling is of secondary importance. One could infer from DeAlessi (1983) that the structure of property rights imposes an additional constraint on the producing firm. Referring to the exchange between Stigler and Leibenstein on X-inefficiency, DeAlessi further comments that 'Stigler argued that if transactions costs are positive (presumably the rights to the use of resources are privately held) then contracts are not fully specified and enforced'. Incomplete labour contracts are recognised as a source of X-inefficiency (Leibenstein 1980). Hence a reason why firms are not producing at minimum cost is that resources are used to enforce contracts. This returns the debate to the original argument made by Alchian (1965) 'that differences in property rights can explain evidence used to support the existence of X-inefficiency'. The conceptual debate between Buchanan and Sisk on a willingness criterion masks a more important issue regarding the link between undesirable rent-seeking and compensated (unwilling) transfers. The existence of a causal link between rent-seeking and X-inefficiency as measures of the cost of the transfer of resources will now be examined.

RENT-SEEKING AND X-INEFFICIENCY

There are many different research avenues within the domain of rent-seeking not covered in this chapter. Our specific interest is in re-appraising Tullock's original rent-seeking diagram. One central question remains unconvincing answered in the literature: is a rent-seeking measure an easily identifiable geometric measure? We reply in the negative, arguing that there may be a possible overlap with other measures of the social costs of monopoly, possibly Leibenstein's (1966) X-inefficiency measure and particularly the Harberger triangle. The overlap with X-inefficiency may sound surprising and be anathema to many economists, since Neo-Classical economics would not afford either measures the luxury of a common theoretical base. That this has occurred is an accident of history which resulted in rent-seeking being identified with the public choice school of thought. The analysis presented in the next section is from McNutt (1993b), who has argued that the (social) cost of rent-seeking as measured is the sum of X-inefficiency as measured and Harberger losses. The argument in his paper is a reaction to Congleton (1988) who argued that the social cost of rent-seeking was the sum of a Harberger triangle and an opportunity cost of rent-seeking

The overlap in the geometric areas in both papers is a possible measure of X-inefficiency identified later in this chapter as (P_1RCP_2) in Figure 6.6. The measure is a subset of Congleton's geometric area, replicated as (P_1ABP_2) in our Figure 6.6. In retrospect, Leibenstein (1966) responded to the Mundell (1962) challenge requesting 'a thorough theoretical examination of the validity of the tools upon which these studies (of losses from monopoly) are founded', by introducing his concept of X-inefficiency. In subsequent analysis X-inefficiency, which required according to Rowley (1987) 'strong assumptions ... concerning stock market inefficiency', was overshadowed by the efficient capital market hypothesis debate during the early seventies. At the same time, the rent-seeking insight, directed by Tullock at the monopoly losses in public markets, became fashionable, but unlike X-inefficiency, it had an inbuilt immune system against neo-classical derision, with its location under the public choice umbrella. The two approaches differ in their interpretation of wasteful competition, but the difference may be superficial or even irrelevant in a partial normative analysis.

Public choice scholars continue to address the normative analysis of rent-seeking within a partial equilibrium framework. Frantz (1988) commented that 'rent-seeking arguments, have tended to allow for the existence of X-inefficiency but to argue that it entails *no welfare loss*' (our italics) (p. 436). By adopting this position public choice theory ignores the fact that if elements of X-inefficiency can be identified as producer's surplus they must feature in a social welfare function. The issue addressed in this section is whether or not geometric measures of rent-seeking and X-inefficiency overlap in the same partial equilibrium framework. We conclude that they do. The possibility of an overlap creates a problem in identifying geometric measures purporting to explain the welfare impact of monopoly outside the bounds of the Harberger triangles. A resolution of this measure identification problem, which is not beyond the capacity of public choice scholars in general and microeconomists in particular, will require, we believe, a rehabilitation of both rent-seeking and X-inefficiency within the modern developments of industrial organisation theory. In the interim, we present our analysis in this section.

Within public choice the higher costs which contribute to allocative inefficiency are due to rent-seeking. Other scholars assume away X-inefficiency either by arguing that (regulated) firms have little incentive to be X-inefficient (Joskow 1978), or by criticising X-efficiency theory because it does not accept maximisation behaviour. McNutt (1993b) discussed the possibility of an overlap in his reaction to Congleton (1988) who had earlier concluded in his paper 'that the social cost of rent-seeking is the Harberger triangle plus the opportunity cost of scarce economic resources utilised in rent-seeking activities'. Naughton and Frantz (1991) have concluded 'that a priori (without empirical evidence), one cannot without assurance', compare the social costs of X-inefficiency and rent-seeking. One possibility is to consider an overlap between the two measures as the Charbydis and Scylla of the social costs of monopoly. In other words, the monopolist divides his profit between both rent-seeking and X-inefficiency.

Although the social costs of monopoly are associated with rent-seeking activity the literature is not particularly clear on either the apportionment of such costs or on the extent of their magnitude. Positive estimates on the social costs of rent-seeking differ widely across the literature. The development of the efficient rents approach represents an attempt to explain incomplete dissipation of rents. Many authors including Buchanan (1980) and Tirole (1988) instead have suggested a typology of rent-seeking costs. For example, Buchanan's 'third party distortions' and Tirole's 'administrative costs' would not be regarded as socially wasteful expenditures. The absence of any reconfiguration of the geometric explanation of the social costs of rent-seeking in the light of such normative developments is a recurrent problem for public choice theorists. Congleton (1988) suggested that the social cost of rent-seeking is the opportunity costs of the real resources used in rent-seeking behaviour. Indeed Tirole's (1988) strategic costs of rent-seeking would include the expenditure of real resources either for long term R&D expenditure to develop a new product or in order to erect entry barriers. The opportunity costs of these resources would amount to the social cost of the rent-seeking activity.

We contend that Congleton's particular treatment of an opportunity cost argument within a partial geometric framework leads to a paradox in that the traditional (geometric) social cost of monopoly, Tullock rectangle plus the Harberger triangle, does *not* obtain. One explanation proffered here is a possible overlap in the geometric interpretation of rent-seeking and X-inefficiency. The essence of the social cost of monopoly within which both X-inefficiency and rent-seeking evolved, is that a price above the long run perfectly competitive price represents a (unwilling) transfer of resources from the consumer to the producer. Quite simply if the monopoly price Pm in Figure 6.6 is realised the trapezoid (PmGAP$_1$) is divided into Tullock's rectangle (PmGEP$_1$) and Harberger's triangle (GEA). The rectangle is the amount that completely dissipates the monopoly rent.

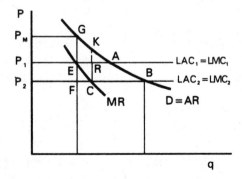

Figure 6.6: Rent-seeking and X-inefficiency

Congleton (1988) identified an opportunity cost of rent-seeking expenditures as a shaded area L in his paper, which he computed by asserting a reduction in the marginal cost of production had resources been spent on the research and development. This is reproduced here in Figure 6.6 as the area (P_1ABP_2). He proceeded eventually to show that the social cost of rent-seeking (denoted by SC in the following equations) was the sum of the Harberger triangle and the opportunity cost of rent seeking L. We suggest that this may not be the case. The social cost of rent-seeking includes the opportunity cost of the real resources used, but the geometric area in Congleton may not be a measure of that opportunity cost. In any analysis of either rent-seeking or X-inefficiency one has to incorporate the marginal revenue curve into the construction. This reinforces the assumption that the monopolist is producing at a profit maximisation output. The significance of this assumption is seldom questioned and not even alluded to by some authors. If the reduced costs of production $(LMC_1 - LMC_2)$ were attainable, the rent-seeking monopolist would move to the profit-maximising point C in Figure 6.6. LMC_1 represents the observed monopoly production costs while LMC_2 represents the unobserved costs, realisable in Congleton's analysis only if resources are diverted to research and development.

In his calculation of the economic cost of monopoly 'through the route of erecting an entry barrier', there is one possible oversight, that is, the direct costs of the resources used to deter entry. These direct costs increase the long run average cost of production. Assuming a constant LAC, we obtain the result LAC = LMC (long run marginal cost of production). This result is the converse to the result that R&D expenditures contribute to a decrease in long run costs. And of direct importance here is the location of the surreal point C which splits the area (P_1ABP_2) into (P_1RCP_2) and (RABC). Had the monopolist deterred entry by adopting an entry deterrent strategy which translates into an overhead cost, the corresponding increase in average costs $(LAC_1 - LAC_2)$ would generate the trapezoid equal to (P_1ABP_2), where (P_1RCP_2) could be interpreted as a measure of X-inefficiency. Since the area $(P_1RCP_2) < (P_1ABP_2)$, it would appear that the social cost of X-inefficiency as measured in this chapter is less than the opportunity cost of rent-seeking as measured by Congleton. A difficulty arises here in the interpretation of the area (P_1RCP_2) as the measure of X-inefficiency.

Let us look closer at the concept of X-efficiency as applied in our analysis. X-inefficiency is directly concerned with costs of production, rent-seeking likewise is concerned with diverting funds away from production. Within the public choice literature rent-seeking behaviour simply assumes away X-inefficiency. For example, Crain and Zardkoohi (1978) have recently argued that a firm which is more X-efficient generates the funds to engage in rent-seeking. They comment that 'X-inefficiency is a linear function of rent-seeking expenditures'. Frantz (1988) interprets the linearity condition to imply that 'even if it (X-inefficiency) exists it is of no consequence' (p. 185). The existence of X-inefficiency, by reducing available rent-seeking funds, creates an opportunity cost, defined in terms of lower profits, for the firm. Entry restriction measures absorb economic resources up to the point where marginal entry deterrent costs are equated with marginal cost savings due to entry restriction. X-inefficiency is inevitable in this non-competitive market and production costs must be higher than the hypothetical level that entry might provide since entry-deterring costs must be accounted for. The representative firm erects an entry barrier by increasing quantity or output in order to saturate the market; a decision which increases the costs of production accruing to the firm.

In looking for an X-environment *a la* Leibenstein (1980) and Frantz (1988) within this firm, we must explore how the entrepreneurs may react in the post-barrier situation? In many respects, the X-inefficiencies are essentially a black box of possible behaviour. In particular, entrepreneurship will no longer be routine while economies of scale will have to be exploited to minimise the higher costs of production. Eventually intra-firm problems will emerge as latent skills have to be motivated and discretionary behaviour is reduced. In this scenario X-inefficiency manifests itself as an overhead cost. The once-off increase in costs reflects the opportunity costs of time and effort in erecting the entry barrier. We are looking at an inefficiency which is not caused by price deviating from the marginal cost. If X-inefficiency affects the level of marginal cost, it is measured by the rectangular area (P_1EFP_2) in Figure 6.6. However, if X-inefficiency manifests itself as an overhead cost, it is measured by (P_1RCP_2), assuming that the average cost inclusive of overhead cost is LAC_1. The area (P_1RCP_2) is equivalent to the loss Wx as described by Comanor and Leibenstein (1969). The area (P_1EFP_2) is also equivalent to the social costs of real X-inefficiency outlined in Formby, Keeler and Thistle (1988).

A priori one must clearly distinguish between X-inefficiency manifesting itself either as an increase in marginal cost which is the position of Congleton and Formby, Keeler and Thistle, or as an increase in overhead costs, the position adopted here in this chapter. In a search for a common denominator between X-inefficiency and rent-seeking in the analysis of the social costs of real resources expended, this distinction in X-inefficiency is crucial, particularly so if both measures are used as mitigating evidence in anti-trust. The rent-seeking acquisition expenditures identified by Formby *et al.* and the confusion between the latter and Naughton and Frantz (1991) on an economically intuitive interpretation of the geometric measure (HBDI) (equivalent to FGKC in our Figure 6.6), as either 'the loss is allocate efficiency' according to Naughton and Frantz, or according to Formby, Keeler and Thistle 'properly a part of X-inefficiency, not allocative inefficiency', can be easily resolved by interpreting X-inefficiency as an overhead cost. Looking at Figure 6.6, the area (FGKC) is the sum of subsets of geometric measures of both X-inefficiency and the Harberger loss triangle. The welfare loss from X-inefficiency is the area

(P_1RCP_2) in Figure 6.6 and this conclusion is based on our interpretation of the analysis in both Crew and Rowley (1971) and Comanor and Leibenstein (1969).

   Theorem 6.2: The social cost of rent-seeking as measured is the sum of a measure of X-inefficiency and the Harberger losses.

   Proof:

$$SC = (H + C) + (L - C) \qquad\qquad 6.1$$
$$L = (PmGFP_2 + GFB) - (PmGEP_1 + GEA)$$
$$C = PmGEP_1, \quad H = GEA$$
$$<=>$$
$$SC = (GEA + PmGEP_1) + (L - PmGEP_1) \qquad\qquad 6.2$$
$$= PmGFP_2 + GFB - PmGEP_1$$
$$= (PmGFP_2 - PmGEP_1) + GFB$$

$$SC = P_1EFP_2 + GFB \qquad\qquad 6.3$$
$$GFB = GEA + ERFC + RABC$$
$$SC = (P_1EFP_2 + ERFC) + GEA + RABC$$

$$SC = P_1RCP_2 + GEA + RABC \qquad\qquad 6.4$$

   The X-inefficiency measure (P_1RCP_2) is a subset of the original Congleton $L = (P_1ABP_2)$, which is central to the conclusion reached in this section. This conclusion however depends on LMC2 being realised (say) before the threat of entry. The corresponding Harberger triangle would be (GFB). If we reconsider Congleton's (1988) SC equation as equation 1 below we outline the steps in arriving at our conclusion.

   But what is the economic intuition behind RABC? We intend to argue that it is a Harberger loss measure. We agree with Congleton that (P_1ABP_2) is a measure of the social costs of rent-seeking, but it is in the composition and interpretation of the geometric area that we disagree; it is we contend the sum of a measure of X-inefficiency and Harberger losses. Consider Figure 6.7. D_1 and D_2 are the Hicksian demand curves for a price fall from Pm to P_1, and D_1 and D_3 are the Hicksian demand curves for the price fall Pm to P_2.

   The corresponding consumer surplus measures are the Marshallian measures ($PmGAP_1$) and ($PmGBP_2$), and the compensating variations are ($PmGRP_1$) and ($PmGMP_2$). The triangular areas (GRA) and (GMB) depend on the size of the income effect (Boadway and Bruce 1984), and if income effects are zero these geometric areas are zero as argued in McNutt (1993b). In Figure 6.7 the Harberger triangles are (GRE) and (GMF) respectively.

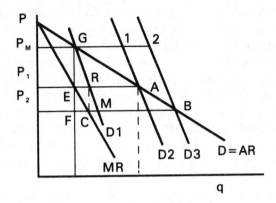

Figure 6.7: X-inefficiency measures

Lemma: If the area (GEA) is minimal, the social costs of rent-seeking and our measure of X-inefficiency coincide.

If GMB = 0 the area RABC approximates zero. Plugging this into our equation 6.4 we can rewrite equation 6.4 as equation 6.5:

$$P_1ABP_2 = P_1RCP_2 + GEA \qquad 6.5$$

And as the area GRA = 0 the area GEA approximates zero. Plugging this into our equation 6.5 we can rewrite equation 6.5 as equation 6.6:

$$P_1ABP_2 = P_1RCP_2 \qquad 6.6$$

Hence the social costs of rent-seeking and our measure of X-inefficiency coincide. As McNutt (1993b) argued: 'the entry deterrent expenditures generate no quasi-rents for the factors of production employed'. Otherwise the social cost of rent-seeking equals the sum of a Harberger loss (GEA), an X-inefficiency measure and a Harberger type area (RABC). When income effects are zero, it is only the area (RABM), a subset of (RABC), that is strictly equal to zero. The smaller triangular measure (RMC) remains positive. And this measure is a subset of the Harberger triangle (GMF). The area (RABC) is a subset of the Harberger loss (G2BF); if points G and 2 coincided (income effects are zero), the triangle (GBF) would be an exact measure of the Harberger loss. Since (RABC) is a subset of (G2BF), it may be interpreted as a Harberger loss measure. There is, we suspect, a problem of measure identification embedded in this analysis which highlights the need to reconsider the micro foundations of rent-seeking and the social costs of monopoly. Congleton may have unwittingly led a Trojan horse into the partial analysis of rent-seeking.

A NOTE ON RENT-SEEKING AND ANTI TRUST

Rent-seeking is now clearly identified in the literature with monopoly acquisition and the ensuing rent-seeking costs are added to the traditional social costs of monopoly. This has attracted the attention of anti-trust regulators who are interested in the regulation of monopolies. The geometric areas identified in this chapter depend on the level of monopoly price Pm in order to furnish accurate measures of the social costs of monopoly. It is imperative that accurate measures are obtained as aspiring monopolists will tend to expend real resources and exert efforts to acquire the monopoly position. Once installed they will continue spending and exerting effort in order to maintain the monopoly position. Tirole (1988) considered both strategic costs and the administrative costs of rent-seeking. The latter include lobbying costs but the strategic costs include expenditure of real resources on developing a patent and the costs of erecting barriers to entry. Existing monopolies, the incumbent firms in an industry, compete in non-price aspects like technology, R&D, advertising and product differentiation. Real resources are devoted to these activities, resources which have a high opportunity cost, and resources which are being used primarily to maintain the monopoly position. The social cost of rent-seeking does include the opportunity costs of resources used in non-price competition. The problem just outlined above is in identifying these opportunity costs.

An interesting dimension to this debate on rent-seeking and the maintaining of a monopoly position is the extent to which the incumbent monopolist, through lengthy and complicated regulatory procedures, attempts to delay the entry of another firm. The incumbent's expenditure on legal fees to protect its acquired monopoly position could be factored into a measure of the social cost of rent-seeking. This institutional barrier to entry evokes an argument by Brock and Evans (1983) that monopoly interference in the regulatory process (an interference referred to as 'regulatory-process predation') may be a pure waste of resources. Predation refers to the 'inducement of exit' - an existing monopolist may set up entry barriers in order to deter entry but may also expend resources to induce the exit of a rival firm. One important micro-economic impact of this is on the tractability of rent-seeking estimates with the consequent unreliability of the existing monopoly price Pm. The incumbent monopolist may alter price and as Tirole (1988) argued: 'if the incumbent is unsure whether he will deter or accommodate entry, it is not clear whether he will charge more or less than the monopoly price'. This apart, the aspiring monopolist once established in the market may engage in anti-competitive behaviour like limit-pricing. If so this will impact on the geometric areas of the rent-seeking in a partial equilibrium diagram.

Type-2 Errors

In particular, incomplete information on the level of monopoly price may invoke what we label as type-2 errors in computation of the geometric measure of the social cost of rent-seeking. Suppose we have the following scenario. Let P_1 be the price used by the regulator to calculate the Tullock rectangle and let Pm be a realistic market price. If the regulator were to assume that $P_1 = Pm$ but in fact $Pm > P_1$, the partial equilibrium estimate of rent-seeking would represent an underestimate of the true amount of rent-seeking. If, on the other hand, she assumes that $P_1 > Pm$ when in fact $Pm = P_1$, an overestimate of rent-seeking will result. Both estimates are indicative of a type-2 error. In other words, the regulator by assuming that an observed price is equal to or greater than a market price, accepts a false hypothesis. This relates directly to our earlier discussions concerning the inaccuracy of the partial geometric measures, which depend on an observable and accurate market price, Pm.

Jadlow (1985), by using different statistical assumptions has argued that the predicted social waste is less than estimated by economists. In other words economists incur type-2 errors. But how does it connect with rent-seeking expenditures *per se*? An incumbent monopolist will expend real resources in an attempt to deter entry. We could approximate this rent-seeking expenditure by arguing that rent-seeking costs includes the opportunity costs of these resources used in non-price entry barriers such as R&D expenditure or on legal fees to delay a regulatory process. Conversely the monopolist may wish to induce exit through price manipulation or deter entry by limit pricing; in either case the regulator would wish to avoid making a type-2 error in estimating the measured area of the social costs of rent-seeking. One could argue that with price barriers the expected loss to the monopolist in terms of monopoly profit will limit the amount of rent-seeking activity conducted. In the limit an incumbent monopolist may expend his entire monopoly profits equal to the area (PmCAPc) in Figure 6.2 earlier, in deterring entry or sacrifice a percentage of the profits to retain market dominance.

Non-Price Barriers

The story may differ in accounting for rent-seeking costs in the case of non-price barriers. In this case the resources used have a clear alternative use and it is their opportunity cost that is added to the cost of rent-seeking. In the case of price barriers, profits are sacrificed (say) in the short run. A (low) price barrier employed by monopolists may induce an overestimate of the partial measure of rent-seeking which could be counterproductive in improving the mitigating circumstances in monopoly regulation. Hence a monopolist in attempting to avoid the type-2 error may use non-price barriers, thus making the regulator's task of estimating the costs of rent-seeking less tractable. In the case of bribes to government officials, the rent-seeking expenditure reduces to a pure transfer which involves no social costs and the social cost of the monopoly could be measured by the usual geometric areas. With price barriers, however, rent-seeking expenditures amount to a diminution in the short run profits of the monopolist (no cost to society), but the usual geometric areas remain inaccurate.

For non-price barriers, however, it is the opportunity costs of the resources used which contribute to the true cost of rent-seeking expenditures. A difficulty with identifying the true cost of rent-seeking is the possible overlap with a measure of X-inefficiency. In the case of non-price barriers the usual geometric areas and the Tullock trapezoid may have to be amended. An effective non-price entry barrier could manifest itself by incumbents either unilaterally or collectively engaging in higher short run production levels. This will signal to the potential entrant a lower than expected residual market share. For example, brand proliferation by dominant firms acts as an effective barrier to entry. At the level of smaller firms, by collectively increasing output marginally they can increase total output substantially. For a profit maximising firm, the non-decreasing output range lies below the mid-point of the industry demand curve. How the required reduction in price in order to absorb the increase in quantity will affect total revenue (TR) depends on the elasticity of the demand curve facing the firm.

The change in total revenue (denoted ΔTR) is composed of two changes: (i) ΔTR due to increase in price at given quantity; and (ii) ΔTR due to increase in quantity at given price. In Figure 6.8 the geometric area (P_1CAPc) represents the ΔTR in (i) and the area (ABqcq1) represents the ΔTR in (ii). These geometric areas are proper measures only if the demand and cost curves are linear. We define ΔTR = ([P_1CAPc) - (ABqcq1)]) and ΔTR > 0 for an inelastic (elastic) demand curve (P_1CAPc) > (ABqcq1) as price increases (decrease). As argued earlier in our discussion on X-inefficiency, the erection of an entry barrier will increase the average costs of production. If the firm is to at least break even it will charge a market price equal to average cost of production (say) P_1 in Figure 6.8. How the higher price affects total revenue will depend on the elasticity of the demand curve.

The geometric area (P_1CAPc) has been identified throughout this chapter as the Tullock rectangle and equals the amount of rent-seeking the monopolist will engage in to secure the franchise. However, for an incumbent monopolist we proffer the area (ABqcq1) as representing an additional amount of real resources the incumbent firm would be prepared to expend in order to protect its market position. The more monopolistic the market the more inelastic the demand curve (say) D* in Figure 6.8 and the smaller the area (ABqcq$_1$);

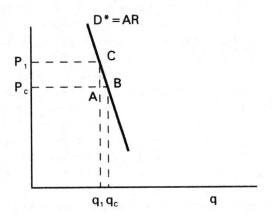

Figure 6.8: Change in total revenue

conversely the less monopolistic the market the more elastic the demand curve in Figure 6.8 and the greater the area (ABqcq1). In the latter case, if the firm is prepared to erect non-price barriers it will incur a short term loss in total revenue. We suggest that the opportunity cost of a non-price barrier is equivalent to a short run loss in total revenue and measured by the area (ABqcq1). In other words, with non-price barriers rent-seeking expenditures are augmented by an amount equal to the short term total revenue of the firm. With non-price barriers the Tullock rectangle underestimates the amount of rent-seeking expenditures by an amount (ABqcq1). This inaccuracy is more likely to hold in those monopolised situations where demand elasticities vary across different product ranges. In precisely these situations the regulator may incur a type-2 error by underestimating the amount of rent-seeking expenditures. Consequently, the accuracy of the regulator's estimate of the amount of rent-seeking expenditures may be invariant with the demand elasticity but monotonic in the potential rents accruing to the monopolist.

Regulation and Rents

The argument could be adapted further if each incumbent firm could deter entry by simply increasing output supply in the market. Each incumbent is producing in the inelastic range of the demand curve, which arises because of the combination of a lower market price and an increased incumbent supply. Our concern here is with the behaviour of incumbent firms in deterring entry by producing at higher output levels. How should a regulator, if at all interested, view this new low price-high quantity configuration, that may be arbitrarily close to the ideal perfectly competitive configuration? As noted earlier, the avoidance of a type-2 error requires accurate information on the level of monopoly price and on the expected level of prices. Neither the incumbent firm nor the regulator can afford a type-2 error. In particular the incumbent monopolist would wish the regulator to err on the side of computing lower social costs. To avoid such an error occurring, the regulator should view the lower price as concomitant to higher short term output deterrent levels and extract the opportunity cost of the real resources used, (ABqcq1), to sustain such a low price. If such real resources can be identified in the partial equilibrium model they could be added to the traditional social costs of monopoly. As a special case in her argument the regulator should not interpret the willingness of a monopolist to be regulated on price (price decrease) independently of the consequential increased output, which may have been the original intention.

The regulator will tend to concentrate on price. Price regulation is associated with a reduction in price to a perfectly competitive price but price reduction should not be viewed as an end in itself, particularly in the special case of incumbent firms facing high elasticity demand curves. Their objective may be to increase output to a level that no longer makes entry profitable for a potential entrant. The search for a lower bound on price for such a firm, equivalent to a marginal cost lower bound, would require the derivation of a regulatory price in terms of the higher output level. The extent to which this lower bound price and the computation of the area (ABqcq1) would contribute to anti-trust investigations, may vary according to the amount of rents being sought. The incentive for particular firms to engage in rent-seeking may abate if anti-trust investigators, as argued by Pittman (1988), maintain 'a vigorous anti-trust policy'. Hence the possibility of a regulator incurring a type-2 error by overestimating the rent-seeking costs under a vigorous anti-trust policy may dissuade the incumbent firm in the long term.

The discussion on price and non-price barriers only highlights the weaknesses in competitive rent-seeking models in evaluating the social costs of monopoly. Earlier in this chapter we had argued that the partial equilibrium model creates ambiguity in the usual geometric areas if it is used to deal with the case of non-price barriers, such as erecting an entry barrier. If the monopolist uses real resources in order to erect non-price barriers, the issue for economists is to explain how the opportunity cost of these resources factor into the traditional geometric social costs of rent-seeking, calculated as the sum of a Harberger triangle and the Tullock rectangle. The discussion on price and non-price barriers weakens the role of competitive rent-seeking models in evaluating accurately the social costs of monopoly. Kahana and Katz (1990) have recently challenged the original Posner (1975) position by arguing that price discrimination cannot increase welfare once rent-seeking is taken into account. If the rent-seeking behaviour uses some of the monopoly profit, then this dissipation of monopoly profit involves no social loss but a transfer from the monopolist to the lobbyist; however if the market for lawyers (say) responds to this redistribution, then there is the additional general equilibrium impact on allocative efficiency. Likewise if non-price barriers require the expenditure of real resources, the opportunity cost of these resources will have to be factored into the rent-seeking estimates. Dilorenzo (1984) in a rather interesting paper addressed the notion accredited to Cowling and Mueller (1978) that non-price competition in a private market represents a legitimate form of rent-seeking. The application of rent-seeking outside the domain of government issued monopoly franchises was supported by Tollison (1982) in his classic review. For Cowling and Mueller (1978) the empirical estimates on the social costs of monopoly were higher than before, when they included non-price competition, particularly R&D and advertising expenditures. The benefits to society of advertising expenditure, R&D and innovation must be included surely in estimating these social costs.

A major point raised by Dilorenzo, which must not be overlooked, is that if one were to acknowledge that competition is best described as a dynamic process rather than a static condition, non-price competition may be reinterpreted as competitive behaviour. Such behaviour, he outlined, increased rather than reduced welfare. Our initial reaction to this literature is that rent-seeking behaviour is omnipresent but that rent-seeking costs remain in abeyance. Benham (1972) had earlier presented evidence to show that legislative restrictions on advertising reduced competitive pressures; this had the impact of raising prices and reducing consumer surplus. It also increases the probability of a regulator making the type-2 error. It is only within a static Neo-Classical perfectly competitive model that advertising expenditures appear to be excessive. Advertising is necessary in order to reduce the market imperfections in information. Dilorenzo (1984) concludes and we concur that 'including advertising and R&D expenditures as part of the social costs of monopoly due to rent-seeking will surely lead to empirical estimates that are, at best, *misleading*' (our italics). It is the possibility of incurring computational errors in the evaluation of rent-seeking that places demands on scholars to re-evaluate the normative foundations of rent-seeking within the accepted partial equilibrium model. In particular, the demands are greatest from the public choice scholars who adamantly use the partial model.

7. Economic Analysis of Clubs

The market is not the only mechanism through which goods and services are provided in a modern political system; we reserve the term, *collective goods*, for those goods and services which are provided wholly through the political process. Otherwise known as public goods, collective goods engage the government in securing a just and equitable distribution of resources which warrant a citizen tax. Within classical public finance theory, the central government finances are directed at the provision of collective goods and services which are provided for each and every citizen within a democratically elected political system. This provision is referred to in the public goods literature as the non-excludability factor which is important in determining the optimal conditions in the provision of collective goods. Earlier chapters have addressed the many factors which influence the level of collective goods and services provided by the government. The allocation of the central funding towards the provision of collective goods illustrates an important role of government as the benevolent dictator in the economic system. As argued in Chapter 6, for example, the direction of that funding may be dictated by the behaviour of rent-seekers.

Market failure not only manifests itself with imperfect competition, incomplete markets and uncertainty but also with public goods and externalities. A primary reason why market failure persists is reflected in the inability of citizens to act co-operatively and it is this lack of co-operation which mandates an allocative role for government in the economy. A Prisoner's Dilemma characterisation of the market failure problem would indicate a Pareto inferior outcome as long as a dominant strategy existed for the individual citizen. The incentive to cheat on collective decisions, otherwise known as the free rider problem, illustrates one dominant strategy which undermines the optimal provision of collective goods. In the classic tradition of public choice, government intervention *per se* would represent an externality. The increasing trend towards local public goods in the provision of public sector output has facilitated the application of club theory which exhibits a co-operative response to the resolution of a local or regional issue.

There are two salient properties pertaining to the provision of collective goods, namely, non-excludability in supply and non-rivalry in consumption. The latter implies that inter-citizen consumption is mutually exclusive, that is, the consumption by one citizen of the collective good will not affect the consumption level of any other citizen. Radio broadcasts, clean air or defence spring to mind as examples of a non-rivalrous collective good. Non-excludability is the hallmark of a political system where the central government funding emanates directly from citizen taxation. However, in the provision of some collective goods, either local public goods or club goods, the citizens often prefer to act independently of government. The property of excludability in the supply of the collective good is the *sine qua non* of club goods. Of particular interest to the theme of this chapter is how local citizens secure an optimal supply of the local collective good.

Buchanan (1965) in his influential paper derived the economic conditions under which an optimal provision of a local public good could be attained. This early work outlined a justification for club analysis in the explanation of why clubs would organise. Both Buchanan and Olson (1965) recognised independently that clubs enable members to exploit economies of scale in the provision of the collective good and to share in the cost of its provision. They each addressed the issue of membership restrictions, with Olson distinguishing between exclusive clubs and inclusive clubs with no membership constraints. The exclusion criterion has since entered the public finance literature as an important hallmark in the analysis of congestion and crowding externalities. In their classic review on the economic theory of clubs, Sandler and Tschirhart (1980) trace the origins of the idea to the work by Pigou (1920) and Knight (1924) on road congestion. The attempt by these early scholars to extract a toll that would limit congestion is the type of exclusion that characterises the theory of clubs.

Likewise, Tiebout (1956) had earlier addressed a club related issue in his work on population mobility and size of local government. His voting-with-the-feet hypothesis has many direct applications in the area of local public goods. Other scholars, notably Schelling (1969) and McGuire (1974) justified club formation on the basis of what has been referred to as a taste for association. This has since been translated in the club literature as the assumption of homogeneity (identical tastes), an assumption which has raised the policy issue as to whether or not mixed clubs are optimal. For example, if mixed clubs are not optimal then the policy of group segregation is optimal whereas the policy of busing, as practised in some US states, is sub-optimal. The issue of optimality, however, is not completely resolved across the club literature. This and other issues in the club literature will be addressed throughout the chapter which is principally concerned with the optimal provision of collective goods. Collective goods by their very nature are unmarketable. The conceptual framework under review will examine the economic nature of collective goods, that is, the provision of pure public goods as defined by Samuelson (1954) and club goods as identified by Buchanan (1965). The latter developed the theory of clubs as one resolution to the recurrent problem of market under-supply of Samuelsonian public goods. Although public goods and club goods represent examples of a collective good the distinctions between them according to Starrett (1988) do 'provide foundations for a normative theory of fiscal federalism' (p. 3). The economic analysis of clubs, however, may be applied to the provision of local public goods, ranging from the supply of decentralised regional public goods (local health boards) to community projects and neighbourhood schemes, such as community sports clubs and residents associations.

PUBLIC GOODS

Public Goods Paradox

Public goods contrast with private goods; public goods are non-excludable and non-rivalrous in consumption while private goods are sold to those who can afford to pay the market price. The market price excludes some consumers while the property of rivalrous consumption ensures that not all consumers who can afford to pay the price, actually purchase the private good. The public goods property of non-rivalry ensures that a provision of the good for consumer A entails a provision for consumer B. Likewise, the property of non-excludability ensures that we cannot exclude consumer B from securing the benefits of the public good, consequently there is no incentive for consumer B to pay the costs of providing the public good. The distinguishing feature of public goods is that provision for one individual entails provision for all and each individual's consumption of the good does not impinge upon others' use on consumption of the good. However there is one issue unresolved in the literature concerning the relative significance of the properties of non-excludability and non-rivalry in the definition of a public good. We shall address this rather intriguing issue later .

To what extent the theory of clubs enables policy makers to escape the under-supply equilibrium in the optimal provision of public goods remains a challenging issue. The interchange between club provision and an interest group provision of a local public good will be developed along with our discussion of the Tiebout (1956) model. Whereas a club provision refers to an excludable goods provision, an interest group provision may refer to the possibility of a non-excludable goods provision. This approach may contribute to the debate on the formation of interest groups particularly at the local neighbourhood level, but how it impacts on the theory of public goods provision ultimately depends on intra-interest group economies of organisation. In other words, the optimal provision of collective goods generally is constrained by what can broadly be defined as the public goods paradox, that is, unless the spoils of the collective good are divisible there is no incentive for the individual to participate in its provision.

Club theory overcomes this problem of non-excludability in that only members of the club use the club good. The non-excludability characteristic of a pure public good in general or a collective good in particular, may constrain the realisation of economies of scale in any interest-group provision of the collective good unless the gains are divisible. Pure public goods as originally defined by Samuelson (1954) have the unique characteristics of non-excludability and non-rivalry in consumption. A lighthouse signal is a classic example of a pure public good. Local radio or community radio, theatre performances and untelevised sports events are interesting examples of a local public good.

Table 7.1: Public goods typology

	Excludable	**Non-Excludable**
Rival	Private good	Public good
Non-Rival	Local public good	Pure public good

The public good in this typology is characterised as non-excludable and rival. In other words, rivalness in consumption is the distinguishing feature between a public good and a pure public good. The good could be described as a common good in the absence of any rival behaviour between citizens; some examples include air quality, frontier land and outer space. Rivalrous behaviour, however, converts the common good into a public good as frontier land is zoned, air quality control becomes necessary and space stations are constructed. Once property rights are established the good eventually becomes an excludable and rival private good. For example, as the uncongested bridge, a rival and non-excludable good becomes a congested bridge with Pigou-Knight tolls, the good becomes a rival and excludable private good.

There are increasingly few examples remaining of a pure public good otherwise defined as a public externality. Medical knowledge is one example but the classic examples of national defence, the environment, outer space and unpolluted air are no longer regarded as pure public goods. To what extent they represent collective goods, thus warranting a citizen tax, depends upon the benchmark of acceptability of the good by the citizenry. For example, should *peaceniks* who may regard defence as an unacceptable public good or Gaelic speakers who may regard the English-language public radio broadcasts as an unacceptable public good, be obliged to pay the requisite fee or charge to have the good supplied? While pollution represents the classic example of an externality, may we suggest pollution control as a modern example of a pure public good. This would include anti-smoking legislation, catalytic converters in car exhausts and CFC legislation. Albeit, the classic lesson from the literature is that an optimal provision of pure public goods will escape the policy maker.

Table 7.2: Collective goods typology

	Excludable	Non-Excludable
Rival	Private good	Private externality
Non-Rival	Club good	Public externality

Private goods are clearly distinguished by the characteristics of rivalrous and excludable consumption, whereas examples of a private externality range from a public good such as optional second-level education, third-level education or a congested bridge to a book in the library. But of direct interest to us is the characterisation of the good defined as non-rival and excludable as both a local public good in the public finance literature and as a club good as suggested by Buchanan (1965). A characterisation of the public good, education, as a private externality is in sharp contrast to the characterisation of the club good in Table 7.1. The optimal provision of the club good will be analysed in detail later but let us turn our attention to the economics underlying a private externality.

Private Externality

In the provision of collective goods there may be non-economic factors at play which undermine the optimal provision of the good. One is reminded of free riders and tax evaders. We suggest that in the provision of some collective goods, particularly education or local authority housing, that family size and low family income may have an important part to play in determining the behaviour of the citizen. The economic behaviour of the citizen may be linked to government efforts to abate the excludability factor. In other words, economic policies which alter the family income constraint, such as food stamps and education vouchers, open a Pandora's box of counter-intuitive behaviour that may be impossible to explain. One possible explanation addressed in this section is a variant of Moffitt's (1990) kinked-budget constraint approach which is 'closely related to economic theory and *to the nature of economic behaviour* of individuals' (our italics) (p. 120).

This section examines the economic reaction of individuals in socio-economic groups to the supply of a private externality. In particular we examine the behaviour of the group when the government provides an income support to help overcome the excludability factor. The private externality in question is the public good, optional second-level education; optional second-level education occurs after a mandatory number of years is attained in school. In our discussion education vouchers represent the income support. Advocates of voucher financing (Seldon 1986), argue that vouchers extend choice to parent-consumers. The San Jose experiments carried out in the US in the 1970s indicated that parents select government programmes which reinforce their class-related social values. Vouchers may enhance parental choice but they may also dissuade some parents from continuing with the education of their siblings. It is not our intention to rehearse the arguments for and against the voucher, but rather to examine this counter-intuitive result within the context of a kinked budget constraint. The policy question that must be addressed is as follows: is it conceivable that voucher financing of optional second-level education would dissuade parents from continuing with their children's education? If so under what circumstance would this occur?

In order to develop an intuitive explanation we extend Moffitt's kinked-budget constraint to a voucher scheme as illustrated in Figure 7.1. Educational expenditure is represented on the y-axis and the number of schoolgoing children is represented on the x-axis. The line (AB) represents the original pre-voucher income constraint of the (smaller) representative family with N_c schoolgoing children. The line (ACD) represents the voucher income constraint. If the representative (smaller) family of size N_c is to be just as well off with or without the voucher the same indifference curve (assuming that indifference curves are applicable here given that the number of children is a discrete variable!) should be tangent to both the (AB) and the (ADC) constraints.

The kink can be explained by the additional costs of a voucher education scheme arising from (say) travelling costs to the preferred school, distance costs imposed by urban and rural geography, and incidental costs like school uniforms and books. It is only possible for the representative family to be no worse off, if the number of schoolgoing children fall from N_F to N_E. Textbook economics would concur with this point. Since vouchers increase the cost of education, that is $(E_4 > E_3)$, for a family size that is larger than K in Figure 7.1, the utility maximising representative family will always reduce the number of schoolgoing children because of the substitution effect. But is there an alternative explanation to the calculated result of the textbook? Is family size an important variable in this story? In other words, is the optimal supply of a collective good constrained by socio-economic conditions which do not factor into the policy maker's equations? We suggest that it is.

Different family sizes give rise to different locations on the voucher constraint (ACD). Moffitt (1990) alluded to precisely this point when he comments: 'different persons in different initial locations (on the constraint) react to changes in parts of the constraint in very different ways' (p. 124). Family size becomes a significant variable in explaining economic behaviour once income compensation is offered to the larger family; and compensation will be necessary in order to buffer the larger family N_F from the increased costs of education. Figure 7.2 illustrates the likely impact of an income supplement on voucher recipients. For example, the parallel line L which passes through the point F represents an income supplement to the N_F family. But the offer of this supplement may be counter-productive in that it may induce the representative (larger) family N_F to decrease the number of schoolgoing children. This captures Samuelson's quasi-substitution effect addressed by Green (1976), 'if price had risen the quasi-substitution effect would require an increase in the budget which would put the consumer on a higher indifference curve than before and the term over-compensation would be appropriate' (p. 123). The higher indifference curve is I_1 in Figure 7.2; the parent-consumer will either remain with N_F schoolgoing children or reduce the number to N_G. If the parent-consumer decides to remain at N_F the quasi-substitution effect is zero, otherwise it is non-zero.

The larger family simply regards the supplement as income *per se* not as a supplement to finance education. By associating large families like N_F with low income groups we may find in Becker and Tomes (1976) a supporting explanation for the possible reduction in the number of schoolgoing children: 'public compensatory education programs essentially increase the endowment of some children in poorer families, (the) increase in the wealth of these families produced by the increase in endowment would induce a redistribution of parental time and expenditures away from the children being compensated and towards the other children and themselves'. The introduction of vouchers may arguably enhance parental choice in the selection of schools but it may hamper the attainment of equal access to education, both inter-family and intra-family access.

In other words, the excludability factor is intensified. The extra cost accruing to larger families will necessitate an income supplement; the supplement dissuades the family from continuing with education. Policy makers intent on avoiding this possible reduction may have to change the relative price of education at the voucher school nearest the (larger) representative N_F family. This could lead to the unacceptable situation of a geographic concentration of low-income families with large numbers of schoolgoing children. Paradoxically the negative externality of geographic concentration, otherwise known as ghettos, may evolve from a failed attempt by government to abate the excludability factor in the supply of a public good. Evidently there is something embedded in 'the nature of economic behaviour' which generates this result; we refer to it as *an endowment effect*, cocooned within an economic analysis with kinked-budget constraints, which is not adequately captured by the traditional Slutsky theorem. Moffitt may find it necessary to estimate this effect in addition to his 'marginal price and income elasticities' (p. 124), while policy makers should take cognisance of this effect in the optimal provision of private externalities.

Free Rider Problem

The provision of collective goods in general and of public goods in particular is constrained by a free rider problem. Individuals are inclined to misrepresent their preferences for the collective good and the consequence is under-provision. Consider the funding of a local swimming pool. The local authority could survey all the potential users, asking them what price (P_i) they would be prepared to pay for a pool. Then the marginal cost (MC) of providing the pool could be determined by the efficiency criterion which equates $MC = \Sigma P_i$. We may regard ΣP_i as a proxy for the marginal social valuation (MSV) of the good, such that if MSV > MC the public good should be provided. However the price (P_i) that each individual reports will have to be paid in order to cover the costs of providing the pool. If this is the case there is an incentive for the jth individual not to reveal the true price. This phenomenon of the free rider implies that a perfectly competitive outcome is not attainable as the price does not reflect the value put on the pool nor the marginal cost of providing it. In other words if equation 7.1 holds:

$$\Sigma Pi \leq MC = (\Sigma Pi - Pj) \qquad\qquad 7.1$$

the resulting divergence between marginal cost and price creates an under-supply equilibrium in the provision of the collective good. It is interesting to note the paradoxical result that although every potential user of the pool will benefit equally not every user will pay equally to have the pool provided. This addresses an important issue in club theory. If exclusion is feasible then the economic analysis is equivalent to a private goods analysis. However, if exclusion is not feasible the public good could be analysed as a common property resource, rival and non-excludable in supply. An interesting example emerges at the theatre, concerts or football matches where the free rider is replaced by his private good equivalent, the ubiquitous ticket tout.

Externalities

Within the public finance literature, public goods are closely related to externalities since the work of both Mishan (1971) and Evans (1970) established that consumption externalities can be analysed as a public good.

Hence equation 7.2 derived below may be applied generally in the treatment of consumption externalities. An interesting example is a public inoculation programme against a common virus; those who did not manage to get inoculated, derive some measure of benefit from those who did. The marginal rate of substitution (MRS) schedule refers to the marginal benefits derived from the ith consumers consumption of the public good (inoculation) which translates into a welfare condition which states that the collective benefits should equate with the marginal rate of transformation (MRT) of providing the inoculation, that:

$$\Sigma MRS = MRT. \tag{7.2}$$

The role of externalities in the provision of public goods cannot be overlooked. The treatment of externalities whether within the consumption-consumption, production-production or the more familiar production-consumption dichotomy is of direct importance to achieving a supply of collective goods. For example, how best to abate the externality of the Pigovian smokey chimney, whether by standards or Pigovian taxes, remains an important area within public finance. If the costs and benefits of externalities are unrecognised when allocative decisions are made a suboptimal provision of the public good is more than likely to occur. For example, a production externality such as pollution, causes a divergence between the private cost of production and the social cost of production. It is only when the costs are computed to include all relevant social costs that an efficient allocation will occur. The economic approach to the pollution problem interprets pollution as an external cost.

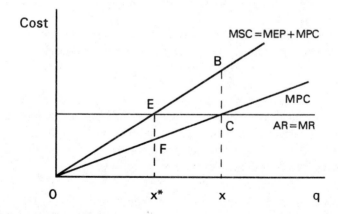

Figure 7.3: External costs of pollution

Figure 7.3 illustrates the costs where (MPC) is the firm's marginal private costs which differ from the marginal social costs (MSC), by an amount equal to the external cost of pollution (MEP). The firm optimum output is X; however external costs of an amount (OBC) are imposed. The social optimum is X* where the product price equates with the marginal social costs. This is reminiscent of equation 1 which was not obtained due to the presence of a free rider. A movement from the firm optimum to the social optimum reduces external costs by an amount (BCEF) but leaves external costs of an amount (OEF). Hence (OEF) is the optimal amount of externality. But how is the firm encouraged to move? If a Pigovian tax T, such that T = (MEP) were imposed, the firm will bear or internalise the external costs in the form of a tax. Of direct interest to public choice scholars is how the internalising of this externality evolves through a number of mechanisms. Apart from Pigovian taxes and subsidies there are bargaining possibilities and legal sanctions.

The Excludability Factor

At this juncture we return to the property of excludability which is the essence of a club theory approach to the provision of public goods. Our earlier definition of non-rivalry as mutually exclusive consumption across citizens indicates the pre-eminence of an excludability factor in club theory. With respect to the property of non-excludability, let us first demonstrate how this property may contribute to market failure and the possible breakdown of the Paretian results. If consumption of the public good is not contingent on payment, individuals have no incentive to reveal their true preferences. The individual becomes a free rider as announced earlier, and if all individuals behave likewise the net result is an absence of effective demand for the good. Where consumption is non-rival exclusion could be easily applied. However, because the marginal cost to previous consumers of adding one extra consumer is zero, the price should be zero. In this case there is no need to exclude. However the administrative costs of the public good provision must be covered somehow and with non-rival consumption in the absence of exclusion, the usual market method cannot determine price.

Musgrave and Musgrave (1980) have argued in favour of the non-excludability characteristic in arguing that with excludability, non-rivalrous goods can be effectively provided by private production. In a different context Ng (1979, p. 190) emphasised the non-rivalrous characteristic, particularly if we do not regard public production as a necessary and sufficient condition for a public good. Since free riders impact on these conditions it is rather difficult to compute exactly the individual's valuation of a public good. And this is particularly difficult if payment is not contingent to a particular preference revelation. The revelation mechanisms introduced independently by Grooves

(1973) and Clarke (1971) and others are attempts to minimise the problem. Another alternative to the market failure result in the provision of public goods is to be found in the general theory of clubs. Tanzi (1972) had shown that welfare costs may be involved in providing public goods which differ with respect to how individuals may be excluded from consuming them. In standard public goods analysis it is assumed that consumption of the public good can be extended to all consumers at a zero marginal cost. It is also assumed that a free rider problem exists or that individuals can only be excluded at some positive cost. Loehr and Sandler (1978) consider the issue of a 'forced rider' in which people 'are forced to consume, whether they like them or not' a range of public goods, for example defence. They further comment that: 'it is entirely possible that the welfare of some individuals might fall when a marginal unit of the public good is provided' (p. 27). The Pareto optimality conditions would have to allow for subsidies for these individuals to ensure that the marginal utility to tax price ratios for all individuals are equal. The forced rider may influence the provision of the public good. This could be extended to local goods and services where forced riders may be involved in decision making.

The costs of providing the public good must include the bargaining costs attributable to the resolution of the ensuing debate on the amount of public good supplied if at all. The treatment of these bargaining costs are a central feature in Buchanan and Tullock (1962) whose framework was used by Loehr and Sandler in considering the impact of bargaining costs in the provision of public goods. We recreate the latter's treatment and allude to *the internal group*, introduced in a later section (see p.199), as a factor in the analysis as applied to local public goods.

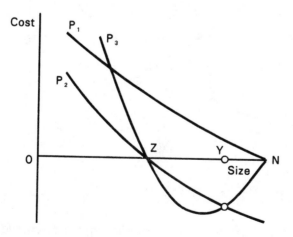

Figure 7.4: Optimal provision of a public good

Figure 7.4 illustrates the net indirect costs imposed on forced riders and the number of individuals required to reach agreement on public provision. The curve P_1 'represents costs imposed upon a person who bears some burden under all decision rules with the exception of unanimity'. In this case if the individual was a forced rider he would agree to the decision only when adequately compensated, that is when net costs are zero at N, where the entire population is in agreement. The cost function is: 'downward sloping since the greater the proportion of the population needed for agreement, the more likely persons similar to himself (but not identical to him) will be wooed by the early proponents of the public action'.

There will be many cost curves; cost curve P_2 for example may become a free rider if greater than OZ/ON individuals are in the decision. A point may be reached where the need to form larger and larger coalitions would force bargains between free riders and forced riders As illustrated P_3 would begin to turn upward after a proportion OY/ON was passed. A particularly interesting point in Loehr and Sandler (1988) in their comment: 'in the case of P_2, the cost curve need not end at zero when unanimity is reached. Some free riders may still exist, even where everyone is in agreement on the policy' (p. 31). Summation of all individual cost curves creates the community cost curve C in Figure 7.5.

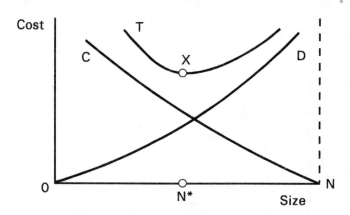

Figure 7.5: Community costs and provision

The curve D indicates that more and more decisive groups would imply a higher cost in terms of effort and bargaining. Both curves are summed into T which has a minimum point X which occurs when a coalition of ON*/ON is reached. Each policy will have different cost curves and the T minimum point will differ. If the decisions have to be made at the point where community costs are at a minimum as indicated in the construction then we are abandoning Pareto optimality. The solution presented represents a second best solution.

The Coase Theorem

Pigou (1920) had suggested that government intervention was necessary in order to abate the externality problem. The transactions costs of grouping concerned citizens together in order to resolve the externality problem was prohibitive. Coase (1960) argued that in the absence of transaction costs, concerned citizens could resolve the problem, independent of government. Theorem 7.1, the Coase theorem, amends the public choice analysis of the externality problem.

   Theorem 7.1: In the absence of transactions costs and bargaining costs, concerned citizens will agree to resolve an externality problem and arrive at a Pareto optimal allocation of resources, independent of government.

   The apportionment of blame and the allocation of property rights, that is, the right to clean air, the right to pollute, proffer an alternative, indeed a complement, to the introduction of Pigovian taxes. The idea behind liability rules was to apportion blame; an alternative to this procedure in tort law is to establish optimal conditions which may prevent the accident or property rights dispute occurring. In Chapter 6 we addressed the issue of property rights and noted that a compromise outcome was attainable if each citizen recognises the interdependence of rights. The traditional response in public finance was either to compensate the offended party or tax the offending party. This required an apportionment of blame which may have induced unnecessary government expenditure and rent-seeking activity. The costs incurred must be weighted against an inter-citizen or club resolution of the initial dispute.

   Let us consider an inter-citizen resolution by adapting an earlier argument in Turvey (1971) who argued that the traditional interpretation of an externality is rather restrictive. How much group B suffers from A's externality depends not only on 'the scale of A's diseconomy but also on the precise nature of A's activity and B's reaction to it' (p. 310). For example, the victim in Pigou's chimney example could reduce the disutility by installing an indoor clothes-line. The Pigovian solution of reducing the amount of smoke contrasts with the alternative solution of either building a higher chimney or using different smokeless fuel. In what follows we show that an inter-citizen solution, if feasible, is a more socially efficient outcome than a government solution. The externality in the local neighbourhood is the number of empty bottles (QB) which are supposed to be deposited by the citizens in government supplied bottle-banks. The government imposes a household tax, TJ, on each Jth household in the community in order to cover the cost of collecting and recycling the bottles. As an alternative the government considers an inter-citizen solution; it offers a price, PJ, for each bottle collected by the citizens. A community net revenue constraint could be expressed as equation 3 as follows:

$$\Sigma PJ - \Sigma TJ = 0 \qquad\qquad 7.3$$

The cost to the community, CJ, of the externality is composed of the government lump sum tax and a transactions cost $P^\wedge$ of co-ordinating all the concerned citizens. The cost equation is:

$$CJ = TJ + P^\wedge \qquad\qquad 7.4$$

As long as $P^\wedge.QB = CJ$ the citizens will continue with the inter-citizen collection scheme. We translate this equation into an inter-citizen constraint which may be expanded as follows:

$$P^\wedge.QB - CJ = 0 \qquad\qquad 7.5$$

$$\Rightarrow \qquad P^\wedge.QB - TJ - P^\wedge = 0 \qquad\qquad 7.6$$

$$\Rightarrow \qquad P^\wedge.(QB - 1) = TJ, \text{ and since } PJ = TJ \text{ by definition} \qquad 7.7$$

$$\Rightarrow \qquad P^\wedge = PJ/(QB - 1) \qquad\qquad 7.8$$

Equation 7.8 shows that with an inter-citizen resolution the cost $P^\wedge$ is less than the government cost of PJ. If citizens can agree on the resolution of an externality problem, the cost to the government of financing the inter-citizen solution may be less than a central government solution. The inter-citizen resolution like the Coase theorem offers an alternative to government action in the resolution of an externality problem. One policy implication of this result applies to traffic congestion in large cities. Rather than impose a tax of (say) TJ on car owners who persist in driving to the city at rush hour, car-users should be encouraged to resolve the externalities of long tailbacks, car emissions and queues by acting collectively. Car pools with special motorway lane access, such as the HOV lanes in the US, would be socially more efficient than allowing as many TJ paying cars to enter the city limits; citizens would prefer to incur a garage parking fee if lower than PJ.

PARETO OPTIMALITY

Within an analysis of Paretian welfare economics three conditions arise which must be met for Pareto optimality to exist. The graphical derivation of the result is illustrated in Figure 7.6.

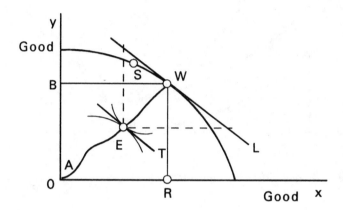

Figure 7.6: Pareto optimality

This diagram contains the production box (BWRA) which is determined by the production technology. The two individuals reach an optimal distribution point at E. For a Pareto optimum to exist the marginal rates of substitution (MRS) across individuals must be equal to each other as at point E and equal to marginal rate of transformation (MRT). The slope of the transformation curve at point W is equal to the slope of the line $L = \Delta Y/\Delta X$; this line is parallel to the line T whose slope is the MRS. In short an economy will not reach a Pareto optimum in the consumption across individuals A and B in the production of goods X and Y unless the following equation holds:

$$MRS^A_{xy} = MRS^B_{xy} = MRT_{xy} \qquad\qquad 7.9$$

Equation 8.9 suggests that each individual's MRS should also equal the MRT. This translates into the graphical requirement that lines L and T run parallel. Consider the point W which corresponds to a point on individual A's indifference curve which is tangent to the transformation curve. If we interpret the transformation curve as individual B's indifference curve we are able to generate the consumption box contained within the L-shaped shaded region. If individual A was at point S, for example, a move to W would not affect the utility of consumer B. Hence the move represents a Pareto improvement and point S is not a Pareo optimum. At point W however, both indifference curves are tangent with a slope equal to the MRT as defined by line L. At point W therefore the optimality condition MRS = MRT obtains.

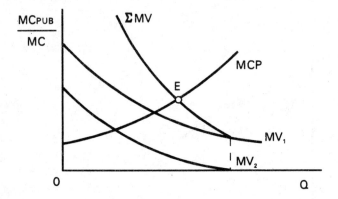

Figure 7.7: Pareto optimality and public goods

One can further establish that a Pareto optimum will exist if prices everywhere are set equal to marginal cost. Hence perfect competition maximises welfare in the sense that it secures a Pareto optimum. This result is more popularly known as the fundamental theorem of welfare economics. However there are some modifications required; product and factor markets are imperfect, economies of scale exist, marginal private cost does not reflect the true cost of production, there are consumption interdependencies, externalities and public goods. The Lipsey and Lancaster (1956) theorem of the second best, in attempting to set as many prices as possible equal to marginal cost, proceeds to develop a rule that set price equal to marginal cost plus marginal external cost. If prices do not diverge from this rule, the second best theorem suggests that price adjustments will be Pareto improving.

The existence of public goods however affect these marginal equivalencies. The condition for Pareto optimality now differs and Samuelson (1954) had shown that it requires the sum of the marginal rates of substitution (MRS) to equal the marginal rate of transformation (MRT), that is, equation 7.2 earlier, which differs from the private goods case in equation 7.9 which required the MRSs to be equal to each other and also equal to MRT. A different construction is required in order to highlight the public goods case. Figure 7.7 illustrates the implication of public goods on the Pareto conditions. The schedule (MC) represents the marginal cost of providing the public good and (MV) represents the individual marginal valuation curves. The MRT is expressed as the ratio of the respective marginal costs of the public goods, denoted by MC_{PUB} and of the private goods, denoted by MC. As each unit of the public good is consumed by each individual we vertically add the MV to acquire ΣMV and equation 7.10,

$$\Sigma MV = MC. \hspace{4cm} 7.10$$

yields the optimal amount of the good, which is illustrated in Figure 7.7 by the point E where ΣMV = MC. An additional concern expressed earlier is the different marginal valuations by each consumer on the same amount of the public good. Imagine two MV curves lying below those illustrated in Figure 7.7 and proceed to sum vertically to get the new ΣMV curve. The new point of intersection with the marginal cost curve will be to the left of E in Figure 7.7. Hence the general conclusion is a market failure result, in that the public good will be undersupplied in an economy which relies on the price allocation mechanism.

Loehr and Sandler (1978) develop the idea of joint products in the provision of public goods. Defence expenditure they suggest produce deterrence which is a pure public good and protection against attack which is an impure public good. The optimal provision of public goods with joint products is a generalisation of the Pareto equation introduced earlier. Since, by definition, joint production requires that the same intermediate input produces one or more public goods and private or impure public goods as outputs, the application of this approach may be important in the provision of local club goods.

CLUB GOODS: TIEBOUT-OATES WORLD

In this section we re-examine the conditions which independently underpin the Tiebout (1956) and Oates (1972) models of local public goods and adapt the Loehr-Sandler model in our search for some common ground in a Tiebout-Oates type world. Refer to Figure 7.8, where the N-axis represents a community where the origin (0,0) represents the individual, hence each point between 0 and N represents different sized groups. For example ON* might represent a county or shire while ON*/2 might be a local community. In considering the provision of a public good and of a local public good in particular, we would like to be able to identify the decisive group, if one exists. In the Loehr-Sander model a decision rule for the optimality provision of the local good is provided. If the outcome of a decision rule reflects the decisive power of an internal group alluded to earlier, who regard a public good as a positive externality, a parallel treatment to the economic theory of clubs in deciding on an optimal provision of a local public good, may emerge.

An additional factor to be considered is who exactly decides on how much of the public good is provided. The decision could be left to majority rule which as a voting mechanism does not remain immune from lobbying and vote-trading. The presence of an internal group may require a selective use of decision rules in order to minimise their power; otherwise the outcome is dictatorial. Aronson (1978) echoes our concern on internal groups when he comments 'that although the pure public good is consumed by all in equal amounts it is not preferred by all in equal amounts' (p. 150). The local public good is still pure in as much as those who consume it consume the same amount. The difference is that the benefits are limited to a geographic area and the forced riders can easily leave the area. Aronson explores the conditions under which there may be an advantage to having local public goods supplied by central government. In developing the argument he comments 'local choice offers the advantage of allowing us to match supply with our preferences. On the other hand, local choice may prevent us from taking advantage of economies of scale' (p. 151). We reproduce his diagram in a later discussion in this chapter as Figure 7.12 which illustrates the welfare gains and costs of joint consumption on the vertical axis and the size of the sharing group on the horizontal axis.

In the interim, the line (OA) in Figure 7.8 shows the potential gain from joint consumption. As Oates (1972) argued the (OA) line reaches a maximum as diseconomies of scale set in with too large a group. The line (OL) indicates the aggregate potential welfare loss of consuming an amount of the good different from the personal choice. (OL) rises steeply at the large group size as a uniform amount is supplied to all including those with extreme preferences. The difference between (OA) and (OL) is captured in the line (OW) which reaches a maximum point at N* which is the optimal group size. Hence central provision of a public good should occur when the potential welfare gains from joint consumption 'are so great that N* is equal to the entire population'

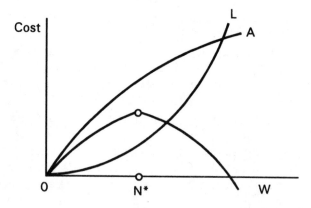

Figure 7.8: Gain from joint consumption

(p. 152). A value less than N* implies the desirability of decentralisation as formalised by Oates (1972) in his decentralisation theorem. Oates theorem supports a system of local choice. The issue still remains whether or not the local authority supplies the local citizens with the local public goods they require.

As alluded to in an earlier discussions individuals, particularly forced riders, can leave the local neighbourhood. This assumes no relocation constraints; crucial to the question posed here is the failure of individuals to reveal their true preference for local public goods. Tiebout (1956) in analysing the efficiency in the supply of public goods acknowledged that voting process was the only recourse to reveal the preferences of the sharing group. The optimal allocation is determined by a voting-with-the-feet exercise. Tiebout presented an earlier framework for the theory of clubs in assuming an infinite number of individuals who form themselves into many clubs of different sizes. Under certain conditions the infinity assumption allows each club to maximise its own benefit without violating Pareto optimality. The Buchanan-Ng framework, outlined in the next section, may be preferable to the Tiebout framework in the case where location of consumers is exogenous, transport is costly and where there are few clubs. In the Tiebout model individuals can vote with their feet, moving to regions according to their preferences for public goods.

Nevertheless, in order to examine this model we note two assumptions of the Tiebout model, *vis-a-vis:* (i) consumer-voters are fully mobile: and (ii) they have full information on the differences on revenue and expenditure in the local areas. These two assumptions depend on the absence of relocation constraints such as employment, house purchase and school availability. It also presupposes a large number of alternative communities with which the consumer can effectively rank order each community. The remaining assumptions include: (iii) there are no external economies or diseconomies of scale in the supply of the public services; (iv) there is an optimal community size for every community service; and finally (v) communities below the optimal attract the new residents. This set of assumptions establish the classic Tiebout model and ensure the global optimality of excludable public goods provision. Mueller (1989, p. 157) outlines an illustrative proof of this global property.

However the new residents can produce congestion in the new area and the resulting congestion costs and possible negative externalities if the community has grown beyond the optimal size, forces Mueller to conclude that in general the Tiebout model will not produce a Pareto optimal outcome. In his illustration he shows quite clearly how a non-Pareto though stable equilibrium can emerge. Empirical evidence to support the hypothesis has been forthcoming. Cebula (1979) showed that inter area differences in welfare benefits influenced migration decisions while Aronson and Schwartz (1973) in their analysis showed that those towns likely to gain in relative population are those that offer residents equal or better services at an equal or lower tax rate.

We offer an alternative interpretation to the global condition in a Tiebout-Oates world by considering the idea of a marginal decision (MD) curve. This differs from the average benefit curve employed by Mueller (1989); while both curves represent benefit, Mueller's curve assumed that benefit was a function of community size. In our alternative presentation illustrated in Figure 7.9 the marginal decision curve is a function of the number of internal members in the sharing group. As illustrated, the MD schedules are mirror images of each other; this reinforces the point that utility in the club is maximised by dividing the club good equally between each group. We extend this concept of an internal group into the formation of alliances in the provision of public goods. In many instances the alliance may form to prohibit the supply of public goods as with defence or environmental quality.

Let us take the example of tulips in a public square. In this characterisation tulips represent a public good, planted in the public square by the local authority. Assume that the tulips offend a sub-group of individuals who spend the day in the square. To this sub-group the tulips represent an externality. The square itself is a public good, but the presence of tulips reduces the utility of this sub-group. Next we introduce the concept of internal member; define the sub-group S of citizens, C, such that there is an issue i which at least one member j of the group regards as an externality, then $j \in S$ is defined as an internal member of the set S. The set S is a proper subset of the set C. If the committee responsible for planting tulips decides against tulips in the square, the internal group is defined as decisive. The significance of an *internal group* is in its ability to rank local public goods in descending order of preference.

The important characteristic of an alliance supplied public good is jointness in supply, that is, the supply includes private benefits as well as public goods. The private good may include cultural or educational benefits but may also include private externalities as with the tulips example. Club theory has to a limited extent overlooked how the members of a sharing group became associated. Apart from similar tastes may we suggest an association by alliance of internal citizens. How this manifests itself is as follows: the sharing group is subdivided into group A which derives exactly half as much utility as group B, the internal group, in any provision of a local public good. Group B as an internal group has a negative impact on the remaining members, $(MD_A) = 1/2$ (MD_B). If the rule is to maximise the utility of the sharing group then emphasis will be in the direction of group B.

Corollary 7.1: The presence of an internal group may reduce the amount of a local public good in order to maximise the utility of the sharing group.

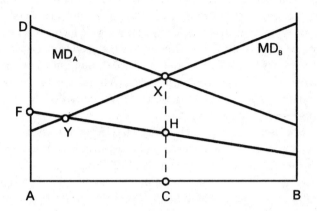

Figure 7.9: Optimal provision of club goods

Figure 7.9 illustrates the respective MD-schedules. Before the internal sub-group formed the optimal provision of the good was X. The new equilibrium provision with the internal group is less than X at Y. Ironically the utility of the A group has decreased from (ADXC) to (AFHC). The dominance of the internal group secures a reduction in the amount of local public good in order to maximise the utility of the sharing group, B. This we identify as the *tulips paradox*, that is, in the local provision of a public good the presence of a decisive internal homogeneous group with identical tastes may reduce the supply of the public good in order to maximise the utility of the sharing group.

Buchanan's Model

There are two basic models across the literature on club theory, the Buchanan (1965) within-club model and the more general Oakland (1972) total economy model which will be developed in a later section. Buchanan's model is the classic treatment of clubs while the Oakland model is more general in extending club theory to include heterogeneous members, discrimination, variations in the utilisation of the public good and exclusion costs. Neither model, however, guarantees Pareto optimality in the provision of local goods, which ironically is the *raison d'etre* of club theory as a methodological study of the allocative efficiency of (impure) public goods. The assumptions underpinning the Buchanan model include the following: (i) individuals have identical tastes for both private and public goods; (ii) the size of the club good (a swimming pool), hence its total cost, is fixed; and (iii) equal sharing of costs. Mueller (1989) has argued that (iii) follows as an assumption from (i). In a simple model Buchanan determines the optimal size of the club membership. Mueller shows that with some algebraic manipulation, by deducting each individual's share (equal shares) of the cost of providing the good from private income to obtain 'net of public good income', and substituting this into an objective function with the amount of public good and club size as explanatory variables, the Buchanan model obtains the Samuelson condition for the efficient consumption of a public good.

The crucial assumption in the Buchanan model and in club theory generally, is the assumption of identical tastes and incomes. The Tiebout model shows that it is inefficient to have individuals of differing tastes in the same club. Intuitively, think of ten left-handed golfers in a golf club of 25 right-handed players. The result here is akin to Pauly's (1967) early result that no stable equilibrium will exist if the left-handed golfers form a winning majority. If the number of left-handed golfers increased, the threat of exit by the right-handed golfers is strong since they could leave and form an alternative club. The dynamics of the situation suggest a small optimal membership, hence there is a limited degree of publicness or alternatively there is an excludability factor. What this implies is that beyond a certain membership size additional members impose a cost on existing members. There is congestion and negative externalities which reduce the utility of existing members. In Buchanan's economic theory of clubs, the variable to be optimised is the number of members or consumers.

According to Ng (1979) the relevant Pareto optimality condition requires 'that any individual in the club must derive a 'total benefit in excess of the aggregate marginal cost imposed on all other consumers in the club' (p. 211). So the Buchanan-Ng theory is to optimise the membership; alternatively Oakland considers the degree of congestion to be important. We did allude to crowding earlier as an important characteristic of club good provision. Club theory has many interesting applications in the analysis of congestion and in establishing the optimal group size for (say) a local golf club or a local community. Buchanan's economic theory of clubs builds on three rather important assumptions: (i) that the benefits and costs are divisible amongst the club members. As more members join, average costs for the provision of the club declines, but marginal benefits begin to fall as more members contribute to congested levels of membership; (ii) it is costless to the club to exclude members. This conveniently removes any distortion should exclusion be deemed necessary in order to attain an optimal (MC = MB) membership. Finally it is assumed that (iii) there is no discrimination across members. This is a rather difficult assumption to defend in practice, as in the case of golf

An analysis introduced by Brown and Jackson (1990), which uses a four-quadrant diagram, is rather helpful for illustrative purposes. The fourth quadrant in their construction (in the SE corner) identifies an intersection point which represents optimal size and optimal quantity. We illustrate a similar point in Figure 7.10. Essentially the function of a club is to provide a public good. The optimal size of the club maximises the net benefits accruing to each member. While average benefits remain intact, average costs decline as membership increases. This classic interpretation would suggest that the bigger the club the better. The assumption which underpins the classic theory is that of perfect jointness, in other words the local public goods are pure public goods. In the real world additional members create congestion and members experience a declining net benefit after a certain size has been achieved.

Figure 7.10 illustrates the costs and benefits for each club member. Note the particular shape of the cost curve C. It is defined as a rectangular hyperbola since the total cost, the area underneath the curve, is exactly the same at different levels. The benefit curve declines in the case of less than perfect jointness. N_1 is the group size for which net benefits are greatest; N_1 is only optimal for the club with costs C_1. A greater club size has higher costs and a different level of optimal membership N_2. The positive correlation between the size of the public facility and the optimal size of the club is illustrated by line X in Figure 7.11. It is rather important to determine the optimal size of facility for clubs of different sizes. Hence the line Z captures the positive relationship between optimal size of the facility and size of the group. The point of intersection between these two lines represents the optimal club size. The point of intersection, C^* in Figure 7.11, is the optimal club.

In Brown and Jackson (1990) this elusive point is arrived at in their figure 3.8 (p. 81) in a similar way. They consider a particular club size S_1 with a corresponding cost curve $C(S_1)$ radiating as a straight line from the origin. The corresponding optimal level of output X_1 is at the level where $MC(S_1) = MB(S_1)$. Hence for each pair a locus of points L is plotted which is equivalent to our line Z. They proceed to extract the optimal size S^*, on the assumption that S^* is given for each level of output X^*. Likewise for each pair (S^*, C^*) a locus of points L^* is plotted which is equivalent to our line X in Figure 7.11. The intersection between L1 and L^* yields the optimal club; in both sets of illustrations the move to the optimal club size is convergent. The important realisation in the provision of club goods, is that for any given amount of the good X, one consumer's utility is functionally dependent on the number of consumers actually consuming X. In the case of the swimming pool, a point is reached where the resource is congested.

The Buchanan-Ng framework on clubs regard the number of consumers as the variable to be optimised. Pareto optimality 'requires that any individual in the club must derive a total benefit in excess or at least equal to the aggregate marginal cost and imposed on all other consumers in the club'. An important assumption in the classic Buchanan theory is the assumption of homogeneity in tastes across the population. If we assume that social preferences treat all homogenous members symmetrically then the indifference curve between any two individuals will be symmetric around a 45 degree line. The policy result is that each member will have equal utility and an equal allocation. This result depends upon the convex property of the utility possibility set. The objective of a utility maximising club in deciding on a club size is to maximise the utility of an individual member. Since everyone in the club gets the same allocation the club cannot do better; however Sandler (1992) argues that 'if the total population is less than the derived efficient club size' (p. 48), the club may not even do as well.

General Models

The general model assumes the existence of a private good and an impure public good, with the private good acting as a numeraire. The members are heterogeneous, non-members are costlessly excluded, and club members determine their utilisation rate of the club good by varying the number of visits (to the public park) and time spent at the club. Optimal provision in this general model, within which both members and non-members are considered in deriving the optimal conditions for a single club, requires according to Sandler and Tschirhart (1980), 'that the marginal benefits from crowding reduction, resulting from increased provision, equal the marginal costs of provision (MRT)' (p. 1489). This is analogous to the earlier Pareto optimal condition (MRS = MRT) for public goods provision, and not unlike the conclusion extracted by Buchanan. The utilisation condition in the general Oakland model requires an equal rate of utilisation for all members, although total toll payments (for utilisation) vary between heterogeneous members.

Oakland's model is identical to the Buchanan model under the following conditions: (i) all members are homogenous and each consumes the available quantity (say) X of the public good, such that $X_i = X_j$; (ii) for the members S the crowding function must be an identity mapping, i.e. $C(S) = S$, this reduces the general Oakland utility function to the Buchanan function $U(Y_1, X_1, S)$, where S substitutes for $C(S)$. The insertion of a crowding function into the utility function is one major difference between the models in club theory. Sandler (1979) argued that by including a crowding function, crowding externalities such as poor view can be considered: in addition (a) increases in the provision of the public good reduces crowding and (b) increases in member use of the good increases crowding, that is $(dc/dx_i > 0)$. It has been argued that the general model implicitly assumes cardinality of the utility function. Sandler and Tschirhart (1980) in their review of club theory comment that since 'the general model requires an ordering of the population based upon club preferences' (p. 1490), cardinality is implicit.

Cardinality may rule out particular functional forms of the utility function, that may be otherwise appropriate for club analysis, for example the transformation W = LogU. In practice, however, populations cannot be ordered; this applied weakness in the Oakland model has been overcome by Hillman and Swan (1979) who proposed an ordinal representation that does not require an ordering of the population. Their model, which we address as a *ceteris paribus* model, maximises an arbitrary members utility subject to the constancy of other members utility levels. Recall that Buchanan maximised individual utility U(Y, X, S) subject to a production:cost constraint F(Y, X, S) = 0. The Hillman and Swan (1979) result is akin to this basic Buchanan model when (i) C(S) = S and (ii) F = U(Y, X, C(S)). The (ii) condition is the Buchanan constraint in the optimisation procedure; an analogy requires that the Hillman and Swan constraint be rewritten as F = U(Y$_1$, X, C(S)) = 0. This may be unlikely but worthy of further research.

In the case of a pure public good (national defence) both properties of non-rivalry and non-excludability are retained. In the general theory of clubs, however, we have collective consumption but with an exclusion principle, for example, the imposition of a membership fee. One can think of club goods as public goods *sans* non-excludability. There are economies of scale in that additional members reduce the average cost of the club good. But additional members also lead to crowding which in the long run could be regarded as the introduction of rivalrous consumption. Indeed the club goods have polar extremes as noted by Mueller: 'for a pure public good the addition of one more member to the club never detracts from benefits of club membership ... (for) a pure private good, say an apple, crowding begins to take place on the first unit' (p. 131). Buchanan was the first to consider the efficiency properties of voluntary clubs.

Both Tiebout (1956) and Oakland (1972) represent alternative frameworks to the approach adopted by Buchanan (1965) in accounting for the under-supply of public goods. Oakland (1972) looked at the degree of congestion while the Tiebout (1956) model is an application of club theory to community size. A Tiebout-Oakland public goods problem would manifest itself for those public goods for which congestion begins at a certain size of community. As the community gets larger, residential density increases (community congestion), reducing the utility of everyone living in the community. Two factors which are important in the context are: (i) that the total number of people may not be an integral multiple of N, the number of workers, i.e. there may be a fixed population as identified by Pauly (1967); and (ii) the number of communities may be fixed; the one exception, alluded to by Atkinson and Stiglitz (1980), is a frontier society. If the communities are fixed (say) to two, an optimal provision of the public good may involve an equal treatment, a result which in Atkinson and Stiglitz (1980) yields a local minimum (maximum) solution with population shortage (excess), hence social welfare could be increased by moving to an unequal treatment. We alluded to this point earlier in our construction of Figure 7.9 in our analysis with marginal decision curves. However, the general theory of clubs with the property of no discrimination of members assumes a group of homogenous individuals. The Tiebout world has heterogeneous individuals sorting themselves out into homogenous populations with homogenous tastes. Hence doctors and lawyers live in the same neighbourhood, and there are golfers in the golf club and swimmers in the swimming club. But is the sorting optimal? In answering this question we have to refer to the concept of homogeneity.

We have come to the conclusion that there are at least two interpretations of homogeneity in the club literature, firstly Tiebout homogeneity as captured in his work where he commented on: 'restrictions due to employment opportunities are not considered' (p. 419). In mixed communities doctors and lawyers do not have equal incomes since the respective income depends on labour supply. Consequently they are not perfect substitutes, and the community needs both; the community is better off if they have the same tastes. And secondly an Atkinson-Stiglitz type homogeneity, which is a weaker version of the Tiebout homogeneity, and argues 'that individuals are [not] always better off forming homogeneous communities with people of identical tastes' (p. 531). In their argument, they consider a third public good produced as a compromise to a merged community forming from the separate communities. In the merged case the individual can enjoy the benefits of the economies of scale associated with three public goods (equivalent to our average cost reductions in the Buchanan model), but when these benefits are weighted against diminishing returns to labour N (equivalent to the declining benefits in a Buchanan model), the individual is better off.

An interesting dimension arises in the context of a heterogeneous population which can be translated into different marginal valuations. If for example the local authority does not tax the individuals according to their respective valuations, by imposing an equal tax, there may not be an optimal provision of the local public good in the merged community. As illustrated in Figure 7.12 those who value the public good less are essentially subsidised by the high value individuals and receive a windfall $W = (0AQ)$ in the provision of the good. The movement from separate communities to a merged community is not a Pareto improvement. Atkinson and Stiglitz (1980) arrive at a similar result, assuming no diminishing returns to labour, in looking at positive benefits, that is 'everyone's taxes [are] cut'. Whether the sorting is optimal or not depends clearly on the assumptions of diminishing returns to labour, the existence of a windfall provision to individuals with lower valuations and on the assumption of homogeneity.

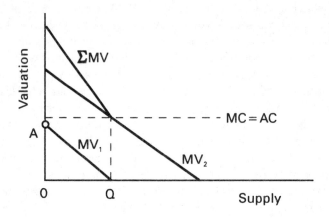

Figure 7.12: Provision with different valuations

Pauly (1970a) and McGuire (1974), in their generalisation of the earlier work of Tiebout, assume an indefinitely large number of individuals, forming clubs of different sizes. Pareto optimality is not violated with the assumption of infinity (uncountable infinity according to Ng (1979)) as each individual can join a club that suits his or her preference, thus maximising the individual (average) benefit or the benefit of the club. The applicability of this infinity framework is according to Ng (p. 212) suitable for the cases where the number of clubs for the same good is large and the population is mobile; he suggests group segregation in housing, the nomadic life and sports clubs. In our typology of public goods presented earlier, we identified the club good as a non-rival excludable public good. A different usage of rivalry has been discussed in the literature by Starrett (1988) in the context of club theory and local communities. The spatial element in local communities, with competing use for a limited (same) space, generates 'club rivalry that is independent from the rivalries we have been discussing' (p. 58). In what he refers to as a 'bare bones model', Starrett concludes with an optimality condition which suggests that efficient size will require that the average provision cost equals the sum of the various marginal rivalry costs.

In the model transport costs play the role of rivalry costs, as Starrett argues 'transportation has no value to the members *per se* but must be incurred if they want to share the collective good' (p. 59). That each individual in the club is an equal distance from the collective good, the assumption of radical symmetry, is dropped in an alternative model which allows for choice in the number of trips to the collective good (public park) and in the amount of residential land held by each individual. The first best solution is an unequal division of land as individuals closer to the public good represent an externality to these further out in the residential area. The latter residents have larger tracks of land. Starrett's unsurprising conclusion is a formulation 'that treats equals equally' (p. 60); the reason, apart from the formal rigour of his model, is that in the real world the political system will impose this constraint on society. Of the Lagrangean optimisation results presented by him the one that is of interest in this chapter is the condition for optimal club size.

Theorem 7.2: The Henry George Theorem states that if public expenditure is fixed and population varies, the population that maximises consumption per capita is such that rents equal the public good expenditure.

The Starrett (1988, p. 62) result which states that the supply of the public good should equal the pseudo land-rent in the optimal spatial club is in many respects similar to the Henry George Theorem as derived by Atkinson and Stiglitz (1980, p. 525). Optimisation on club size leads to the Starrett result. In the Henry George world each citizen had identical tastes, an assumption which is imported by Buchanan into his original club model. Since club rivalry involves spatial separation the marginal cost of rivalry is reflected in the marginal premia on limited space. Starrett concludes 'that in our bare-bones model this premia could be measured in terms of transport costs, (but) differential land rents turns out to be the right measure in broader contexts' (p. 62). The measure is right, relatively speaking, in that it secures an optimal club size. The different approaches within the general theory of clubs highlight the many different characteristics of a club and of a club good. The general theory of clubs offer a solution to the optimal provision of public goods. The public good is not a pure public good, but rather there is an element of congestion as individuals consume the good up to its capacity constraint.

What arises then is some exclusion mechanism in order to charge consumers a price for the provision and use of the good. And as Brown and Jackson (1990) comment, the purpose of a club 'is to exploit economies of scale, to share the costs of providing an indivisible commodity, to satisfy a taste for association with other individuals who have similar preference orderings' (p. 80). For Buchanan-Ng the main club characteristic is membership or numbers of consumers, and it is this variable that has to be optimised. For Tiebout an assumption of infinity of individual consumers presupposes costless exit from one region to another and the formation of many clubs. Oakland considered the degree of congestion as an important characteristic in the provision of a club good. There is room for all of the characteristics in a general theory of clubs that seeks to determine a Pareto optimal distribution of public goods. What has not been examined in this context is the interpretation of an individual's income elasticity of demand as a proxy for tastes for a public good. In the Tiebout world high income individuals may migrate to the same area which leaves relatively poorer individuals consuming only the public goods which they themselves can afford to provide.

No one really objects to club membership when the public good is tennis courts, squash courts or golf clubs. To avoid congestion in the club and to achieve economies of scale, a Pareto efficient outcome is arrived at by introducing an exclusion principle. But a Tiebout world of clubs, in which right-handed golfers exit to form an alternative club, is quite different to the world in which high income individuals migrate to one area and low income individuals to another area. As Mueller (1989) pointed out 'the voluntary association approach is likely to affect the distribution of income' (p. 144). If individuals can vote with their feet and have positive income elasticities of demand for public goods they can benefit from being in a community with incomes higher on average than their own. But for the poorer individuals transport and mobility is costly and for the higher income individuals the formation of interest groups (e.g. regional or local environmental lobby) is a concomitant to the provision of the public good. Each militate against an egalitarian distribution of the public good. Any attempt to transfer across from rich to poor 'runs directly into the issue of the proper bounds of the polity, and the rights of citizenship' according to Mueller (p. 144).

SOME CONTROVERSIES

In this final section we look at some of the more recent controversies which have arisen across the literature on club theory. Many of the issues have an important bearing on the optimal provision of local public goods and consequently on local public finance. Membership homogeneity has emerged as one of the more controversial issues within the club literature, particularly from a public policy perspective. For example, if mixed clubs with heterogeneous membership are found to be non-optimal, as outlined in our earlier discussion, serious policy implications for group housing or education schemes may arise. The literature is divided on the optimality of mixed clubs, with Ng (1973) and Oakland (1972) arguing for the optimality of clubs and Berglas and Pines (1978) Helpman (1979), McGuire (1974) and Stiglitz (1977) arguing in favour of homogenous clubs. The latter group, according to Sandler and Tschirhart (1980) 'have recognised that mixed clubs may be desirable when strong scale economies require a larger membership than possible with homogeneity' (p. 1492). Mixed clubs however are not Pareto optimal due to an important assumption, the equal cost sharing assumption which states that in a mixed club, albeit all members pay the same membership fee, those members with higher valuations of the public good have a higher total payment as they use (visit the park) the good more frequently. Conversely mixed clubs are shown to be efficient when there are no second best constraints imposed. Hence by invoking second best constraints requiring all members to share club costs equally, as alluded to in our argument on windfall gains or requiring all members to use the club equally irrespective of tastes as in McGuire (1974) and Porter (1978), mixed clubs can always be shown to be less desirable than homogenous clubs.

Neither the within-club Buchanan model nor the Oakland economy model, ensure Pareto optimality. As Sandler and Tschirhart (1980) conclude '(within-club) may fail when the membership size is large relative to the entire population, (general model) will fail when multiple clubs are desirable' (p. 1493). The multiple clubs translates into a variable number of clubs and this requires that both the optimal number and optimal size of clubs be determined simultaneously. A rather different slant on the optimality controversy is whether or not Buchanan in his original article, failed to consider Pareto optimality. Ng (1973) has argued that Buchanan did fail to give Pareto optimal conditions in maximising the 'average net benefits instead of total net benefits' (p. 294); Ng (1979) in defending his position has reiterated that his analysis aims 'at Pareto optimality or maximising total benefits of the whole population' (p. 212). Both Berglas (1976) and Helpman and Hillman (1977) criticised Ng's (1973) attack on Buchanan and questioned whether or not Ng (1973) had maximised total benefits of one club, which in general is non-Pareto optimal.

The Buchanan-Ng framework on clubs which concentrates on each particular club is preferable, according to Ng (1979), to 'the more general model [wherein] *these* conditions are not satisfied' [our italics] (p. 212). The conditions referred to are generally the infinity conditions outlined in our discussion. In contrast Berglas (1976) defended Buchanan on optimality. The debate continues and Helpman and Hillman (1977) suggest that the issue is very much dependent 'on a recognition of the different types of club problems analysed' (p. 295), and a realisation of the difference between maximising average net benefits (for the members) and maximising total net benefits for the club. Buchanan proceeded with the former, whereas Ng proceeded with the latter 'in maximising total net benefits for the entire economy' (p. 1493), according to Sandler and Tschirhart (1980). Other scholars have considered the issues arising from exclusion costs, member discrimination and the analysis of an efficient membership fee or toll for optimal club provisions. The interested reader is directed to the review by Sandler and Tschirhart (1980) and Mueller (1989) and the bibliographies contained therein.

Game theory is beginning to shed some light on the issues raised in the club literature but Pauly (1967) to whom we referred earlier, had defined the optimum club size as that size for which average net benefits were maximised. This early example of a game theoretic result remains at variance with the non-game arguments by Ng (1973), Helpman and Hillman (1977) and the

Oakland general model. A direct comparison between the game and non-game outcomes is complicated by the different assumptions used. In particular the game theoretic approach does not admit the interdependency between the membership and the provisions which characterises the classic Buchanan type model; nor does it consider a simultaneous solution to membership, provision of the good and finance. In many cases the club fee is decided ex-post. The approaches do converge on the optimum number of clubs in the homogenous case. Pauly (1970) divided a mixed population into homogenous groups, with each group divided into multiple clubs where average net benefits are maximised. He proves that the core is non-empty and exists 'if the clubs consist of identical members with equal payoffs and that clubs with higher average pay-offs have fewer members' (p. 60).

However there are two more recent controversial developments to which we would like to turn our attention. The first concerns the issue of profit maximising clubs, alluded to in the classic survey by Sandler and Tschirhart (1980). Berglas and Pines (1978) have demonstrated that a perfectly competitive industry with identical firms (each firm acts as a club) supplying the shared club good would achieve the same efficiency conditions as those of a private co-operative. Hillman (1978) found that the non-discriminating monopolist provided smaller output and charged a higher price and operated more crowded facilities than the non-profit co-operative. In contrast Hillman and Swan (1979) have shown that a discriminating monopolist will always achieve an efficient outcome. Ng (1974) argued that a government was necessary in order to achieve the efficient outcome, defined as maximising total benefits. He continued to argue, in the spirit of our earlier discussions that since members under a monopolist will maximise net benefit rather than total benefit, an efficient outcome is not attained in the absence of a centralised government. Ng apparently underestimated the impact of short-run political objectives in guiding a government-run club, as later outlined by Sandler (1979).

Scotchmer (1985) has argued that with a homogenous population profit maximising clubs will achieve an equilibrium that is 'within epsilon' of being efficient. There is entry in response to profits, and with incumbent clubs making a conjectural variation on 'the price and facility response in other clubs when it changes its strategy' (p. 39), the number of clubs will be too large. The strategy space is defined by facility X and price P, not facility X and the member N. With the strategy space (X, P) each club believes that it can get more clients at the expense of other clubs. The set of strategies is a Nash equilibrium if no club can charge (X, P) such as to make more profit, with the zero conjectural variation assumptions. The strategy space (X, N) is abandoned because the Nash equilibrium requires the assumption, deemed unlikely by Scotchmer (1985), that 'the other [clubs] will change their prices in whatever manner necessary to maintain the clientele' (p. 27). The early profit-maximising club literature explored by Berglas (1976) and Wooders (1980) had assumed that there was an efficient size sharing group, and the conclusion has been that provided entry forces profits to zero, a club equilibrium will be efficient. However these firms are competitive in the sense of being a 'utility-taker', whereas Scotchmer (1985) departs from this in arguing that firms take as fixed the strategies of other firms. It is essentially a non co-operative game and the equilibrium is cast as a Nash equilibrium. For members the utility available in other clubs will change as membership changes.

The second development is the idea of a multi-product club, footnoted by Sandler and Tschirhart (1980, p. 1513) in the wake of new material on contestability theory. In particular they suggest a role for the concept of economies of scope defined simply as complementarity in production. Within the literature, however, some scholars have considered this issue, although the joint products include a private good and an impure (or indeed pure) public good. Our discussion of the Samuelson constraint and the Henry George Theorem is testament to that. However in the area of local government, where communities and cities share multiple club goods, this application may prove to be useful. Berglas and Pines (1978) did however present a multi-product club model, but did not consider the concept of economies of scope. The essence of this assumption in the industry analysis is that the two products cannot independently be provided at a cheaper cost than joint production.

It is important to recall that the relationship in the club literature between the average cost curve and the number of clubs is related to the definition of a single product monopoly. The condition of sub-additivity in the cost function had already been used in the club literature by Pauly (1970a) in his argument that 'club characteristic functions may be sub-additive' (p. 55). The many variants to the economic analysis implicit in Buchanan's original model have advanced our understanding of club theory and have helped to incorporate club theory into the economic analysis of local public finance. The economic theory of clubs represents an attempt to explain the under-supply equilibrium of a public goods provision. It raises many different and controversial issues which impinge on government policy in the public sector. In many respects, a club provision proffers an alternative to a central government provision of local public goods. The salient characteristic of a club, the excludability factor, may militate against an equal and democratic distribution of the club good. At the level of voluntary clubs, with which Buchanan was originally concerned, club theory can appraise the efforts at achieving optimal membership of the club and the maximum utility of club members. A proper typology for public goods has to be established before all the remaining issues in club theory are adequately dealt with by public choice scholars. A decision on the relative

8. Democracy and Voting

The initial problem about voters which political economists must inevitably face, and one of the most frequently studied behavioural questions, is the question of why people vote. This behaviour is difficult to understand because the expected gains of voting are very small, whereas the act of voting has clear personal costs. This argument assumes that people's behaviour is motivated by personal self-interest. While the assumption may hold in the choice of what house to buy, it should be noted that the assumption that self-interest governs behaviour has been questioned in recent research (Kahneman, Knetsch and Thaler 1986). That people vote, for example, is less difficult to explain if people are viewed as motivated by altruistic gain, as long as non-voting does not appear to have immediate costs for specific groups in society. Therefore all citizens will try to vote. 'The democratic method is the process of participation, specifically through voting, in the management of society, where voting is understood to include all the ancillary institutions (like parties and pressure groups) and social principles (like freedom and equality) that are necessary to render it significant' (Downs 1957, p. 8).

In the public choice tradition attempts are made to answer the question, 'why bother to vote?'; the emphasis in this chapter on who precisely governs in a democracy, is borrowed from the title of Dahl's (1961) classic study, 'who governs?'. It captures the essence of voting in a modern democracy. Scholars admit that voters are influenced by different motives such as party loyalty, apathy, habit, sense of duty or public spiritedness. The problem for the voter introduced earlier in Chapters 2 and 3, is how to use her very limited power effectively. The situation is different in a marginal constituency, in by-elections or in single issue referenda. And the crucial issue is whether or not voting in democratic societies best delivers the outcomes for which you as a selfish rational voter-citizen wish or vote. Citizens have the right to vote in a legitimate political order, one that is 'sanctioned by its population' (Held 1987, p. 238) and as voters we are expected to 'act rationally in politics ... each citizen casts his vote for the party he believes will provide him with more benefits than any other' (Downs 1957, p. 36).

However, increasingly more citizens in democracies across the world are opting not to vote. We contend that both actions, voting and what we shall call *voluntary non-voting* are rational 'for people who prefer better choice alternatives in the future to present participation in the selection of a government' (Downs, p. 49).

In particular, non-voting is rational for those who feel acutely unrepresented in the political system and their cynicism, scepticism and their detachment from the legitimate political system mirrors their inherent distrust of that system. Inevitably their detachment confers legitimacy to a political sub-order wherein new political movements originate and causes are popularised by vociferous interest groups and anarchists. Is it simply legitimacy or the presence of (rational) voters that provides the proverbial glue that cements the liberal democratic polity or is it what has been called 'strategies of displacement' (Offe 1984), that is, strategies that 'disperse the worst effects of economic and political problems onto vulnerable groups while *appeasing* those able to mobilise claims more effectively' (Held 1987, p. 240) [our emphasis].

Such strategies are only credible provided 'those able to mobilise' are in a position to return the incumbent government at the next election. It is against this background that we are in the position to entertain such questions as how is the political order held together? what does voting mean in a real world democracy? Everyone accepts that democracy requires some form of political representation. For whatever family of reasons, be it 'the fear of the possible chaos of direct democracy' (Schofield 1993), 'the impossibility of persuading millions of voters to pay attention to the minutiae of decision making', fairness or justice, the electorate must choose political representatives to act on their behalf. We should recall that Hobbes's 'Leviathan' was conceptualised as an all-powerful autocratic figure needed to regulate the behaviour of citizens as organised groups. Voting is the hallmark of a democracy and many of us would question the imposition rather than the election of government. The US Founding Fathers' need for representation to protect against what the late Bill Riker called 'the tyranny of the majority', was reiterated recently by Wilson (1990) in an honorary lecture: 'To paraphrase a twentieth century commentator, man is good enough to make republican government possible but bad enough to make it necessary'.

But if we cast our minds back to the real world - in 1994 the world's press carried photographs of an event that many thought they would never witness as millions of South Africans of all races and creeds queued patiently for their most basic of democratic rights, the right to vote. In contrast scholars decry the low and declining voter turnout across democracies. The voter turnout as measured in McNutt (1995) averaged 72 per cent across OECD democracies in recent national elections for the electoral period 1988-1992. But we have to be very careful here in distinguishing between the *right* to vote and the *obligation* to vote. In many democracies individuals and groups are disenfranchised, lack empowerment and have no effective participation in the democratic political system in which they are citizens. There is a hint in the statistics that voting is relatively less important in the more developed economies, plausibly less important as a catalyst for the delivery of their share of government expenditure and public goods.

More citizens are opting for indirect participation as reflected in the overall number of interest groups which has taken a sharp increase in recent years. Schlozman and Tierney (1986) and Walker (1983) found that over 30per cent of the lobbying organisations in their studies were founded after 1960. Baumgartner and Walker (1988) found that 90 per cent of the citizens in a pilot study of political participation were involved with interest groups. Many social perspectives have been suggested to reverse the decline in voter turnout but few advocate the legal sanction of compulsory voting. One-sixth of the one hundred and eighty or so democracies in the world have made voting a legal obligation not merely a social responsibility. The effect of compulsory voting on turnout is inevitable. However, the reluctance of reformers to cross the line from social responsibility to legal sanction reflects a difference in the interpretation of the maxim: one person, one vote; from one person one *can* vote to one person one *must* vote, a difference in interpretation within which is cocooned a different property rights regime.

In other words, by eliminating the right not to vote or by constraining the right to vote ownership within the electoral process is redefined, raising 'issues of democratic order and limits to voluntary choice' (Crain and Leonard 1993). Within many democracies the plethora of institutions and bureaucracies, and in particular the structure of civil society - including private ownership of productive property, sexual, religious and racial inequalities and discrimination - do not create conditions for what Dahl (1979) defines as a 'fully democratic political system', that is, equal votes, effective participation, enlightened understanding and equal control of the political agenda. It is equally possible to argue that existing institutions in the polity may be unjust and need to be changed; in such a case the emphasis will be on the conditions under which noncompliance would lead to political instability and ultimately to the formation of new institutions, more just and representative of the populace. Consequently new ideals of enfranchisement, empowerment, governance and legitimacy replace representativeness, majority rule, government and fairness respectively as scions of an ancient and noble tradition of voting.

The Tyranny of the Majority

So was Lipset (1963, p. 32) correct when he argued that 'political apathy may reflect the health of a democracy'. The answer really does depend on the socio-economic grouping and political persuasion of the citizen. While democrats may agree with this sentiment, they interpret voting in rather different ways. In the liberal view, *a la* Madison, 'the function of voting is to control officials, and no more'. Madison, the original American scholar of liberal democracy, defined a republic as 'a government that derives all its powers directly or indirectly from the great body of the people, and is administered by people holding their offices during pleasure, *for a limited period,* as during good behaviour' [our italics].

While the liberal remedy of an election may elect a new government - and not necessarily the voters' choice - it more than likely returns the same politicians; such 'tenured incumbents' may curry favour with particular interest groups (McNutt 1995), supporting unpopular policies that benefit their constituent group and not the group of the individual citizens, that is, society. According to a populist view of voting *a la* Rousseau 'participation in rule-making is necessary for liberty'. The problem here as identified by Riker is that 'populist voting is logically correlated with coercion' (p. 13). This is evident from either the history of civil rights struggles or referenda both of which reflect the dichotomy of majority rule *versus* minority rights.

Populism can be traced back to the fundamental notion of Rousseau's social contract and the general will of the people. Scholars have tried to reconcile this with Locke's version of majority rule and his presumed belief that right is what the majority wills. Riker sounds some alarms bells: 'All one has to do is to find that a majority (perhaps a putative or even a wholly imaginary and nonexistent majority) has willed some version of self-mastery. It then becomes both reasonable and necessary to impose that version of liberty by coercion' (p. 13).

The populist view of voting can be used to justify coercion in the name of temporary majorities. Therefore in the populist view of voting the opinions of the majority must be right and 'must be respected because the will of the people is the liberty of the people'. In the liberal view, however, there is no such identity, voting is just a decision and has no particular moral character. Against this background there are two competing hypotheses at work attempting to explain the decline in voter turnout in modern democracies. The (rent-seeking) interest group theory of government argues that public policy is driven by the demands of competing pressure groups and that any asymmetry in costs and benefits means that pressure groups have greater incentives to organise and expend real resources on lobbying than (say) a random taxpaying citizen.

Alternatively we could begin with the premise borrowed from Crain and Leonard (1993), that voters and non-voters are different. In this hypothesis the set of citizens that vote voluntarily is not representative of the entire electorate. Likewise when a compulsory voting rule brings in those voters who would not vote voluntarily, this changes the demographic composition of the electorate. Specifically the set of non-voters tend to be 'poorer, less well educated, younger and disproportionately higher in minority or discriminated groups' than the set of voluntary voters. In short, voluntary non-voters are plausibly net recipients of government services, however, the ex-ante prejudice that more inclusive democracy will expand the size of government growth is not supported empirically (Crain and Leonard 1993).

From a contractarian perspective we should really ask: is it irrational or inconsistent behaviour for the voluntary non-voter to favour a compulsory voting rule? The answer is no, if we treat such a rule as an institutional mechanism to reduce the asymmetry in incentives facing organised groups (G-groups *vide* p. 223) and atomistic individuals. A voluntary non-voter may prefer a mandatory rule if the extra cost to the individual (in the form of registering and going to the polls) is more than offset by the extra benefit (in terms of lower wealth transfers to the gatekeeper and effective participation), if everyone were required to vote. A variety of institutional conditions influence this outcome in addition to the opportunity cost argument just outlined. They may include the opportunity of empowerment, the fiscal capacity of the economy to redistribute income to the poor, and institutional characteristics of the political process which determine the probability of party-specific tenure.

The typical inefficiencies associated with democracy, independent of the voting rules, are often the consequence of classical principal-agent problems where hidden action enable the agents (the elected parliamentarians) to exploit the principals (the voters). However in modern democracies where increasingly more citizens are classified as voluntary non-voters and more citizens are marginalised or disenfranchised, the approach may be somewhat misguided. A different perspective which focuses on voluntary non-voters, the marginalised and the disenfranchised and their respective responses to legitimating their unelected representatives is introduced later in this chapter.

The Ideal of Democracy

An important feature of any representative political institution,whether it be a government or a committee, is the formal set of rules that govern the voting procedure. The voting process, as noted in Chapter 2, by which a democratic society composed of individuals with different preferences decide upon a course of action, has been analysed since the earliest writings of Borda, Condorcet and Dodgson in the eighteenth century. Majority rule and variants thereof remain pre-eminent in the choice of voting rule, and although political scientists have been aware of the instability of the rule from these earlier contributions it was not until Arrow's original formulation of 'the voting paradox', which highlighted the absence of a rule or method of aggregating individual preferences, that disturbing questions about voting were raised.

In many of his pamphlets on voting, Dodgson, better known for Alice in Wonderland, referred to a tendency of voters to adopt 'a principle of voting which makes an election more a game of skill than a real test of the wishes of the electors' (1876, p. 10). This is equally true today. The game of skill is also played in committees where individual committee members adopt a rule or strategy on how to vote. Farquharson (1969), who pioneered the idea of sophisticated voting, introduced the sophisticated voter as one who 'makes the best use of his vote, to attempt to predict the contingency likely to rise: that is to say, how the others are likely to vote' (p. 38).

Having acknowledged sophisticated voting and voluntary non-voting we now ask the inevitable question: why have government? If we challenge the basis of elected government we challenge the ideal of democracy. Stevens (1993) has argued that government can be 'done' in a variety of ways; although economic developments in recent years across free-world democracies have indicated a heavy reliance on the market, the existence of public goods, such as policing, defence and the law, require more government. Historically 'the Leviathan' was necessary in order to avoid anarchy. Free riders roam the black economies of our democracies, courts intervene where transaction costs are high and the law supplants user-demand functions in relegating the rights of the citizen to the courts. Consequently, too much of the public good may be produced (pollution and crime) or indeed too little may be produced (education and income redistribution to the poor). The logic of economic self-interest with free riding and high transaction costs is that inefficiency in the supply of the public goods will obtain in the absence of some degree of government intervention.

The principle of democracy is founded on voting procedures. In other words, voting and the process of voting is central to democracy. Arrow's impossibility theorem was a direct challenge to the theory of democracy, and the controversy which it unfolded, deserves a central place in any public debate on voting. The theorem had an important impact on liberal democratic political thought. Quite simply, it ruled out populism, which is best illustrated in a political system by a referendum which reflects the Roussean will of the people. The stark conclusion of the impossibility of a collective outcome attacked the very fundamentals of the political process, a process with which public choice theorists are becoming increasingly identified. Riker (1982) envelopes voting with the conceptual and ideological meaning of democracy, proffering voting as a method *a la* Downs (1957) by which citizens in a democracy can 'seek self respect and self control' (p. 8). The Arrovian perspective on the voting paradox is crucial to an understanding on how voting actually works.

We embarked on the Arrovian adventure in Chapters 2 and 3 earlier. The majority rule criterion in many respects evokes the tyranny of the majority (Riker 1982). This translates into a concern for the welfare of the minority, the 49 per cent or less who may have preferred the alternative to the majority outcome. In some of the examples in Chapters 2 and 3, the choice is simply between a number of voters rule outcome and an outcome arrived at by strategic manipulation of the votes. However, there is a subtle difference: strategic manipulation invests decisive power in an elite G-group while the social outcome based on (say) the number of voters rule, NVR, is more unanimous. But it is not as simple and straightforward as this surely; if it were there would have been no need to develop an entire literature on voting rules and a companion set of acceptable properties that they must satisfy.

Perfect Democracy

The democracy and growth theme has been rehabilitated in the literature[1] by the desire amongst scholars to explain the economic success of developing economies. What did these economies have in common? One answer, in varying degrees, is undemocratic government. What if we compare East Asia with Eastern Europe and the former Soviet Union, where democracy apparently arrived before economic reform. Democracy can be defined with respect to free and fair elections, protection of civil liberties, multi-party legislatures, freedom of press and of speech - the political geography of the world's democracies shows that the richest countries are democratic and nearly all of the poorest countries are not. Albeit, the claim that authoritarian regimes favour development, based solely on the East Asia miracle, is the exception not the rule. Historically as economies evolve, vociferous and well organised G-groups evolve and prosper with the concomitant security of property rights and the enforcement of contracts rather than with the right to vote. Democratic governments secured these rights; but there is little hard evidence to decipher whether it is the emerging prosperous groups that demand democracy or whether democracy fosters prosperity.

The relevance of the debate to voting is to ascertain whether democracy, that is, the right to vote, is sufficient to ensure the prosperity of the citizenry. In many democratic systems, economic power manifests itself with the emergence of the G-groups which either complement government or supplant the role of government. For example, endogenous government behaviour, whereby the government is open to manipulation and wont to manipulate the economy in order to relax the re-election constraint, has been recognised by macroeconomics scholars of the political business cycle school. Such government behaviour becomes the norm as the democracy evolves and hierarchical systems develop which rank-order the citizens; the first ranking which is the very hallmark of democracy is between the elected parliamentarian and the voter, the principal-agent characterisation alluded to earlier in this chapter.

Within the set of parliamentarians there is the government and the opposition parties; across the voters there are those who voted for the government and those who voted for the opposition parties; across the citizens there are voters, the disenfranchised and voluntary non-voters. Institutions evolve with the democracy providing public good and private good services. As the economy develops, citizens are further sub-divided by different classes of work; industrial, agricultural and services; and by socio-economic groupings, creed and race. In other words, as the democracy evolves an inherent hierarchical division of the citizenry becomes embedded in the system and institutions continue to emerge which reinforce the hierarchy. The implications of this development is that the user-demand function for many services is absent. This facilitates the creation of institutional groups which are able to usurp public good information and in so doing acquire command over the amount of economic resources. With such a characterisation of economic power, a perfect democracy *a la* Dahl, independent of the right to vote, does not obtain.

Within this evolutionary scheme of things information is transformed from a public good to a private good and G-groups evolve to define legal rights, to pronounce the state of your health, and to protect and police your private property, to determine your right to vote and inevitably to determine your share of economic resources. Citizen sovereignty is violated without the citizen being aware of it; citizens no longer know their rights without recourse to (say) a lawyer and in general citizens of the democracy become disenfranchised by the hierarchical nature of institutions. This facilitates the further creation of institutional G-groups which are able to usurp public good information and in so doing acquire command over the distribution of economic resources within the democracy.

The Anarchy of Legitimacy

The description of the voting paradox in Chapters 2 and 3 reveals the impossibility of arriving at a transitive social choice. However with vote-trading a majority decision emerges. If we nominate one representative voter, we can further illustrate her preferences across a pair of issues on a measurable distance, either left: right or conservative: liberal. In such a representation each voter has an ideal point x^* which may coincide with the status quo $x0$ on the issue as illustrated in Figure 8.1. Finally allow for a limited set of points called *the win set*, that is acceptable to the citizen as being better than the status quo. Suppose that a group of representative citizens with an ideal point x^* have been designated to propose change in the status quo. One possible rule to adopt is the closed rule which allows this group of citizens to propose a single change which the other citizens cannot change. If the Chairman of the privileged group (for example, a Cabinet minister, or Prime Minister), the *agenda setter*, is extremely optimistic then his best proposal is his own ideal point $x1$. However this will not be accepted by the other citizens in a majority

vote as being better than the status quo. Only points in the win set will be
accepted and since x1 is not in the win set the proposal will be defeated.

Alternatively the agenda setter may spend some time determining the
preferences of his fellow citizens and locating the dimensions of their respective
win sets. Rather than attempt to detail how one can determine the actual win
set, given a history of political order, legislation and institutional rules in a
polity, we will arbitrarily specify the win sets. In the case at hand only points
in W(x0), the win set relative to x0, will be accepted by enough of the citizens
for agreement. Since the agenda setter has abandoned x1, he opts for x2 having
consulted with the fellow citizens and coming to a reasonable expectation as
to the location of the win sets as illustrated in Figure 8.2. If he knows this set
exactly then he can behave more sensibly and propose the best change subject
to the constraint that it is accepted, that is, subject to being in the win set
W(x0). Suppose now that the agenda setter with ideal point at x1 is the Prime
Minister of a political party that has jurisdiction over policy in a polity.

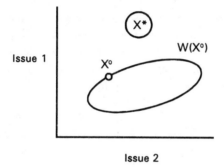

Figure 8.1 The win set, I

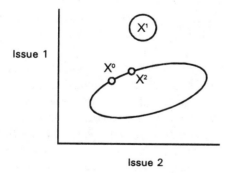

Figure 8.2 The win set, II

In Shepsle's (1979) model changes must come from the party - if the party makes no proposals then the outcome is inevitably the status quo x0. However in its more general terms the *agenda-access* model suggests that outcomes will be tilted in favour of those with access to the issue at hand - G-groups, for example - and that changes in agenda-access will change the equilibrium and deliver an outcome in the win set. This outcome must be submitted to the citizens but they have no agenda-access for the purpose of amending the proposal. This requirement operates just like a closed rule within a Shepsle legislature, with the exception in our analogous case that the citizens will enjoy access through ratification of the outcome by a popular referendum. Access is not denied the citizen's representatives - the fact that their elected and unelected representatives can materially affect the proposal that is tailored by the agenda setter, should ensure that it is likely to 'pass muster among the citizens'.

The Institution of Indirect Initiatives

As illustrated in Figure 8.3 a second win set, Wp(x0), is shown which represents the set of changes that a majority of unelected representatives think is better than the status quo. If we assume that a popular referendum is mandatory then the agenda setter's best proposal is no longer x2 but rather x3, the best proposal accepted by both the elected and unelected representatives and the citizens. The pivotal role of the unelected representatives is imperative in arriving at this outcome by a process which we call the *institution of indirect initiatives*. The elected representatives opt for an outcome that secures re-election of their members and satisfies the ideal point of the median voter. The unelected representatives, however, seek legitimacy, requiring an outcome that will be acceptable to the majority of the electorate. The stability of the equilibrium point x3 can be considered in the context of a few difficult analytical properties to do with win sets. We can either focus on an institutional setting which best describes electoral competition between the unelected representatives or between the unelected and elected representatives (the gatekeepers) and government.

We opt for the latter. So we have two parties which compete for the disjoint set of votes of the electorate by adopting policy positions across a vector of issues $X = (x1, x2, ..., xn)$. Once the parties announce their positions, say x1 and x2, all the citizens vote according to their own ranking over $(x1, x2)$. In the more traditional positive social choice models one would differentiate between: (i) parties interested in winning elections which we refer to as the *gatekeepers;* and (ii) parties interested in maximising the vote which we refer to as the *harriers*. We have a representation of three voters across the triple (a,b,c) with the gatekeeper party's preference profile represented as $a > b > c$

and the harrier party's preference profile represented as c > a > b.

An application of the Holler-Steunenberg (1994) model ascribes a utility function to each player Ui = Ui(m,p) with a probability of winning (1/2, 1) and a set P = (a,b,c) describing a discrete set of alternatives. Given the preference ranking, player g will always win a majority of votes and thus defeat x by choosing some x^ if player h chooses x first and player g knows x when choosing x^. In a variant of the Holler-Steunenberg game, player h decides on policy xn by solving the decision problem of player g for alternatives to xn, represented by (a*,b*,c*). If player h selects (c*), for example, and player g selects (b), then voters 1 and 2 will vote for (b) with the pair (c*,b) illustrated in Figure 8.4. We proceed and player h selects (b*) and g selects (a) then voters 1 and 3 will vote for (a); continuing with player h selecting (a*), player g choosing (a), spanning a set of *indirect initiative pairs* = ((c*,b), (b*,a), (a*,a)) until we are able to describe the *best reply set* of player g and the *best proposal set* of player h in the lower panel of Figure 8.4.

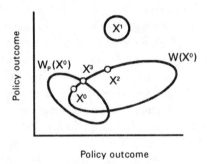

Policy outcome

Figure 8.3 Intersecting win sets

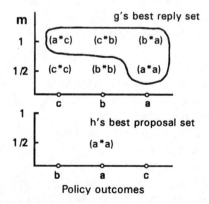

Figure 8.4 Reply and response

In our particular illustration the best response set is a singleton. The agenda setter is able to determine the location of the win set by the revelation of each indirect initiative pair and opt for that pair which delivers x3:

$$x3 = f(a^*,a) => (a^*,a) = f^{-1}(x3)$$

The pair (a^*,a) indicates an outcome that offers both players a one in two chance of winning an election.

Government and Governance

Effective participation, captured by f^{-1}, by marginalised or disenfranchised groups in a polity is assured as their representatives engineer the calculus of voting and voting procedures in order to locate outcomes in the win set. As Riker (1982) so eloquently put it: 'what makes all this so democratically unpalatable is that, apparently, the only way to make 'society' choose coherently is to impose a dictator' (p. 18).

At this juncture, we return to the Downsian question: why bother to vote? In a very real sense there is an opportunity cost to the citizen in the location of the win set. Alternative (x0) may have been the preferred citizen choice but alternative (x3) was the compromised alternative agreed by negotiation by the representatives of the citizens. The gain, denoted by G(x3) and computed (say) in terms of political stability by returning (x3) must be weighted against the high opportunity cost of (x3), denoted by C(x3), from the citizen's perspective. The lesson of the 1798 French Revolution, is that representatives, no matter how dictatorial, cannot afford to disregard the Bastille constraint in Chapter 2, that is, C(x3) > G(x3). In other words, no compromise on voting rules to secure a majority outcome should be tolerated in a democratic system. The fact that the Bastille constraint has been relaxed in modern democracies reflects more on the citizens and their demands and expectations from a democracy than on the political system *per se*. But as expectations increase across groups of voluntary non-voters and disenfranchised voters, the institution of indirect initiative may have to take precedence in order to secure a negotiated voting outcome in a win set.

There is a 'radical distinction' Mill (1951, p. 229) argued between 'controlling the business of government and actually doing it'. While voting is the kernel of democracy, voting at elections is not really required for 'skilled government' - a dictatorship, for example, represents a political system in which citizens do not vote. Albeit, the international literature is undecided on whether or not democracy or dictatorship best delivers higher levels of economic growth and equality. The democracy-development debate which has appeared in the economic literature raises many disturbing questions like 'why democracy'? which inevitably leads to the Downsian question: why vote? The question, however, must be understood from the perspective of an earlier point that voting is exercised to gain some benefit, but in many instances disregarding the type of political regime, particular socio-economic G-groups do better than others. Political parties align themselves to the different socio-economic groups and part of the mechanics of voting for a citizen is in voting habitually without regard for the election of government.

How differently would an individual voter behave if, for example, on election day, in addition to the list of candidates, there was a probability weight attached to each candidate indicating the probability of being in government or if the alternatives were negotiated win set alternatives, in contrast to Mill who recommended a complex plural voting system: 'so that the masses, the working classes, the democracy, would not have the opportunity to subject the political order to what he labelled simply as ignorance'. In his complex system 'the wiser and more talented should have more votes than the ignorant and less able' (p. 324).

What if the political system adopts a plural voting system where the lower socio-economic groups and disadvantaged groups are awarded two or three votes per voter. By not voting, lower socio-economic groups signal a lack of identification with the modern democracy whereas in contrast the low turnout of the higher socio-economic groups signals a recourse to rent-seeking. Schumpeter (1976) argued that democracy is important because it legitimates the position of authority. The interesting questions here are: (i) does a no vote signal acquiescence in the political system; and (ii) does an occasional vote legitimate a political system? Schumpeter assumed that voting entails a belief that the political system or the political institutions are accepted, that is, legitimated.

However, scholars are now of the opinion that Schumpeter's concept of legitimacy failed to distinguish between different grounds for accepting or complying with the political system or the institutions. We have in this chapter referred to non-voting; Mann (1970) and Habermas (1976) list different 'normative agreements' as to why individuals do what they do. In addition, one doubts whether participation by voting should be equated with 'legitimacy' at all. Political systems through time create the conditions of its own legitimacy (Held 1987). But the intriguing question is to unravel the circumstances under which the citizens confer legitimacy, that is, the circumstances under which citizens do things because they think them right, correct, justified or worthy. This is the essence of the institution of indirect initiative.

It can be said that if a political system is implicated in the creation and reproduction of systematic inequalities of power, of wealth, income and opportunities will rarely enjoy sustained legitimating by G-groups other than those whom it *directly benefits*. However, Schumpeter did not examine the issue of non-participation; effective participation in a political system, he argued, does depend upon the political will but also, we would argue, upon having the actual capacity (the resources and skills) to pursue different courses of action, for example, revolution, anarchy or terrorism. In his democratic system the only full participants are the members of political elites in political parties and in public office. The 'role of ordinary citizen is not only highly delimited, but it is frequently portrayed as an unwanted infringement on the smooth functioning of 'public' decision making'.

Furthermore, the idea that individuals are 'free and equal' in liberal democracies is questioned by many New Left writers. In modern democracies great numbers of individuals are restricted systematically from participating actively in political life - inequalities of class, sex, religion and race substantially hinder the extent to which it can legitimately be claimed that individuals are free and equal. As Pateman (1985, p. 171) put it : 'the free and equal individual is, in practice, a person found much more rarely than liberal theory suggests'.

If government is independent of the gatekeepers and rent-seeking classes, then the New Left would concur that it is plausible for the citizen to obey and respect it; however, if the government inevitably and the state inescapably is locked into the reproduction of the inequalities of everyday life, then 'the whole basis of its claim to allegiance is in doubt'.

Why then bother to vote? Why not employ the resources and skills to pursue different courses of action. If people are poorly represented they are likely to believe that only rarely will their views and preferences be taken seriously - they realise that democracy represents periodic involvement in elections. However, if people are systematically marginalised they realise that their views are taken seriously with terrorist and anarchic activities. Grounds for accepting or legitimising the unelected terrorist or anarchic representatives could be found in the Mann-Habermas 'pragmatic acquiescence' as identified in Held (1987, p. 182) 'although we do not like a situation (it is not satisfactory and far from ideal), we cannot imagine things being really different and so we accept what seems like fate'.

The ground for compliance is analytical; in real life different types of agreement are often fused together into a win set and we have to analyse the different meanings of acceptance entailed by an act like voting or tacit support for terrorists. Concessions to unelected representatives or anarchic groups should not be misunderstood. In the first instance, it is only if the unelected representatives of the marginalised voters have the opportunity directly to participate in decision-making at the local level; and secondly, and more importantly, the opportunity for extensive participation in areas which would radically alter the context of national politics. The unelected representatives would have to learn about economics and budgeting, political representation, operating within a parliamentary or congressional structure: 'complemented and checked by fully self-managed organisations in the workplace and in the local community. Only such a political system, in Macpherson's view, would actually realise the profoundly important liberal democratic value of the equal right of self-development' (Held 1987, p. 258).

Their constituents are likely to believe that participation is now worthwhile but for self-determination to be achieved, democratic rights need to be extended from the polity to the economy and to other central institutions. The structure of the modern corporate world makes it essential that the political rights of the citizens be complemented by a similar set of rights in the sphere of work and community relations. The transition from government to governance takes place thus reducing a sense of estrangement from power centres and nurturing a concern for collective problems, thus legitimising governance. Analogous to a New Left model of participatory democracy - which makes democracy count in people's everyday life by extending the sphere of democratic control to those key institutions in which most people live out their lives - the legitimate issue is: 'how can individuals be free and equal, enjoy equal opportunities to participate in the determination of the framework which governs their lives, without surrendering important issues of individual liberty and distributional questions to the uncertain outcomes of the democratic process?' (Held 1987, p. 264).

Our reply, which underpins the theme of this chapter, is that non-participation by marginalised or disenfranchised groups - who in many democracies are now in a position to legitimate their unelected representatives - may be juxtapositioned with anarchy in modern political systems.

Conclusion

What does voting accomplish? - the election of a government not of your choice and acquiescence in the conduct of government. From the liberal perspective the outcome is both tangible and transparent to the citizen, voting elects a government. However, voting rules, which convert individual votes into an outcome do bias that outcome. For example, plurality or first-past-the-post rule, under the Westminster model of government, militates against the smaller political parties. And there are many special interests that stand between the people and the general will, the G-groups which include tenured politicians, gatekeepers, bureaucrats, organised interest groups and corporations. The accomplishment may be in electing a government but a greater accomplishment would be in revealing and unmasking who really governs. Citizens inevitably govern by effective participation.

The theory of social choice raised disturbing questions about voting rules; the historic Condorcet voting paradox reveals that simple majority rule applied to three voters will not return an agreed (transitive) majority outcome from their three alternatives. But in everyday voting arenas from small committees to national decision making, majority rule is applied and decisions are made.

Unless there is unanimity, majority rule fosters disagreement and bifurcates the issue into the majority opinion and the minority opinion. The antagonism and dislike and the polarisation of citizens which accompanies the application of majority rule is easily observed around the time of populist referenda, particularly on moral and political issues. Negotiation through the institution of indirect initiatives locates an outcome in a win set, abating any antagonistic response.

The majority rule problems as indicated in the voting paradox can be resolved in the traditional way by allowing representatives to compete for elected office by forming coalitions or packaging sets of issues to appeal to voters, including minority voters, with intense preferences. These elected representatives could also exercise agenda control which would restore stability to majority rule voting. The use of legislative committees to deal with different types of legislation is the quintessential example of agenda control; certain committees have substantial power over labour, health for example and unelected representatives are increasingly enjoying agenda-access in political systems across the world. In the free world democracies such is the power, writes Norris (1990, p. 42), 'of mass-media misrepresentation and simulated ideological consensus that there appears no longer to exist any gap between what the people want (as reflected in opinion polls, electoral surveys) and what their leaders promise (as likewise manufactured through this highly elaborated feedback mechanism)'.

Albeit, while voting is a hallmark of a free-world democracy it does not guarantee that the citizens' preferences are represented. Effective participation of the citizens through consultation on the dimensions of a possible win set does ensure that preferences are represented. The demise of the communist regimes across Eastern Europe is compared to the liberal democracies of Western Europe as command economy is replaced by the free-market capitalist enterprise. The UK with a degree of selective coercion exercised by government under the Thatcher administration has striven to enforce free-market doctrine through the curtailment of union activities, the extension of police power to intervene in industrial disputes, the withdrawal of numerous welfare provisions from those acutely in need and the redistribution of tax benefits and wealth in order to create an ever widening gap between the highest and lowest income groups.

We must reflect on whether we as citizens are witnesses to the unrepresentable activities of elected officials, or are we opting out of the direct democratic process, realising tangible benefits through indirect participation in the democratic process. And for the denizens of once communist East European democracies, does voting take place in a vacuum as their economies are rescued by massive loans with crippling interest repayments and their political systems reconstructed 'along lines laid down by multinational corporate interests' (Norris 1990, p. 41). In newly emerging democracies, indeed across old crusty democracies, once marginalised and disenfranchised groups are beginning to enjoy agenda-access as their unelected representatives are consulted by the gatekeepers and legitimated in a new political order, a fully democratic political system wherein *negotiation first and voting second* on a range of issues is the norm. In such a political system voting may be good for your political health.

NOTES

1. The interested reader should look at *The Journal of Economic Perspectives*, 1993, Vol.7, No.3, and the symposia paper on 'Democracy and Development', contained therein.

References

Alchian, A.A. (1965), 'Some economics of property rights', *Il Politico*, Vol. 30, pp. 816-29.

Alesina, A. (1988), *Macroeconomics and Politics*, MIT Press, Cambridge.

Alesina, A. (1991), *'Political Business Cycles'*, Paper Presented at the Annual Meeting of the European Public Choice Society.

Alesina, A. and Roubini, N. (1992), 'Political Cycle in OECD Economies', *Review of Economic Studies*, Vol. 59, pp. 663-688.

Applebaum, E. and Katz, E. (1987), 'Seeking rents by setting rents', *Economic Journal*, Vol. 97, pp. 685-699.

Aronson, J.R. (1978), *Public Finance*, McGraw-Hill, New York.

Aronson, J.R. (1982), 'Political inequality: An economic approach', in Ordershook, P. and Shepsle, K., (op. cit.).

Aronson, J.R. and Schwartz, E. (1973), 'Financing public goods and the distribution of population in a system of local government', *National Tax Journal*, June.

Arrow, K.J. (1950), 'A difficulty in the concept of social welfare', *Journal of Political Economy*, Vol. 58, No. 4, pp. 328-46.

Arrow, K.J. (1951), *'Social Choice and Individual Values'*, 2nd Edition, John Wiley & Sons, New York.

Arrow, K.J. (1963), *Social Choice and Individual Values*, 2nd Edition, Yale University Press, New Haven.

Arrow, K.J. (1969), 'Tullock and an existence theorem', *Public Choice*, Vol. 6, pp. 105-112.

Atkinson, A.B. and Stiglitz, J.E. (1980), *Lectures in Public Economics*, McGraw-Hill, New York.

Auster, R.D. and Silver, M. (1979), *The State as a Firm: Economic Forces in Political Development*, Kluwer, Boston.

Axelrod, R. (1984), *The Evolution of Cooperation*, Basic Books, New York.

Baldwin, R.E. (1985),*The Political Economy of US Import Policy*, Cambridge, MIT Press.

Bandyopadhyay, T. (1986), 'Resolution of paradoxes in social choice' in Samuelson, L. (ed), *Microeconomic Theory*, Kluwer-Nijhoff.

Banks, J.S. (1985), 'Sophisticated voting and agenda control', *Social Choice and Welfare*, Vol. 4, pp. 295-306.

Banzhaf, J.F. (1965), 'Weighted Voting Doesn't Work', *Rutgers Law Review*, Vol. 19, pp. 317-42.

Baumgartner, F.R. and Walker, J. (1988), 'Survey research and membership in voluntary associations', *American Journal of Political Science*, Vol. 32, pp. 908-928.

Baumol, W.J. (1959), *Business Behaviour, Value and Growth*, Macmillan, New York.

Baumol, W.J. (1967), 'Macroeconomics and unbalanced growth: The anatomy of urban crisis', *American Economic Review*, Vol. 57, No. 3, pp. 414-26.

Baumol, W.J., Panzar, J.C. and Willig, R.W. (1982), *Contestable Markets and the Theory of Industry Structure*, Harcourt, Brace, Jovanovich, Inc., New York.

Baysinger, G. and Tollison, R.D. (1980), 'Evaluating the social costs of monopoly and regulation', *Atlantic Economic Journal*, Vol 8. pp.22-26.

Beauchamp, T.C. and Bowie, M.E. (1983), *Ethical Theory and Business*, Prentice Hall, New York.

Becker, G. (1983), 'A theory of competition among pressure groups for for political influence', *Quarterly Journal of Economics*, Vol. 98, pp. 371-400.

Becker, G. and Tomes, N. (1976), 'Child endowments and the quantity and quality of children', *Journal of Political Economy*, Vol. 84, No. 4(2), pp. 143-62.

Bendor, J. (1988), 'Formal models of bureaucracy', *British Journal of Political Science*, Vol. 18, July, pp. 353-95.

Benham, L. (1972), 'The effects of advertising on the price of eyeglasses', *Journal of Law and Economics*, Vol. 15, No. 2, pp. 327-36.

Benson, B. (1984), 'Rent-Seeking from a property rights perspective', *Southern Economic Journal*, Vol. 51, No. 2, pp. 388-400.

Berg, S. (1985), 'Paradox of voting under an urn model: The effect of homogeneity', *Public Choice*, Vol. 47, No. 2, pp. 377-87.

Berg, S. (1990), 'The ambiguity of power indices', University of Lund, Sweden, *Mimeo*.

Berglas, E. (1976), 'On the theory of clubs', *American Economic Review*, Vol. 66, AEA Papers and Proceedings, pp. 116-21.

Berglas, E. and Pines, D. (1978), *Clubs, local public goods and transportation models: A synthesis*, Working Paper 32/78, Foerder Institute, Tel-Aviv, Israel.

Bhagwati, J.N. (1980), 'Lobbying and welfare', *Journal of Public Economics*, Vol. 14, pp. 355-63.

Bhagwati, J.N. (1982), 'Directly unproductive profit seeking activities', *Journal of Political Economy*, Vol. 90, No. 5, pp. 988-1002.

Bhagwati, J.N. (1983), 'DUP activities and rent-seeking, *Kyklos*, Vol. 36, No. 4, pp. 634-37.

Bhagwati, J.N. and Srinivason, T.N. (1980), 'Revenue seeking a generalisation of the theory of tarriffs', *Journal of Political Economy*, Vol. 88, No. 6, pp. 1069-87.

Binmore, K. (1992), *Fun and Games: A Test of Game Theory*, D.C. Heath & Co., Lexington, MA.

Black, D. (1948), 'On the rationale of group decision-making', *Journal of Political Economy*, Vol. 56, No. 7, pp. 23-24.

Black, D. (1958), *The Theory of Committees and Elections*, Cambridge University Press, Cambridge.

Black, D. (1969), On Arrow's Impossibility Theorem', *Law and Economics*, Vol. 12.

Blais, A. and Dion, S. (1988), 'Are bureaucrats budget maximisers', Unpubilshed mimeo quoted in Dunleavy, P. (1991), *(op. cit.)*

Blau, J.H. (1957), 'The existence of a social welfare function', *Econometrica*, Vol. 25, No. 2, pp. 303-13.

Blau, J.H. and Deb, R. (1977), 'Social decision functions and veto', *Econometrica*, Vol. 45, pp. 871-79.

Boehm, R.H. (1976), 'One fervent vote against wintergreen', *Mimeo*, University of San Francisco.

Bonner, J. (1986), *Politics, Economics and Welfare, An Elementary Introduction into Social Choice*, Harvester-Wheatsheaf, Brighton.

Borcherding, T. (1977), *Budgets and Bureaucrats, The Sources of Government Growth*, Duke University Press, Durham.

Borda, J.C. (1781), 'Memoire sur les elections au scrutin', English translation by Grazia (1953), *Isis*, Vol 44.

Bowen, H.R. (1943), 'The interpretation of voting in allocation of resources', *Quarterly Journal of Economics,* Vol. 58, pp. 27-48.

Brams, S.J. (1977), 'When is it advantageous to cast a negative vote?' in Henn, R. and Moesschlin, O. (ed), *Mathematical Economics and Game Theory,* Springer Verlag, New York.

Brams, S.J. and Fishburn, P.C. (1978), 'Approval Voting', *American Political Science Review,* Vol. 72, September, pp. 831-47.

Brams, S.J. and Fishburn, P.C. (1983), *Approval Voting,* Birkhauser, Boston.

Brandt, F. (1967), 'Public and private values: A reply to Arrow' in Hook, S., *Human Values and Economic Philosophy,* NYU Press, New York.

Brennan, G. and Buchanan, J.M. (1980), *The Power to Tax,* Cambridge University Press, Cambridge.

Brennan, G. and Buchanan, J.M. (1984), 'Voter choice: Evaluating political alternatives', *American Behavioral Scientist,* Vol 28, No. 2, pp. 185-201.

Brennan, G. and Buchanan, J.M. (1985), *The Reason of Rules,* Cambridge University Press, Cambridge.

Brennan, G. and Flowers, M. (1980), 'All Ng Up on clubs: Some notes on the current status of club theory', *Public Finance Quarterly,* Vol. 8, No. 2, pp. 153-70.

Breton, A. (1974), *The Economic Theory of Representative Government,* Macmillan Press, London.

Breton, A. and Wintrobe, R. (1982), *The Logic Bureaucratic Control,* Cambridge University Press, Cambridge.

Broadway, R. and Bruce, N. (1984), *Welfare Economics,* Blackwell, Oxford.

Brock, W. and Evans, D.S. (1983), 'Predation, A Critique of the Government Case in US v AT&T' in Evans, D.S. (ed), *Breaking Up Bell, Essays in Industrial Organisation and Regulation,* North-Holland, New York.

Brown, D.J. (1975), 'Aggregation of preferences', *Quarterly Journal of Economics,* Vol. 89, pp. 457-76.

Brown, C.V. and Jackson, P.M. (1990), *Public Sector Economics,* Basil Blackwell, Cambridge.

Buchanan, J.M. (1949), 'The pure theory of government finance: A suggested approach', *Journal of Political Economy,* Vol. 57, December, pp. 496-505.

Buchanan, J.M. (1954), 'Individual choice in voting and in the market', *Journal of Political Economy,* Vol. 62, No. 4, pp. 334-43.

Buchanan, J.M. (1965), 'An economic theory of clubs', *Economica,* Vol. 32, February, pp. 1-14.

Buchanan, J.M. (1975), *The Limits of Liberty,* Chicago University Press, Chicago.

Buchanan, J.M. (1978), *Freedom in Constitutional Contract,* A&M Press, Texas.

Buchanan, J.M. (1980), 'Rent-seeking and Profit-Seeking' in Buchanan, J.M., Tollison, R.D. and Tullock, G. (ed), *Toward a Theory of Rent-Seeking Society,* A&M Press, Texas.

Buchanan, J.M. (1983(a)), 'Fairness Hope and Liberty' in Skurski (ed), *New Directions in Economic Justice,* University of Notre Dame Press, Notre Dame.

Buchanan, J.M. (1983(b)), 'How can constitutions be designed so that politicians who seek to serve "Public Interest" can survive?', *Constitutional Political Economy,* Vol. 4, pp. 1-6.

Buchanan, J.M (1993), 'Rent-seeking, noncompensated transfers and the law of succession', *Journal of Law and Economics,* Vol. 71, pp. 26-32.

Buchanan, J.M. (1996), 'Foundational concerns: A critique of public choice' in Paredo, J. and Schneider, F., *Current Issues in Public Choice* (op. cit.).

Buchanan, J.M. and Brennan, G. (1980), *The Power to Tax,* Chicago University Press, Chicago.

Buchanan, J.M. Tollison, R.D. and Tullock, G. (1980), *Toward a Theory of the Rent-Seeking Society*, A&M Press, Texas.

Buchanan, J.M. and Tullock, G. (1962), *The Calculus of Consent, Logical Foundations of Constitutional Democracy*, University of Michigan Press, Ann Arbor.

Buchanan, J.M. and Tullock, G. (1977), 'The expanding public sector: Wagner Squared', *Public Choice*, Vol. 31 pp. 147-50.

Cawson, A. (1982), *Corporatism and Welfare, Social Policy and State Intervention in Britain*, Heineman Educational Books, London.

Cebula, R.J. (1979), 'A survey of the literature on the migration of state and local government policies', *Public Finance*, Vol. 34, No. 1, pp. 69-82.

Chamberlin, E.H. (1933), *The Theory of Monopolistic Competition*, Harvard University Press, Cambridge, MA.

Chernoff, H. (1954), 'Rational selection of decision functions', *Econometrica*, Vol. 22, No. 4, pp. 423-43.

Clarke, E.H. (1971), 'Multipart pricing of public goods', *Public Choice*, Vol. 11, pp. 13-33.

Coase, R. (1960), 'The problem of social cost', *Journal of Law and Economics*, Vol. 3, pp. 1-44.

Colarder, D.C. (1984), *Neoclassical Political Economy: The Analysis of Rent Seeking and DUP Activities*, Ballinger, Cambridge, MA.

Coleman, J.S. (1971), 'Control of Collectives and the Power of a Collectivity to Act' in Lieberman (ed), *Social Choice*, Gordon Breach, New York.

Comanor, W.S. and Leibenstein, H. (1969), 'Allocative effeciency, X-efficiency and welfare losses', *Economica*, Vol. 36, pp. 304-09.

Condorcet, J.A. (1785), *Essai sur l'application de l'analyse a la probabilite des decisions rendues a la pluralite des voix*, Imprimerie Royale, Pairs.

Congleton, R.D. (1988), 'Evaluating rent-seeking losses: Do welfare gains of lobbyists count?', *Public Choice*, Vol. 56, No. 2, pp. 181-84.

Coughlin, P.J. (1992), *Probabilistic Voting Theory*, Cambridge University Press, Cambridge.

Coughlin, P, and Nitzan, S. (1981), 'Electoral outcomes with probabilistic voting and Nash social welfare maxima', *Journal of Public Economics*, Vol. 15, pp. 113-22.

Cowling, K. and Mueller, D. (1978), 'The social costs of monopoly power', *Economic Journal*, Vol 88, No. 3, pp. 727-48.

Crain, W.M. (1977), 'On the structure and stability of political markets', *Journal of Political Economy*, Vol. 85, No. 4, pp. 829-42.

Crain, W.M. and Leonard, M. (1993), 'The right versus the obligation to vote: Effects on cross country government growth', *Economics and Politics*, Vol. 5, pp. 43-52.

Crain, W.M. and Zardkoohi, A. (1978), 'A test of property rights of the firm: Water untilities in the United States', *Journal of Law and Economics*, Vol.21, pp.395-408.

Crane, W. (1968), *State Legislative Systems*, Prentice-Hall, Englewood Cliffs.

Crew, M.A. and Rowley, C.K. (1971), 'On allocative efficiency: X-Efficiency and measurement of welfare loss, *Economica*, Vol. May.

Grier, K. (1991), 'Congressional influence on monetary policy', *Journal of Monetary Policy'*, Vol. 28, pp. 202-220.

Dahl, R.A. (1961), *Who Governs? Democracy and Power in an American City*, Yale University Press, New Haven.

Dahl, R.A. (1979), 'Procedural Democracy' in Laslett, P. and Fishkin, J. (ed), *Philosophy, Politics and Society*, 5th Series, pp. 97-133, Yale University Press, New Haven.

d'Aspremont, C. and Gevers, L. (1977), 'Equity and informational basis of collective choice', *Review of Economic Studies*, Vol. 44, pp. 199-210.

Davis, O.A. and Hinich, M.J. (1967), 'A Mathematical Model of Policy Formation in a Democratic Society' in Bernd, H. (ed), *Mathematical Applications in Political Science III*, University of Virginia, Charlotteville.

Davis, O.A., Hinich, M.J. and Ordershook, P.C. (1970), 'An expository development of a mathematical model of the electoral process', *American Political Science Review*, Vol. 64, pp. 426-49.

DeAlessi, G. (1983), 'Property Rights, Transaction Costs and X-Inefficiency: An essay in economic theory', *American Economic Review*, Vol. 73, pp. 64-81.

De Nardo, J. (1985), *Power in Numbers: The Political Strategy of Protest and Rebellion*, Princeton University Press, Princeton.

Demsetz, H. (1988), *Ownership, Control and the Firm*, Blackwell, Oxford.

Denzau, A. and Katz, A. (1977), 'Expected plurality voting equilibria and social choice functions', *Review of Economic Studies*, Vol. 44, pp. 227-33.

DiLorenzo, T.J. (1984), 'The domain of rent-seeking behaviour;private or public choice', *International Review of Law and Economics*, Vol .4, pp. 185-97.

Dodgson, C.L. (1870), 'A method of taking votes on more than two issues', reprinted in Black (1958), *(op. cit.)*.

Doran, G. and Kronick, R. (1977), 'Single transferable vote: An example of a perverse social choice function', *American Journal of Political Science*, Vol. 21, pp. 303-11.

Downs, A. (1957), *An Economic Theory of Democracy*, Harper and Row, New York.

Downs, A. (1967), *Inside Bureaucracy*, Little Brown, Boston.

Dreeze, J. and Sen, A.K. (1989), *Hunger and Public Action*, Clarendon Press, Oxford.

Dubey, P. and Shapley, L. (1979), 'Mathematical properties if the Banzhaf power index', *Mathematics of Operations Research*, vol. 4, pp. 99-131.

Dummett, M.A. (1984), *Voting Procedures*, Clarendon Press, Oxford.

Dunleavy, P. (1991), *Democracy Bureacracy and Public Choice, Economic Approaches in Political Science*, Harvester-Wheatsheaf.

Dunsire, A. and Hood, C. (1989), *Cutback Management in Public Bureaucracies*, Cambridge University Press, Cambridge.

Durden, G. (1990), 'The effects of rent-seeking on farming income levels', *Public Choice*, Vol. 67, pp. 285-92.

Dworkin, A. (1976), *Our Blood: Prophecies and Discourses on Sexual Politics*, Harper & Row, New York.

Eggertsson, T. (1990), *Economic Behaviour and Institutions*, Cambridge University Press, Cambridge.

Ellingsen, T. (1991), 'Strategic buyers and the social cost of monopoly', *American Economic Review*, Vol. 81, No. 3, pp. 648-57.

Enelow, J.M. and Hinich, M.J. (1984), *The Spacial Theory of Voting*, Cambridge University Press, Cambridge.

Elster, J. and Hylland, A. (1986), *Foundations of Social Choice Theory*, Cambridge University Press, New York.

Evans, A.W. (1970), 'Private good: Externality, public good, *Scottish Journal of Political Economy*, Vol. 17, pp. 79-89.

Fair, R.C. (1976), 'The effect of economic events on votes for President', *The Review of Economics and Statistics*, Vol. 60, pp. 159-73.

Farquharson, R. (1969), *Theory of Voting*, Blackwell Press, Oxford.

Feldman, A.M. (1980), *Welfare Economics and the Social Choice Theory*, Lattague, Martinus, Nijoff, Boston.

Ferejohn, J.A. and Grether, D.M. (1977), 'Weak path independence', *Journal of Economic Theory*, Vol 14, pp. 19-31.

Fiorina, M.P. (1991), 'Elections in the Economy in the 1980s', in Alesina, A. and Carliner (ed) *Politics and Economics in the Eighties*, University of Chicago Press, Chicago.

Fishburn, P.C. (1973(a)), 'The social costs of monopoly and regulations: Posner reconsidered', *Journal of Political Economy*, Vol. 93, No. 2, pp. 410-16.

Fishburn, P.C. (1973(b)), 'Transitive binary social choice and interprofile conditions', *Econometrica*, Vol. 41, pp. 603-15.

Fisher, F. (1985), 'The social costs of monopoly and regulation: Posner reconsidered', *Journal of Political Economy*, Vol. 93, No. 2, pp. 410-16.

Formby, J.P. Keeler, J.P. and Thistle, P.D. (1988), 'X-Efficiency, rent-seeking and social costs', *Public Choice*, Vol. 57, No. 2, pp. 115-26.

Frantz, R. (1985), ' X-inefficiency theory and its critics', *Quarterly Review of Economics and Business*, Vol.25, pp. 38-58.

Frantz, R. (1988), *X-Efficiency: Theory Evidence and Application*, Kluwer Academic, Boston.

Forte, F. and Peacock, A.T. (1985), *Public Expenditure and Government Growth*, Blackwell, Oxford.

Gehrlein, W.M. and Fishburn, P.C. (1976), 'Condorcet's paradox and anonymous preference profiles', *Public Choice*, Vol. 26, pp. 1-18.

Gibbard, A. (1973), 'Manipulation of voting schemes: A general result', *Econometrica*, Vol. 41, No. 4, pp. 587-601.

Gibbard, A. (1986), 'Interpersonal comparisons: Preference greed and the intrinsic reward of life' in Elster, J. and Hyland, A., *(op. cit.)*

Glennerster, H. (1979), 'The determinant's of public expenditure' in Booth, T. (ed) *Planning for Welfare, Social Policy and the Expenditure Process*, Blackwell, Oxford.

Goodwin, B. (1980), 'Utopia defended against the liberals', *Political Studies*, Vol. 28, pp. 384-400.

Graff, W. (1965), *Unpublished notes on the probability of cyclical majorities*, in Sen (1983), Cambridge Churchill College.

Grandmont, J.M. (1978), 'Intermediate preferences and majority rule', *Econometrica*, Vol. 46, No. 2, pp. 317-30.

Green, H.A.J. (1976), *Consumer Theory* (Revised Edition), Macmillan Press, London.

Greir, K. (1991), 'Congressional influence on monetary policy', *Journal of Monetary Economics*, Vol. 20, pp. 202-20.

Groves, T. (1973), 'Incentives in teams',Vol. 41, pp. 617-33.

Habermas, J. (1976), *Legitimation Crisis*, Heinemann, London.

Hammond, P.J. (1976), 'Equity, Arrow's condition and Rawls' difference principle', *Econometrica*, Vol. 44, No. 4, pp. 793-804.

Harberger, A.C. (1954), 'Monopoly and resource allocation', *American Economic Review*, AEA Papers and Proceedings, Vol. 44, May, pp. 77-87.

Hart, H.L.A. (1973), 'Rawls on liberty and its priority', *University of Chicago Law Review*, Vol. 40, Spring, pp. 534-55.

Hartle, D. (1983), 'The theory of rent-seeking: some reflections', *Canadian Journal of Economics*, Vol. 16, No. 4, pp. 539-54.

Hayek, F.A. (1945), 'The use of knowledge in society', *American Economic Review*, Vol. 35, pp. 519-30.

Hayek, F.A. (1960), *The Constitution of Liberty*, Routledge & Keegan Paul, London.

Henrekson, M. (1991), *Wagner's Law-A Spurious Relationship?*, Paper Presented to the 1991 Public Choice Conference, Djion, France.

Held, D. (1987), *Models of Democracy*, Polity Press, Cambridge.

Helpman, E. (1979), 'On optimal community formation', *Economics Letters*, Vol. 1, pp. 289-93.

Helpman, E. and Hillman, A.L. (1976), *On optimal club size*, Working Paper 91/76, Foerder Institute, Tel-Aviv, Israel.

Helpman, E. and Hillman, A.L. (1977), 'The remarks on optimal club size', *Economica*, Vol. 44, pp. 293-6.

Her Majesty's Treasury (1984), *The next ten years: Public Expenditure and Taxation into the 1990s*, HMSO, London.

Higgins, R.S. and Tollison, R.D. (1988), 'Life among the triangles and trapezoids: Notes on the theory of rent seeking', George Mason University, *Mimeo.*

Hillman, A.L. (1978), 'The Theory of Clubs: A Technological Formulation' in Sando, A. (ed), *Essays in Public Economics: The Kiryat Anavim Papers,* Lexington Books, Lexington.

Hillman, A.L. and Katz, E. (1984), 'Risk adverse rent-seekers and the social cost of monopoly power', *Economic Journal,* Vol. 94, No. 373, pp. 110.

Hillman, A.L. and Riley, J. (1989), 'Politically contestable rents and transfers', *Economics and Politics,* Vol. Spring.

Hillman, A.L. and Samet, D. (1987), 'Dissipation of contestable rents and small numbers of contenders', *Public Choice,* Vol. 54, No. 1, pp. 63-82.

Hillman, A.L. and Swan, P.L. (1979), 'Club participation under uncertainty' M*imeo.*

Hinich, M.J. (1977), 'Equilibria in spacial voting', *Journal of Economic Theory,* Vol. 16, pp. 208-19.

Hirshleifer, J. (1976), 'Comment (on Peltzman, 1976), *Journal of Law and Economics,* Vol. 19, August, pp. 241-44.

Hirshleifer, J. (1989), 'Conflict and rent-seeking success functions: Ratio vs difference models of relative success', *Public Choice,* Vol. 63, No. 2, pp. 101-12.

Hirshleifer, J. and Riley, C. (1978), *Auctions and contests,* UCLA Working Paper, No. 118B.

Holler, M.J. (1994), 'Regulatory policymaking in a parliamentary setting: Comment', *Jarbuch fur Neue Politische Okonomie,* Vol. 13, pp. 66-71.

Inada, K. (1969), 'On the majority decision rule', *Econometrica,* Vol. 37, No. 3, pp. 490-506.

Jackson, P.M. (1982), *The Political Economy of Bureaucracy,* Philip Allen, Deddington, Oxford.

Jadlow, J. (1985), 'Monopoly rent-seeking under conditions of uncertainty', *Public Choice,* Vol. 45, No. 1, pp. 73-87.

Joskow, P.L. (1978), *Competition and Regulation in the Property/Casualty Insurance Industry,* MIT Press, Cambridge, Mass.

Joskow, P.L. and Klevorick, A.K. (1979), 'A framework for analysing predatory pricing policy', *Yale Law Journal,* Vol. 89, No. 2, pp. 213-68.

Kahana, N. and Katz, E. (1990), 'Monopoly price discrimination and rent-seeking', *Public Choice,* Vol. 64, No.1, pp. 93-100.

Kahneman, D., Knetsch, J. and Thaler, R. (1986), 'Fairness as a constraint on profit-seeking: Entitlement in a Market', *American Economic Review,* Vol. 76, pp. 728-41.

Kaldor, N. (1939), 'Welfare propositions of economics and interpersonal comparisons of utility', *Economic Journal,* Vol. 49, pp. 549-52.

Kau, J. and Rubin, P. (1981), 'The size of government', *Public Choice,* Vol. 37, No. 2, pp. 261-74.

Kemp, M.C. and Ng, Y.K. (1976), 'On the existence of social welfare function: Orderings and a social decison function', *Economica,* Vol. 43, pp. 59-66.

Kimenyi, M. (1989), 'Interest groups transfer seeking and democratisation', *American Journal of Economics and Sociology,* Vol. 48, No. 3, pp. 339-49.

Knight, F. (1924), 'Some fallacies in the interpretion of social cost', *Quarterly Journal of Economics,* Vol. 38, pp. 582-606.

Kramer, G.H. (1973), 'On a class of equilibrium conditions for majority rule', *Econometrica,* Vol. 41, pp. 285-97.

Kramer, G.H. (1975), 'Theory of Political Processes' in Intriligator, M.D. (ed), *Frontiers of Quantitative Economics,* North Holland, Amsterdam.

Kramer, G.H. (1977), 'A dynamic model of political equilibrium', *Journal of Economic Theory,* Vol. 16, pp. 310-34.

Krueger, A.O. (1974), 'The political economy of the rent-seeking society', *American Economic Review*, Vol. 64, No. 3, pp. 291-303.

Laband, D. and Sophocleus, J. (1988), 'The social costs of rent-seeking: First estimates', *Public Choice*, Vol 58, No. 3, pp. 269-75.

Lafay, J.D. (1991), *The Silent Revolution of Probabilistic Voting*, Paper presented to the 1991 Public Choice Conference, Djion, France.

Landes, W.M. and Posner, R.A. (1975), 'The independent judiciary in an interest group perspective', *Journal of Law and Economics*, Vol. 18, No. 3, pp. 875-902.

Laver, M. (1993), *Theory Institutions and and Government Formation*, Pleanary Lecture at the 1993 Public Choice Conference, Portrush, Northern Ireland.

Laver, M. and Schofield, N.J. (1990), *Multiparty Government: The Politics of Coalition in Europe*, Oxford University Press, Oxford.

Laver, M. and Shepsle, K. (1990), 'Government coalitions and intraparty politics', *British Journal of Political Science*, Vol. 20, pp. 489-507.

Leyard, J.O. (1984), 'The pure theory of large two-candidate elections', *Public Choice*, Vol. 44.

Lee, D. (1985), 'Marginal lobbying cost and the optimal amount of rent-seeking', *Public Choice*, Vol. 45, No. 2, pp. 207-13.

Leech, D. (1990), 'Power indices and probabilistic voting assumptions', *Public Choice*, Vol. 66, pp. 293-99.

Le Grand, J. and Winter, D. (1987), 'The middle classes and the welfare state under conservative and labour governments', *Journal of Public Policy*, Vol. 6, pp. 399-430.

Leibenstein, H. (1966), 'Allocative Efficiency and X-Efficiency', *American Economic Review*, Vol. 56, pp. 392-415.

Leibenstein, H. (1976), *Beyond Economic Man: A New Foundation for Microeconomics*, Harvard University Press, Cambridge.

Leibenstein, H. (1980), *Beyond Economic Man*, Harvard University Press, Boston.

Lepelley, D. (1986), *Some results on the probability of electing the Condorcet loser*, Paper Presented to the 1986 Meeting of European Public Choice Society.

Lindahl, E. (1929), *Just taxation-A positive solution*, first published in German, Lund, English translation in Musgrave, R.A. and Peacock, A.T. (1958), pp. 168-76.

Lindblom, C. (1977), *Politics and Markets: The World's Political Economic Systems*, Basic Books, New York.

Lipset, S.M. (1963), *Political Man*, Doubleday, New York.

Lipsey, R. and Lancaster, K. (1956), 'The general theory of the second best', *Review of Economic Studies*, Vol. 24, pp. 11-32.

Loehr, W. and Sandler, T. (1978), *Public Goods and Public Policy*, Sage Publications, New York.

Luce, R.D. and Raiffa, H. (1958), *Games and Decisions: Introduction and Critical Survey*, John Wiley & Sons, New York.

Mac Crimmon (1968), 'Descriptive and Normative Implications of the Decision Theory Postulates' in Borch, K.H. & Mossin, J. (ed.), *Risk and Uncertainty*, Macmillan, London.

Machiavelli, N. (1952), *The Prince*, Dent, Dutton, Luton.

Madison, J. (1787), *The Federalist*, No. 39-51, in Riker, W. (1982), (op. cit.).

Mann, M. (1970), 'The social cohesion of liberal democracy', *American Sociological Review*, Vol. 35, pp. 423-39.

Margolis, H. (1982), *Selfishness, Altruism and Rationality*, Chicago University Press, Chicago.

Marris, R. (1964), *The Economic Theory of Managerial Capitalism*, Free Press, New York.

Mas-Colell, A. and Sonnenschein, H. (1972), 'General possibility theorems for group decisions', *Review of Economic Studies*, Vol. 39, pp. 185-92.

May, K.O. (1952), 'A set of independent, necesary and sufficient conditions for simple majority rule', *Econometrica*, Vol. 20, No. 4, pp. 680-84.

Mayston, D.J. (1974), *The Idea of Social Choice*, Macmillan, New York.

McCormick, R.E. and Tollison, R.D. (1978), 'Legislatures and unions', *Journal of Political Economy*, Vol. 86, No. 1, pp. 63-78.

McCormick, R.E. and Tollison, R.D. (1981), *Politicians, Legislation and the Economy: An Inquiry into the Interest Group Theory of Government*, Nijhoff-Kluwer, Boston.

McGuire, M.C. (1974), 'Group segregation and optimal jurisdiction', *Journal of Political Economy*, Vol. 82, No. 1, pp. 112-32.

McGuire, T. (1981), 'Budget maximising governmental agencies: An empirical test', *Public Choice*, Vol. 36, pp. 313-22.

McKee, M. and West, E. (1981), 'The theory of second best: A solution in search of a problem', *Economic Inquiry*, Vol 19, No. 3, pp. 436-48.

McKee, M. and West, E. (1984), 'Do second best considerations affect policy decisions, *Public Finance*, Vol. 37, No. 4, pp. 246-60.

McKee, M. and West, E. (1987), 'Further perspectives and the theory of second best', *Public Finance*, Vol. 42, No. 1, pp. 147-51.

McKelvey, R.D. (1976), 'Intransitivities in multidimensional voting models and some implications of agenda control', *Journal of Economic Theory*, Vol. 16, pp. 472-82.

McLean, I. (1987), *Public Choice: An Introduction*, Basil Blackwell, Oxford.

McNutt, P.A. (1988), 'A note on altruism', *International Journal of Social Economics*, Vol. 15, pp. 62-64.

McNutt, P.A. (1992), 'Mapping Fairness', *Pure Mathematics and Applications*, Vol. 3, pp. 175-185.

McNutt, P.A. (1993(a)), 'A note on calculating Condorcet probabilities', *Public Choice*, Vol. 75, pp. 357-61.

McNutt, P.A. (1993(b)), 'On rent-seeking and X-inefficiency', *Public Choice*, Vol. 75, pp. 371-78.

McNutt, P.A. (1995), 'Rent-seeking and political tenure: First estimates', University of Ulster, *Mimeo*.

Meltzer, A.H. and Richard, S.E. (1981), 'A rational theory of the size of government' *Journal of Political Economy*, Vol. 89, No. 5, pp. 914-27.

Migue, J.L. and Belanger, G. (1974), 'Towards a general theory of managerial discretion', *Public Choice*, Vol. 17, pp. 27-43.

Milgrom, P. and Roberts, J. (1990), 'The efficiency of equity in organisational decision processes', *American Economic Review*, Vol. 80, No.2, May, pp. 154-59.

Mill, J.S. (1951), 'Considerations in Representative Government' in Acton (ed) *Utilitarianism, Liberty and Representative Government*, Dent & Sons, London.

Miller, E.G. (1988), *Voting*, Palgrave Dictionary, Macmillan Press, London.

Miller, G.J. (1977), Bureaucratic compliance: A game on the unit square', *Public Choice*, Vol. 29, pp. 37-52.

Miller, N.R. (1980), 'A new solution set for tournaments and majority voting, *American Journal of Political Science*, Vol. 24, pp. 68-96.

Miller, N.R., Grofman, B. and Field, S. (1986), *Cycle Avoiding Trajectories in Majority Voting Tournaments*, Paper Presented at the 1986 European Public Choice Meeting.

Mishan, E.J. (1969), The relationship between joint products, collective goods and external effects', Journal *of Political Economy*, Vol. 77, No. 2, pp. 329-48.

Mishan, E.J. (1971), 'The postwar literature on externalities: An interpretative essay', *Journal of Economic Literature*, Vol. 9, No. 1, pp. 329-48.

Moffitt, R. (1990), 'The econometrics of kinked budget constraints', *Journal of Economic Perspectives*, Vol. 4, No. 2, pp.1 19-39.

Moulin, H. (1982), *Game Theory for the Social Sciences*, New York University Press, New York.

Mueller, D.C. (1979), *Public Choice,* Cambridge University Press, Cambridge.

Mueller, D.C. (1989), *Public Choice II,* Cambridge University Press, Cambridge.

Mueller, D.C. and Murrell, P. (1985), 'Interest Groups and the Political Economy of Government Size', in Forte, F. and Peacock, A.T (op. cit.).

Mueller, D.C. and Murrell, P. (1985), 'Interest groups and the political economy of government size', in Forte, F. and Peacock, A.T. (ed), *Public Expenditure and Government Growth*, Blackwell, Oxford.

Mueller, D.C. and Murrell, P. (1986), 'Interest groups and the size of government', *Public Choice*, Vol 48, No. 2, pp. 125-45.

Mundell, R.A. (1962), 'The review of Jansen's free trade protection and customs union', *American Economic Review*, Vol. 52, No. 3, pp. 621-22.

Murakami, Y. (1961), 'A note on the general possibility theorem of the social welfare function', *Econometrica*, Vol. 29, pp.244-246.

Murrell, P. (1984), 'Examination of the factors affecting the formation of interest groups', *Public Choice*, Vol. 43, No.2, pp. 151-71.

Musgrave, P.B. (1938), 'The voluntary exchange theory of public economy', *Quarterly Journal of Economics*, Vol. 35, pp. 213-37.

Musgrave, P.B. and Musgrave, R.A. (1980), *Public Finance in Theory and in Practice*, Mc Graw-Hill, London.

Musgrave, R.A. and Peacock, A.T. (1958), *Classics in the Theory of Public Finance*, Macmillan, Basingstoke.

Naughton, M. and Frantz, R. (1991), 'X-Effeciency, rent-seeking and social costs, a comment', *Public Choice*, Vol. 68, No. 1-3, pp. 259-65.

Ng, Y. (1973), 'The economic theory of clubs: Pareto optimality conditions', *Economica*, Vol. 40, pp. 291-98.

Ng, Y. (1974), 'The economic theory of clubs: Optimal tax/subsidy', *Economica*, Vol. 41, pp. 308-21.

Ng, Y. (1975), 'Bentham or Bergson, Finite sensibilty, utility functions and social welfare functions', *Review of Economic Studies*, Vol. 42, pp. 545-69.

Ng, Y. (1978), 'Optimal club size: a reply', *Economica,* Vol. 45, pp. 407-10.

Ng, Y. (1979), *Welfare Economics, Introduction and Development of Basic Concepts*, Macmillan, London.

Ng. Y. (1987), 'The role of economists and third best policies', *Public Finance*, Vol. 42, No. 1, pp. 152-55.

Nicolaides, C. (1990), 'Positive and normative conflicts in the expanding domain of economics', *Methodus*, Vol. 2, pp. 8-16.

Niskanen, W. (1971), *Bureaucracy and Representative Government*, Aldine Atherton, Chicago.

Niskanen, W. (1987), 'Bureaucracy' in Rowley, C.K. (ed) *Democracy and Public Choice*, Blackwell, Oxford.

North, D.C. and Wallis, J.J. (1982), 'American government expenditures: A historical perspective', *American Economic Review*, Vol. 82, pp. 336-40.

Norris, C. (1990), *What's Wrong with Post Modernism*, John Hopkins University Press, New York.

Nozick, R. (1974), *Anarchy State and Utopia*, Basic Books, New York.

Nurmi, H. (1983), 'Voting procedures: A Survey Analysis', *British Journal of Political Science*, Vol. 13, pp. 181-208.

Nurmi, H. (1987), *Banks, Borda and Copeland: A comparison of some solution concepts in finite game*, Paper Presented at the 1987 European Public Choice Conference.

Oakland, W.H. (1972), 'Congestion, public goods and welfare', *Journal of Public Economics*, Vol. 1, pp. 339-57.

Oates, W. (1972), *Fiscal Federalism*, Harcourt Brace Jovanovich, London.

Offe, C. (1984), *Contradictions of the Welfare State*, Hutchinson, London.

Olson, M. (1965), *The Logic of Collective Action*, Harvard University Press, Cambridge.

Oppenheimer, J. (1985), 'Public choice and three ethical properties of politics', *Public Choice*, Vol 45, No. 3, pp. 241-55.

Ordeshook, P. (1986), *Game Theory and Political Theory: An Introduction*, Cambridge University Press, New York.

Ordershook, P. and Shepsle, K. (1982), *Political Equilibrium*, Kluwer Academic, Amsterdam.

Ouchi, W.G. (1980), 'Markets bureaucracies amd clans', *Administrative Science Quarterly*, Vol. 25, pp. 129-41.

Oxley, H. (1991), 'Whatever happened to the public sector?, *OECD Observer*, Vol. 169, pp. 31-36.

Parish, R.M. and Ng, Y.K. (1972), 'Monopoly, x-inefficiency and the measurement of welfare loss', *Economica* , Vol. 39, pp. 301-08.

Parkin, F. (1967), 'Working class conservatives: A theory of political deviance', *British Journal of Sociology*, Vol. 18, pp. 278-90.

Pardo, J. and Schneider, F. (1996), *Current Issues in Public Choice*, Edward Elgar, UK.

Pateman, C. (1985), *The Problem of Political Obligation*, Polity Press, Cambridge.

Pathirane, L. and Blades, D.W. (1982), 'Defining and measuring the public sector: Some international comparisons', *Review of Income and Wealth*, Vol. 28, pp. 261-289.

Pattanaik, P.K. (1968), 'A note on democratic decisons and the existence of choice sets', *Review of Economic Studies*, Vol. 35, pp. 1-9.

Pauly, M. (1967), 'Clubs, commonality and the core', *Economica*, Vol. 34, pp. 314-24.

Pauly, M. (1970(a)), 'Cores and clubs', *Public Choice*, Vol. 9, pp. 53-65.

Pauly, M. (1970(b)), 'Optimality, public goods and local government', *Journal of Political Economy*, Vol. 78, No. 3, pp. 572-86.

Peacock, A.T and Rowley, C.K. (1974), *Welfare Economics*, Martin Robertson, London.

Peacock, A.T. and Wiseman, J. (1961), *The Growth of Public Expenditure in the United Kingdom*, Princeton University Press, Princeton.

Pearce, D.W. (1977), *Environmental Economics*, Longman, London.

Peltzman, S. (1976), 'Toward a more general theory of regulation', *Journal of Law and Economics*, Vol. 19, No. 2, pp. 211-40.

Peltzman, S. (1980), 'The Growth of Government, *Journal of Law and Economics*, Vol. 23, pp. 209-88.

Persson, T. and Tabellini, G. (1990), *Macroeconomic Policy, Credability and Politics*, Harwood Academic Press, New York.

Persson, T. and Tabellini, G. (1994), *Monetary and Fiscal Policy*, Vol. I, MIT Press, Cambridge.

Pittman, R. (1988), 'Rent-seeking and market structure: A comment?', *Public Choice*, Vol. 58, pp. 173-86.

Pigou, A.C. (1920), *The Economics of Welfare*, Macmillan, London.

Plott, C.R. (1969), 'Recent Results in the Theory of Voting', in Intriligator, M.D. (ed), *Frontiers of Quantitative Economics*, *(op. cit.)*.

Plott, C.R. (1967), 'A notion of equilibrium and its probability voter moagnitude', *American Economic Review*, Vol. 57, pp. 788-806.

Plott, C.R. (1973), 'Path independence rationality and social choice', *Econometrica*, Vol. 41, No. 6, pp. 1075-91.

Plott, C.R. (1976), 'Axiomatic social choice theory', *American Journal of Political Science*, Vol. 20, No. 3, pp. 511-17.

Polsby, N.W. (1963), Community Power And Political Theory: Yale Studies in Political Science, Yale University Press.

Porter, R.C. (1977), 'On the optimal size of underpriced facilites' *American Economic Review*, Vol. 67, No. 4, pp. 753-60.

Porter, R.C. (1978), 'The economics of congestion: A geometric review', *Public Finance Quarterly*, Vol. 6, pp. 23-52.

Posner, R.A. (1974) 'Theories of economic regulation', *Bell Journal of Economics and Management Science*, Vol. 5, No. 2, pp. 335-58.

Posner, R.A. (1975), 'The social costs of monopoly and regulation', *Journal of Political Economy*, Vol. 83, No. 4, pp. 807-28.

Powell, G.B. (1981), 'Party systems and political system performance', *American Political Science Review*, Vol. 75, No. 4, pp. 861-79.

Rae, D.W. (1975), 'The limits of consensual decision', *American Political Science Review*, Vol. 69, December, pp. 1270-94.

Rawls, J.A. (1971), *A Theory of Justice*, Harvard University Press, Cambridge, Mass.

Riker, W. (1982), *Liberalism Against Populism*, Freeman Press, San Francisco.

Rogerson, W.P. (1982), 'The social costs of monopoly and regulation: A game theoretic analysis', *Bell Journal of Economics*, Vol. 13, No. 2, pp. 391-401.

Rose, R. and Mackie, T.T. (1980), 'Incumbency in government asset or liability?', *Studies in Public Policy*, 54, University of Strathclyde.

Rose, R. (1983), 'The programme approach to the growth of government', *Studies in Public Policy*, 120, University of Strathclyde.

Russell, K.P. and Wilkinson, M. (1979), *Microeconomics*, John Wiley & Sons, New York.

Rowley, C.K. (1987), *Democracy and Public Choice*, Blackwell, Oxford.

Rowley, C.K., Tollison, R.D. and Tullock, G. (1988), *The Political Economy of Rent Seeking*, Kluwer Academic, Boston.

Samuels, W. and Mercuro, N. (1984), 'A critique of rent seeking theory' in Colarder, D.C., *Neoclassical Political Economy (op.cit.)*.

Samuelson, P.A. (1954), 'The pure theory of public expenditure', *Review of Economic Statistics*, Vol. 36, pp. 387-89.

Samuelson, P.A. (1977), 'Reaffirming the existence of reasonable Bergson-Samuelson social welfare functions', *Economica*, Vol. 44, pp. 81-88.

Samuelson, P.A. (1986), *Microeconomic Theory*, Kluwer-Nijhoff, Amsterdam.

Sandler, T. (1977), 'Impunity of defence: an application to the economics of alliances', *Kyklos*, Vol. 30, No. 3, pp. 443-60.

Sandler, T. (1978), 'Public goods and the theory of the second best', *Public Finance*, Vol. 33, No. 3, pp. 331-43.

Sandler, T. (1992), *Collective Action, Theory and Applications*, Harvester Wheatsheaf, London.

Sandler, T. and Tschirhart, J.T. (1980), 'The economic theory of clubs: an evaluative survey', *Journal of Economic Literature*, Vol. 18, No.4, pp. 1481-1521.

Satterthwaite, M.A. (1975), 'Strategy proofness and arrow's conditions', *Journal of Economic Theory*, Vol. 10, No. 1, pp. 187-208.

Savage, L.J. (1954), *The Foundations of Statisics*, Wiley & Sons, New York.

Schelling, T.C. (1969), 'Models of segregation', *American Economic Review, AEA Papers and Proceedings*, Vol. May, pp. 488-94.

Schick, F. (1969), 'Arrow's proof and the logic of preference', *Philosophy of Science*, Vol. June, pp. 127-144.

Schofield, N. (1993), *Political Economy: Institutions, Competition and Representation*, Cambridge University press, Cambridge.

Schlozman, K.L. and Tierney, J. (1986), *Organized Interests and American Democracy*, Harper & Row, New York.

Schumpeter, J.A. (1954), *History of Economic Analysis*, Harper & Row, New York.

Schumpeter, J.A. (1976), *Capitalism, Socialism and Democracy*, Allen & Unwin, London.

Schwartz, J. (1972), 'Rationality and the myth of the maximum', *Nous*, Vol. 6, pp. 97-118.

Schwartz, T. (1977), 'Collective choice, separation of issues and vote trading', *American Political Science Review*, Vol. 71, pp. 999-1010.

Scotchmer, S. (1985), 'Profit maximising clubs', *Journal of Public Economics*, Vol. 27, No. 1, pp. 25-45.

Selby, S.M. (1965), *CRC Standard Mathematical Tables*, Chemical Rubber Co., Cleveland.

Seldon, A, (1986), *The Riddle of the Education Voucher*, Hobert Paperback 21, Institute of Economic Affairs, London.

Self, P. (1980), 'Public expenditure and welfare' in Wright, M. (ed) *Public Spending Decisions*, Allen & Unwin, London.

Self, P. (1993), *Government by the Market*, Macmillan Press, London.

Sen, A.K. (1969), 'Quasi transitivity, rational choice and collective decisions', *Review of Economic Studies*, Vol. 36, pp. 381-93.

Sen, A.K. (1970(a)), *Collective Choice and Social Welfare*, Holden Day, San Francisco.

Sen, A.K. (1970(b)), 'The impossibility of a paretian liberal', *Journal of Politcal Economy*, Vol. 78, No. 1, pp. 152-56.

Sen, A.K. (1973), *On Economic Inequality*, Oxford University Press, Oxford.

Sen, A.K. (1977), 'Social choice theory: A re-examination', *Econometrica*, Vol. 45, No. 5, pp. 1539-71.

Sen, A.K. (1981), 'Poverty and Famines: An Essay on Entitlement and Deprivation', Clarendon Press, Oxford.

Sen, A.K. (1982), 'How is India doing?' *New York Review of Books*, Vol. 29, pp. 41-45.

Sen, A.K. (1986), 'Social Choice Theory' in Arrow, K. and Intriligator, D.H. (ed), *Handbook of Mathematical Economics*, Vol. III. North Holland, Amsterdam.

Sen, A.K. (1987), *On Ethics and Economics*, Blackwell, Oxford.

Sen, A.K. and Pattanaik, P.K. (1969), 'Necessary and sufficient conditions for rational choice under majority decision', *Journal of Economic Theory*, Vol. 1, No. 2, pp. 178-202.

Shapiro, N. and Shapley, L.S. (1978), 'Values of large games: A limit theorem', *Mathematics of Operations Research*, Vol. 3, pp. 290-307.

Shapley, L.S. and Shubik, M. (1954), 'A method of evaluating power in committee systems', *American Political Science Review*, Vol. 48, No. 3, pp. 787-92.

Shepsle, K.A. (1970), 'A note on Zeckhauser's majority rule', *Quarterly Journal of Economics*, Vol. 84, pp. 705-9.

Shepsle, K.A. (1979), 'Institutional arrangements and equilibrium in multidimensional voting models', *American Journal of Political Science*, Vol. 23, pp. 787-92.

Shepsle, K.A. (1986), 'The positive theory of legislative institutions: An enrichment of social choice and spacial models', *Public Choice*, Vol. 50, pp.135-78.

Sisk, D.E. (1985), 'Rent seeking: Non-compensated transfers and laws of succession, property rights view, *Public Choice*, Vol. 46, No. 1, pp. 95-102.

Sraffa, P. (1926), 'The law of returns under competitive conditions', *Economic Journal*, Vol. 36, pp. 535-50.

Starrett, D.A. (1988), *Foundations of Public Economics*, Cambridge University Press, Cambridge.

Stevens, B.J. (1993), *The Economics of Collective Choice*, Westview Press, New York.

Stibbard, P. (1985), 'Measuring public expenditure', *Economic Trends*, No. 382, pp. 94-111.

Stigler, G.J. (1971), 'The theory of economic regulation', *Bell Journal of Economics and Management Science*, Vol. 2, No. 1, pp. 3-21.

Stigler, G.J. (1972), 'Economic competition and political competition', *Public Choice*, Vol. 13, pp. 91-106.

Stigler, G.J. (1976), 'The size of legislatures', *Journal of Legal Studies*, Vol. 5, No. 1, pp. 17-34.

Stiglitz, J.E. (1977), 'The Theory of Local Public Goods' in Feldstein and Inman (ed), *The Economics of Public Services*, Macmillan, London.

Straffin, P.D. (1977), 'Homogeneity, independence and power indices', *Public Choice*, Vol. 30, pp. 107-118.

Straffin, P.D. (1980), *Topics in the Theory of Voting*, Birkhauser, UMAP Monograph.

Sugden, R. (1981), *The Political Economy of Public Choice*, Martin Robertson, Oxford.

Sugden, R. (1986), *The Economics of Right, Cooperation and Welfare*, Blackwell, Oxford.

Sugden, R. (1989), 'Spontaneous order', *Journal of Economic Perspectives*, Vol. 3, No. 4, pp. 85-97.

Suppes, P. (1966), 'Some formal models of grading principles', *Synthese*, Vol. 16, pp. 284-306.

Suppes, P. (1969), *Studies in the Methodology and Foundations of Science*, Reidel, Dordrecht.

Tanzi, V. (1972), 'A note on exclusion: Pure public goods and pareto optimality', *Public Finance*, Vol. 27, No. 1, pp .75-79.

Taylor, M. (1976), *Anarchy and Cooperation*, Wiley & Sons, New York.

Taylor, M. (1987), *The Possibility of Cooperation*, Cambridge University Press, Cambridge.

Tiebout, C. (1956), 'A pure theory of local expenditures', *Journal of Political Economy*, Vol. 64, No. 5, pp. 416-24.

Tirole, J. (1988), *The Theory of Industrial Organisation*, MIT Press, Cambridge.

Titmuss, R. (1970), *The Gift Relationship*, Allen & Unwin, London.

Tollison, R.D. (1982), 'Rent-seeking a survey', *Kyklos*, Vol. 35, No. 4, pp. 575-602.

Tollison, R.D. (1987), 'Is The Theory of Rent-Seeking Here to Stay?' in Rowley, C. (ed), *Democracy and Public Choice*.

Tosini, S. and Tower, E. (1987), 'The Textile Bill of 1985', *Public Choice*, Vol. 54, No. 1, pp. 19-25.

Tullock, G. (1965), *The Politics of Bureaucracy*, Public Affairs Press, Washington DC.

Tullock, G. (1967(a)), 'The welfare costs of tariffs monopolies and theft', *Western Economic Journal*, Vol . 5, pp. 224-32.

Tullock, G. (1967(b)), 'The general irrelevence of the general possibility theorem', *Quarterly Journal of Economics*, Vol. 81.

Tullock, G. (1980), 'Efficient Rent-Seeking' in Buchanan, J.M. Tollison, R.D. and Tullock, G. (ed), *Toward Theory of the Rent-Seeking Society*, Texas A&M.(*op. cit.*).

Tullock, G. (1974), 'Dynamic hypothesis on bureaucracy', *Public Choice*, Vol. 19, pp. 127-31.

Tullock, G. (1985), 'Back to the bog', *Public Choice*, Vol. 46, No. 3, pp. 259-63.

Tullock, G. (1990), *The Economics of Special Priveleges and Rent-Seeking*, Kluwer Academic, Amsterdam.

Turvey, R. (1971), 'Demand and Supply', Allen and Unwin, London.

Van Winden, F.A.A. (1983), *On the Interaction Between State and Private Sector: A Study in Political Economics*, North Holland, Amsterdam.

Varian, H.R. (1976), 'On the history of the concepts of fairness', *Journal of Economic Theory*, Vol. 13, No. 3, pp. 486-87.

Varian, H.R. (1989), 'Measuring the deadweight costs of DUP and rent-seeking activities', *Economics and Politics*, Vol.1, pp. 81-95.

Varian, H.R. (1992), *Microeconomic Analysis*, Norton & Co., New York.

Wagner, R.E. (1890), *Finanzwissenschaft*, Vols. I & II, C.F. Winter, Leipzig.

Walker, J. (1983), 'The origins and maintenance of interest groups in America', *American Political Science Review*, Vol. 77, pp. 390-406.

Weber, M. (1947), *The Theory of Social and Economic Organization* in Parsons, T. (ed) Free Press, New York.

Williamson, O.E. (1963), *The Economics of Discretionary Behaviour*, Prentice Hall, Englewood Cliffs, NJ.

Wilson, J.Q. (1990), 'Why James Madison would have never won the James Madison award', *American Political Science Review*, Vol. 77, pp. 558-62.

Wittman, D.A. (1984), 'Multi-candidate equilibria', *Public Choice*, Vol. 43, No. 3, pp. 287-291.

Wright, M. (1980), *Public Spending Decisions* , Allen & Unwin, London.

Wooders, M. (1980), 'The tiebout hypothesis, near optimality in local public good economies', *Econometrica*, Vol. 48, No.6, pp. 1467-85.

Author Index

Adonis, A., 81
Alchian, A., 165
Alesina, A., 72, 73, 140
Apple, 9
Aronson, J.R., 196-197, 198
Arrow, K.J., 1, 11, 19, 21-35, 47, 48, 49, 52
Atkinson, A.B., 121, 205-206
Auster, R.D., 130
Axelrod, R., 131

Baldwin, R.E.
Bandyopadhyay, T., 28
Banzhaf, J.F., 41
Baumol, W., 81, 103, 134
Baysinger, G., 150, 156
Becker, G., 143, 186
Belanger, 135-136
Bendix, 109
Bendor, J., 131
Benham, L., 177
Benson, B., 142, 159, 160
Berg, S., 41, 65
Berglas, E., 209, 210-212
Bhagwati, J.N., 139, 145, 153
Binmore, K., 35
Black, D., 1, 21, 34, 45, 48, 69
Blades, 78
Blais, 131
Blau, J.H., 35, 52
Boehm, 63-64
Bonner, J.
Borcherding, T.
Borda, 20-21, 29
Bowen, H.R.
Brams, S.J., 63-64
Brennan, G., 47, 119, 134, 152
Breton, A., 119, 134
Brock, W., 172-173

Brown, C.V., 9, 101, 102, 116, 126-128, 132-133, 202-203, 208
Buchanan, J.M., 1-4, 6, 9, 12-13, 18, 22, 24, 25, 27, 47, 71, 103-104, 119, 134, 137-139, 145, 160, 166, 180-181, 183, 190, 200, 205

Cawson, A., 124
Cebula, R.J., 198
Chamberlin, K., 162
Chernoff, H., 28
Clarke, E.H., 189
Coase, R.H., 192
Coleman, J.S.,
Comanor, W.S., 61, 169-170
Condorcet, J.A., 20, 21, 27, 29
Congleton, R.D., 150, 165-166, 167-168, 170
Coughlin, P., 61
Cowling, K., 138, 177
Crain, W.M., 104, 168

Dahl, R.A., 111, 213, 215, 220
d'Aspremont, C., 55
Davis, O.A., 61
DeAlessi, 162, 164, 166
De Nardo, J.
Denzau, A., 61
DiLorenzo, T.J., 177
Dion, 61
Dodgson, C.L., 21, 218
Doran, 57
Downs, A., 1, 2, 7, 13, 17, 20-21, 45, 57, 59, 71, 99, 105, 108, 110-111, 213, 218
Dubley, 41
Dummett, M.A., 54, 66-68
Dunleavey, P., 9, 99, 111, 123-124, 130-131, 133
Dunsire, 133

Durden, G.C., 140
Dworkin, A., 5

Edgeworth, F.Y., 13
Eggertsson T., 159, 160
Ellingsen, T., 151-152
Elster, J., A., 60
Enelow, J.M., 61
Evans, A.W., 187
Evans, D.S., 172-173

Farquharson, F., 21, 62, 218
Feldman, A.M., 33, 44, 47, 48
Ferejohn, J.A., 28
Fiorina, M.P. 72, 74
Fishburn, P.C., 40, 61, 64-65
Fisher, F., 149, 151
Frantz, R., 166, 169

Gehrlein, W.V., 64, 65
Gevers, L., 55
Gibbard, A., 13, 32, 33, 46, 60
Gleenerster, H., 89
Graff, 49
Grandmont, J.M., 49
Green, H.A.J., 186
Grether, D.M., 28
Grooves, T., 189

Habermas, J., 225
Hammond, P.J., 54
Harberger, A.C., 155
Hart, H.L.A., 163
Hartle, D., 140
Hayek, F.A., 47
Held, D., 213, 214, 225, 226-227
Helpman, E., 209, 210
Henrekson, M. 104
Higgins and Tollison, R.D., 138
Hillman, A.L., 150-151, 204, 210, 211
Hinich, M.J., 61
Hirshleifer, J., 150, 156
Holler, M.J., 223
Holtermann,
Hood, 133
Hylland, A., 60

Inada, K., 45

Jackson, P.M., 9, 101, 102, 116, 126-128, 132-133, 202-203, 208

Jadlow, J., 173
Joskow, P.L., 166

Kahana, N., 177
Kahneman, D., 213
Kaldor, 164
Kats, A., 61
Katz, E., 151, 177
Keeler, T.E., 169
Kemp, M., 46
Knetsch, J., 213
Knight, F., 180
Kronick, 57
Krueger, A.O., 137, 142, 149

Lancaster, K., 195
Landes, W.M., 104
Laver, M., 39, 147
Ledyard, 61
Lee, D., 104
Leibenstein, H., 141-142, 165, 169
LeGrand, 89
Lindblom, C., 112-113
Lipsey, R., 195
Loehr, W., 190-191, 196
Luce, R.D., 41

Machiavelli, 109
Mackie, T.T., 141
Mann, M., 225
Margolis, 14
Marris, R., 134
Martin, D., 9, 82
Mas Colell, 33
May, K.O., 21, 28, 34, 48, 66, 69
Mayston, D.J., 45, 49-50
McCormick, R.E., 104, 146
McGuire, M.C., 129, 180, 207, 209
McKee, M., 154
McKelvey, R.C., 12, 61
McLean, I., 4, 14, 164
McNutt, P.A., 14, 47, 65, 66, 75, 105, 140, 146, 150, 165, 166, 170-171, 214 215, 216
Meltzer, A.H., 92-93, 103
Mercuro, 143
Migue, J.L., 135-136
Milgrom, P., J., 139, 163
Mill, J.S. 224
Miller, E.G., 19, 39, 42, 69, 134
Mishan, E.J., 187

Moffitt, R., 183, 186, 187
Moulin, H., 39
Mueller, D.C., 34, 81, 102-103, 104, 113,
    116, 119-120, 121, 126-128, 134, 135,
    138, 146, 151-152, 156, 163, 177, 198-
    199, 200-201, 205, 208-209, 210
Mundell, R.A., 143, 148, 165
Murakami, 46
Musgrave, P.B. 100-101, 104, 111, 162,
    189
Musgrove, R.A., 100-101, 104, 111, 162,
    189

Naughton, M., 166, 169
Ng, Y., 24, 26, 45, 46, 52, 57, 66, 154,
    159, 169, 202, 207, 209-210, 211
Nicolaides, 140, 153
Nitzan, S., 61
Nurmi, 39, 40
Niskanen, W., 9, 99, 104, 105, 107-108,
    109-110, 115-116, 131, 135
Norris, 228-229
Nozick, 5, 16

Oakland, W.H., 200, 205, 209
Oates, N., 196
Offe, 214
Olson, M., 1, 4, 9, 18, 104, 180
Ordeshook, P., 25, 31, 35, 36, 38, 57, 59,
    61, 68-69
Ouchi, W.G., 131
Oxley, 82

Parkin, F.
Parks, R.P., 56
Pateman, C., 226
Pathirane, 78
Pattanaik, P.K., 45, 47
Pauly, M., 202, 205, 207, 210, 212
Peacock, A.T., 16, 103
Peltzman, S., 93-96, 103, 104, 122, 155
Pigou, A.C., 13, 14, 180, 192
Pines, 209, 211, 212
Pittman, 176
Plott, C.R., 28, 47, 49, 59
Polsby, N.W.,
Porter, R.C., 209
Posner, R.A., 104, 137, 143, 149, 161,
    177
Powell, G.B., 107

Rae, D.W., 163
Raiffa, H., 41
Rawls, J., 5, 16, 55, 163
Reisman, 7
Richard, S.E., 92-93
Riker, W.H., 19, 20, 22, 26, 27, 31, 40, 44,
    48, 57, 62, 64, 216, 218-219, 224
Riley, J., 150
Roberts, J., 139, 163
Rose, R., 141
Rowley, C., 16, 165, 170
Russell, K.P., 123

Samet, D., 150-151
Samuels, 143
Samuelson, P.A., 3, 45, 180, 195
Sandler, T., 18, 180, 182, 190-191, 196,
    203-204, 209, 210-211
Satterthwaite, M.A., 60
Savage, L.J.
Schelling, T.C., 180
Schick, 47
Schlozman, 215
Schofield, N., 147, 214
Schumpeter, J.A., 2, 140, 225
Schwartz, E., 25, 198
Scotchmer, S., 211
Selby, S.M., 66
Seldon, A, 185
Self, 90
Sen, A.K., 12, 30-32, 34, 35, 45, 46, 49,
    52-53, 54-55, 57, 91, 163
Shapiro, P., 41
Shapley, L.S., 41-42
Shepsle, K.A., 72, 222
Shepsley, 61
Shubik, M., 41-42
Silver, M., 130
Sisk, D.E., 139
Sonnenschein, 33
Sraffa, 142
Srinivason, T.N., 145, 153
Starrett, D.A., 181-207
Steunenberg, 223
Stevens, B.J., 218
Stibbard, 80
Stigler, G.J., 89, 104, 105, 142-143, 171,
    155
Stiglitz, J.E., 121, 205-207, 209
Straffin, P.D., 42-43, 51, 62
Sugden, R., 4, 16, 27, 51, 62, 154

Suppes, P., 54
Swan, 204, 211

Tanzi, V., 190
Taylor, M., 4, 6, 14
Thaler, R., 213
Thistle, 169
Tiebout, C., 180, 181, 196, 198, 205-206
Tierney, 215
Tirole, J., 152, 155, 157-158, 166, 167,
    172
Titmuss, 14
Tollison, R.D., 104, 136, 138, 145, 146,
    150, 148, 156, 177
Tschirhart, J.T., 18, 180, 204, 209, 210-
    211
Tullock, G., 1-4, 6, 9, 12-13, 24-25, 47,
    49, 99, 103-105, 106-107, 108, 109,
    110, 137, 138, 140, 142, 148, 149,
    150-151, 154, 160, 190
Turvey, 192

Van Winden, F.A.A., 105
Varian, H.R., 139, 143, 145, 156, 159
Von Mises, H., 108, 109-110, 135

Wagner,, 88, 103
Walker, J. 215
Weber, M., 99, 108, 109
West, E., 154
Wilkinson, 123
Williamson, O.E., 134
Wilson, 214
Winter, 89
Wintrobe, R., 134
Wiseman, 103
Wittman, D.A., 61
Wooders, M., 211

Zardkoohi, A., 168

Subject Index

α–Property, 46
agenda-access model, 222, 229
agenda setter, 221-222
altruism, 75
anarchy, 14, 16, 18, 71, 163, 220-222
anonymity, 46, 48, 56
approval voting, 64
Arrow's impossibility theorem, 1, 2, 6, 12, 20-23, 27-35, 43, 46-49, 50, 51, 218
  extensions to, 17, 31-35, 46
  and independence property, 49
  (see impossibility theorems)

β–property, 46
Banks set, 39-40
Banzhaf-Coleman index, 42-43

bastille constraint, 25, 44, 224
Baumol's disease, 103
Baumol effect, 81-82, 88
Bergson-Samuelson SWF, see social welfare function (Bergson-Samuelson)
bliss point, 57
Borda count, 50-51, 68-69
Borda method, 50-51, 70
Borda outcome, 24, 34, 65
Borda paradox, 68
Borda winner, 27-30, 39-40, 70
brand proliferation, 174
Brown's theorem, 46
bureaucracies
  and bureau shaping strategy, 123-125
  Breton, Brennan, Buchanan-model, 119-121
  budget, 130-131
  bureaucratic behaviour effect, 122-123
    and bureaucratic fat, 116
    and bureaucrats, 101, 134-135
  control costs, 128-129
  Downs-Lindblom model, 110-113

Dunleavy model, 123-126
  efficiency of, 102
  and government size, 102-103, 107-108
  and life cycle, 107, 111, 118
  and interest groups, 103-106, 115, 122
line management, 99, 130-131
Niskanen model, 113-117
public choice approach, 108-122
Tullock hypothesis, 117-119

characteristic function, 41
Chernoff condition, 28
clubs
  and externalities, 187-189, 201
  formation, 179-181, 204-209
  and game theory, 210
  and homogeneity, 206-207, 209, 213
  mixed clubs, 210
  multi-product clubs, 210
  optimal provision of, 198-200, 201, 207-208, 212
  and profit maximisation, 210-211
  for redistribution, 192-193, 196-209
  theory of, 5, 18, 179-213
Coase theorem, 192-193
collective choice rule, 27, 28-30, 52
collective goods, 179, 182, 185, 207
committee procedure, 69
  and decisions making, 73-74
compensation, 163-164
concept of finite sensibility, 52
Condorcet criterion (condition), 23, 26
Condorcet loser, 62-64. 65
Condorcet paradox, 2, 22, 26, 64, 65, 227
Condorcet winner, 11, 25, 26,-30, 35, 40, 55, 58, 59, 61, 73
contractarianism, 5
  in welfare economics, 16, 51-52

Coombs exhaustive procedure, 69
cooperative games, 38
copeland winner, 39-40
counter cyclical policy, 9
    and government expenditure, 97

dead-weight loss, 148, 156-157, 170
democracy
    ideals of, 217-219
deterministic voting, 61
directly unproductive profit-seeking, 18
    and rent-seeking, 145, 153-154
Directors' Law, 142-143
domain restrictions, 49
double peakedness, 34
Down's paradox, 11
    and expected utility income, 19
    and voting procedure, 21

Edgeworth contract curve, 15, 44, 48, 53, 58
endownment effect, 187
entry barriers, 167-168, 172, 176-178
excludability, 189-192
externalities, 2, 5, 183-189

forced rider, 190, 197
free rider, 5, 6, 135, 187, 189

G-groups, 18, 219-220, 222, 225
Gibbard-Satterwaite theorem, 12
government expenditure, 76, 78-80
    and displacement effect, 103
    composition of, 83-87
    and relative price effect, 80-83
government growth, 61, 76-98, 99-136
government output, 99-136
    re-election constraint, 99
    interest groups and rent-seeking, 104-105
group contraction lemma, 33

Hammond's Axiom E, 54-55
Henry George Theorem, 207

impossibility theorems, 10-13, 19-43
    and axioms, 10-11, 27-35
    and utility, 11
    and welfare, 16
independence condition, 29-30
independence of irrelevant alternatives (IIC), 49

interest function approach, 105
interest groups, 5, 18, 25, 92, 103-106
    and club theory, 181, 208-209
    and rent-seeking, 141, 150, 154, 159-160, 162
    in voting, 215, 216
inverted order paradox, 68-69
iso-support curves, 95-96

Janus complex, 100

Kaldor-Scitovsky compensation tests, 16, 44

Leviathan model of government, 16, 17, 71, 214
log-rolling, 7, 9, 12, 31, 50, 73

majority voting, 6
    and majority rule, 6, 19, 23, 25, 36, 29, 31, 34, 44, 45, 48-49, 50, 70, 72, 215, 217, 218, 227-228
    fairness of, 66-67, 215
majority winner, 70
marginal theft, 161-162
median voter, 1, 8, 31, 58-59, 61, 92-93, 222
    and bureaucrats, 102
    and redistribution, 103
market failure, 179, 190
merit goods, 85

Nash equilibrium, 38, 61, 211
national income accounts (NIA), 79
net compliments, 100, 103
neutrality, 27, 34-35, 49
new welfare economics, 13
non-cooperative games, 12, 35-36
non-dictatorship property, 29-30
non-price barriers, 174-176, 177
Nordhaus cycle, 73
normative criteria, 13-18

Oates theorem, 197-198
oligarchy, 28, 46
ordering conditions, 28

paratian liberal, 52-53
Pareto conditions, 11, 13, 29-30, 33-35, 45, 48, 193-196
Pareto optimality, 3, 38, 61, 193-196
    and externalities, 192-193

and public goods, 195, 198
 and rent-seeking, 147, 163
Pareto set, 39
participatory democracy, 227
path dependency, 12
Pigovian criterion, 14-15
plurality voting, 62
plurality winners, 30
political business cycle 8, 73-74, 219
 and government, 9
 and rent-seeking, 140
populism, 216
pork-barrel politics, 24
preference profiles, 65
preponderence scores, 67
principal agent, 9-10
 in bureaucracy, 99-136
 and rent-seeking, 152-153
 in voting, 217, 219
prisoners' dilemma, 4-6, 38-39, 134-135,
 179
private goods, 181, 183-187
probabilistic voting, 60-66
property rights, 4
 and rent-seeking, 18, 153-154, 159-
 164
public expenditure, 78-80
 and demand-side, 88-91, 97, 134
 and supply-side, 9, 80, 91-96, 97,
 106-108, 134
public goods, 6, 18, 85, 93, 126-133, 179,
 180-183
 and congestion, 204-209
 and externalities, 187-189
 internal group, 190, 199, 202
 optimal provision, 190-191, 196-199
public sector borrowing requirement
 (PSBR), 83

rational actor model, 8
Rawl's maximin rule, 54
redistribution
 and political dominance, 94-95
 and government intervention, 92-93
re-election constraint, 99, 219
rent seeking, 18, 25, 134, 136, 225, 226
 and anti-trust, 172-178
 competitive outcomes, 150-151
 defined, 137-138
 dissipation of rents, 144-145, 155-
 156,176-178

and economies of scope, 159
 frozen market perspective, 146-147
 theory of 139-141, 147-159
 and third-party distortions, 146, 167

Schwartz theorem, 12, 25
Sen's weak equity axiom, 14-15
separable preferences, 50
Shapley-Shubik index, 41-43
Shelby relations, 64
simple majority rule, 55, 59, 64, 227
sincere preference, 25, 50, 73
single cavedness, 45
single peakedness, 34, 45, 48, 55
 and WSP, 45, 57, 58, 65
single transferable vote, 57
social choice
 and Pareto optimality, 27
 and voting, 19-43, 227-228
social choice paradox, 16
social indifference curves, 44
social welfare functions,
 Arrow, 29
 Bentham, 26, 52
 Bergson-Samuelson, 1, 29, 53
 and maximisation, 16
 and rank-dictatorship, 55
sociotropy, 75
sophisticated voting, 12, 24, 31, 35, 59, 61,
 219
standard national accounts (SNA), 78
strategic voting, 12, 24, 31, 35, 59, 61,219,
 and interest groups, 106
strategies of displacement, 214

truncated-point total paradox, 69
type-2 errors
 in rent seeling, 173, 176

universal domain, 45
unrestricted domain, 30
untilitarianism, 11, 13, 14, 52, 107

V-set, 38-39
value restrictions, 45
vote maximising model (Downs), 8
voting paradox, 11, 13, 19-26, 28-30, 46,
 60, 67, 71, 72, 217-218, 220
voting power, 40-43
voting theory, 20-26, 213-225
vote trading, 7, 12, 17, 24-26, 31-33, 49,

50, 71, 72, 73, 75, 220
    and budgetary allocation, 8
    and pareto efficiency, 8
    and democracy, 20, 213-225
voting systems, 6-8, 66-72
voting-with-the-feet, 198
vouchers, 185-186

Wagner's Law, 9, 88
weak majority preference, 45, 52
welfare economics, 14-15
win set, 220-224, 226

X-inefficiency, 9, 18, 110, 133-136, 153
    and rent-seeking, 153, 164, 165-172